ARCHIE VENTERS

BRONZE IN MY BLOOD

To Milly
In Memoriam

Bronze in my Blood

The Memoirs of

Benno Schotz

GORDON WRIGHT PUBLISHING
55 MARCHMONT ROAD, EDINBURGH, EH9 1HT
SCOTLAND

ISBN 903065 37 1

The publisher acknowledges the financial assistance of the Scottish Arts Council in the publication of this volume.

Typeset by Image Services (Edinburgh) Ltd.
Printed by Alna Press Ltd., Broxburn
Bound by James Joyce & Duffin Ltd., Edinburgh

Contents

Acknowledgements

My thanks go to the members of my family who were involved in helping to produce this book.

My sister-in-law, Mrs. Margaret Parry, typed it twice, my brother-in-law, Asher Stelmach and my son Amiel read it for mistakes, and my nephew David Parry designed the jacket.

But my greatest thanks must go to my daughter, Mrs. Leonard Crome, who edited the manuscript, retyped the final draft, corrected the proofs and prepared the index.

Without so much support and encouragement this book might never have been completed.

Benno Schotz

Preface

For some years before she died my wife Milly would say to me from time to time, "Benno, since no one seems interested in writing a monograph about you, why don't you write one yourself?" I would smile and ask, "Do you really think I could?" "Of course," she would say, "Living with you all these years and hearing you express your ideas, I know you can". She would sometimes enlarge on the subject, "I have listened to your lectures; to you opening exhibitions; I have watched the many calls on your time and energy in the service of others, so why not spend some on yourself?"

However, I was fully engrossed in my sculpture and considered that I dared not divert my energy into a different channel. Yet, when Milly died, my mind was filled with thoughts of her, and her hopes for me, and I decided to do at last what she had asked of me.

Milly had taught me to use basic English, short sentences as opposed to the long ones I had learnt in Russia, and she knew that my simple style would be no hindrance. I thought I remembered little of my beginnings, but as I began to search into my past and write it down, so many visions of those far off days filled my eyes that the constraints disappeared.

As usual, Milly was right. I was able to put down my story and my ideas, and if the soul survives the mortal body, as I truly believe it does, she knows that at last her wish is fulfilled.

Benno Schotz

Prologue

We came to Pärnu when I was about two years old. The final part of
our journey had to be made by road, for as yet there was no railway
linking Pärnu with the rest of the country. I have a faint recollection of
being shaken about in some sort of vehicle, but remember nothing of
our arrival. I had probably fallen asleep. However, the picture that
remains in my mind, and the one I seem to associate with our arrival, is
seeing the next morning, through the window of our house, a child's
desk on a laden cart, sitting at a rakish angle, ready to topple at the
least movement. The cart disappeared the following day.

There was a large plot of grass in front of the house. Ours was a
rather humble dwelling, consisting of one large room into which
protruded the famous Russian stove, almost dividing it in two. Our
front door led into a fairly large entrance hall which gave our home
some additional character. There was a separate kitchen and an inside
lavatory to accommodate four people at once!

The road from the centre of the town passed by the side of the
house, towards the river a couple of hundred yards beyond. There was
another house behind ours. We had a common yard between us with a
broad open gate fronting the street, and various outhouses. Our
neighbours were also Jews, by the name of Lewin (Levine), with children
of our own ages.

Many a driver would stop on the grass plot, unhitch the horse, and let
it graze. Often the men would lift us up on to a horse's back and give us
a ride. They were quite friendly to us tots when they saw us playing
there. We and our neighbour's children played harmoniously together,
except for the occasional squabble.

One day, my brother Maxie and one of our neighbour's boys each
wanted the same spade. One held it at the handle, the other at the
blade, each pulling as hard as possible, while I stood looking on eager
to see the outcome of the struggle. As a child I was already a keen

observer, but this time I was standing too close, and when my brother suddenly let go of the blade end, it sailed through the air, swung and caught my nose, almost severing a nostril. To this day I carry the mark of my 'nosiness'.

My father, Jacob Schotz, was born in Yelock, a village in Lithuania, and was sent to study in the *Yeshiva* of Telsh, a famous Talmudic Seminary that prepared students for the Ministry and the Rabbinate. Our family name derives from the initial letters of the Hebrew phrase '*Sholiach Tsibbur*'. This means literally 'messenger of the congregation', and refers to the Cantor of a Synagogue. But although my father was a fine scholar, he did not wish to enter the Ministry, — a family tradition. Nevertheless, he used to tell us with pride, that when the famous poet and teacher Judah Leib Gordon came to the *Yeshiva* to examine the students, he received from him a *knip* — a pinch of the cheek — in appreciation of his answers. This was considered a great honour, and the memory of it was treasured for a long time.

My father did not want to remain in the 'Pale' — the Ghetto — with its stultifying atmosphere and was therefore apprenticed to a watchmaker, as was his brother Elias, who later emigrated to the United States of America. In their day it was a more skilful craft than today, for a watchmaker had not only to be able to repair all types of clocks and watches, but also to make all the parts, including the smallest toothed wheels and spindles. In later life, although his hands shook badly, he was able to take apart and assemble the smallest lady's watch by holding his wrists against the work bench, steadying his hands.

My mother, Cherna Tischa Abramovitz and her family lived in Hasenput, a small town near Libau, where my maternal grandfather was a Cantor in the Synagogue. My father had gone to work there when he became a journeyman, met my mother, fell in love and married her. Their elder children were born in Hasenput. Then they decided to move to Arensburg. This was a town on the island of Oesel in the Baltic Sea, at the entrance to the Gulf of Riga. It was, perhaps, a strange decision to settle in such a remote and isolated town, but they were young, full of life, love and adventure. There was no other watchmaker on the island, and here was an opportunity for my father to provide a service to the gentry and to the general public who previously had to go to the mainland to have their timepieces repaired. It was only when my eldest brother, Jeannot, reached school age, that our parents began to think about our general education, and this compelled them to return to the mainland.

My father must have decided that Pärnu was a growing town and could meet the needs of himself and his family. The magnet was the two *Gymnasia*, High Schools, one for boys and one for girls. My parents were keen to give their children a proper education, and there were not many such schools in Russia. At that time she had only ten universities for a population of nearly two hundred million, while Scotland, with a population of five million, could then boast of four.

We moved several times, each time to a larger house, but it was of our first home in Pärnu that I have my happiest memories. There we children made a vegetable garden, planting cucumbers, carrots, radishes, and potatoes. Carrots grew well in the sandy soil, and it was great pulling one out of the ground, dusting it against one's shirt, and enjoying its delicious freshness and flavour. I grew sunflowers at the back, and used to watch them turning their 'faces' towards the sun. When they were ripe I would cut off their heads and eat the dried seeds. We were all young, and life was full of enchantment, exploration and discovery.

We became aware of sex in a natural way from watching our animals. One day when two dogs were copulating in front of our open back door, my mother flung a pail of water over them. The dogs tried to run in opposite directions, but could not, and it took them some time to disengage themselves. I must admit that we laughed heartily at the sight of it.

We kept a dozen or so hens and a cock to have eggs for the table. Once when we had two cocks they began to fight for supremacy and we had to do away with one of them. When our mother wanted to replace the older hens she would buy special eggs from a local farm. The male eggs are longer and more pointed in shape than the female eggs, and she would select two that might produce cockerels, and about a dozen rounder ones for female birds. Then a broody hen would be placed on them in a basket and put under our parents' bed for heat and comfort.

To see the newly hatched chicks after they became dry, a bundle of yellow fluff was a sight to fill our hearts with delight. We were even able at times to watch the chick pecking its way out of the shell, the mother hen sometimes helping it with its beak.

On one occasion our entrance hall was transformed into a baker's shop. Jews in Russia were compelled to live in Ghettos prescribed by the Government. Only university graduates, and artisans like my father were exempt from this restriction, and many subterfuges were adopted in the fight to retain their religious identity.

A new Minister had been engaged by our small Jewish community. He had to perform the duties of Rabbi and Cantor in the Synagogue; he had to teach the children Hebrew and the Jewish religion; he also had to perform the ritual killing of the animals and poultry for our food. This was the most important part of his duties. This was not considered a trade as such, and he was therefore liable to be deported at the whim of the authorities. To make his stay legal he had to be given a trade. My father, who was one of the leaders of the community, thought that it would be a good idea if the Minister adopted the role of a baker. Shelves were erected in our entrance hall, and my mother baked loaves of bread of various kinds which were displayed on them. Should the question of his trade arise, here was proof that our Minister was also a baker!

I was born in Arensburg in 1891, the youngest of seven children. The date in my passport is given as 28th. August, according to the Julian calendar, but I would not swear to its veracity. I had three living brothers and two sisters. Jeannot was the eldest, my second eldest brother, Pesach, died before I was born, then came my sister Elsa, my brothers Kuciel and Moses, or Maxie as we used to call him, and my sister Hesse.

When my brother Pesach died in infancy, from meningitis, his death was never registered, forgotten perhaps, because at the time my father was away from home, although his birth had been registered. When the time came for his call-up to military service, my father could not produce him. To the authorities this could have meant that he had absconded, and father would have been in great trouble. So with some diplomacy Jeannot was saddled also with his younger brother's name, as at that time he was already a university student and had deferment from the army.

When Kuciel had to present himself for military service I learnt that he was not a real brother but an adopted one. His family had emigrated to Glasgow and to New Zealand, and as he was apprenticed to father and living with us, it was decided that he should stay behind meantime. When he returned from his call-up, having been exempted, this discovery made no difference, and we thought no more about it.

Pärnu lay on both sides of the river which ran into the Gulf of Riga, the town being at its estuary. It seemed a wide river to me, though it was probably only a little wider than the River Clyde at Glasgow. It was spanned by a wooden bridge built on pontoons, perhaps two feet, if that much, above the water. It was wide enough to let two vehicles pass one another with room to spare. There was a moveable section in the centre long enough to allow a steamer to pass up or down stream, and this section would be pulled out, moved to the side, and meanwhile all the traffic across the river would have to stop. Occasionally, when I happened to be on the bridge and a steamer was about to pass, I would marvel how neatly the captain manoeuvred his ship with just a few inches to spare on either side of the open section.

In winter the river froze up for at least four months. With the approach of spring the bridge would be dismantled and stored at the side of the river, firmly tied up to protect it from being carried away when the ice broke and flowed down the river to the sea. We would seldom know beforehand when the ice would begin to break up and flow. The melting snow would swell the river, and it, in turn, would

14

heave the ice up and lift it free of the river banks. The breaking up of the ice was accompanied by noisy explosions, not unlike cannon fire, and it would begin to move with loud crunching noises, as one large slab of ice would mount on top of another in its dramatic drive to the sea. The river, freed from the containing ice would rise and overflow, the water at times almost reaching our house. It was a wonderful sight, and the people would turn out to see the majestic and irresistable power of nature. It would take a few days for the ice to flow down to the sea, and at least a week for the river to subside. In the meantime, while there was no bridge to connect both sides of the town, a boat would ferry the inhabitants across.

Downstream, there was a properly built pier. A steamer plied between our town and Riga, and periodically a steamer with a red hand on its funnel would arrive from abroad. Father told us a tale he had heard that the owner of a steamship company had two sons, and when the time came for him to retire, he asked them to take identical boats and row to an island some distance away. He said he would leave his ships to the one whose hand first touched the island. When one of the sons saw that he was losing, he chopped off his hand and threw it on to the island, and in this way fulfilled his father's condition to inherit.

The story made a deep impression on me. I was astounded that some people would go to any lengths to attain their goal, whether for financial gain, or to get the better of their fellow men, even one's brother. Although we were brought up in a modest home we were never indoctrinated with the value of riches, and were never urged to go in for a profession because it might prove to be lucrative.

On the opposite side of the river, a little upstream, there was a large forest, and periodically trees would be cut down for export to Britain, principally for pit props. They would be floated downstream and tied together like a huge raft just in line with our house. I forget how they were tied, though I believe the bark of the trees was used for this purpose, but some would spring loose, or become unfastened. The rafts reached out to the middle of the river and we children would often try to walk on top of them and if possible reach the farthest end. This was dangerous, as we had to scamper from one loose log on to a stable one to get a firm footing, for the loose logs would often begin to turn and sink. It was easy to slip and fall into the water, and we took great care that our parents knew nothing of this game.

One day, having nothing better to do, I decided to go fishing. I took my home-made angling rod — a long thin birch branch — and decided to scramble over the logs on the river to fish there. Having had plenty of practice in this sport I reached the end of the raft, and as luck would have it, I caught quite a big fish. I proudly scampered home with my prize. When my father saw it, there was trouble, for he asked me where I had been fishing; then told me of the danger I had been in and scolded me soundly. He was so angry that he broke my fishing rod to teach me a lesson, and made me promise not to go there again. I was most upset, and ran away crying. Later however, I had the satisfaction of hearing that mother had fried the fish I had caught, and that both of them had enjoyed it.

Our parents hardly ever chastised us physically. I only remember one occasion when my father birched me. The reason for the birching, and the pain, were forgotten very quickly, but I still see myself weeping bitterly when I was made to kiss the tool of my punishment. It must have been the memory of this humiliation and indignity, not the punishment itself, which impressed itself upon me.

During the summer I would often hire a boat and row with my sister Hesse for hours. Strange, when I think of it, it never occurred to me to fish from the boat — to row was the thing, and it was most exhilarating. Perhaps I owe the strength in my arms to this youthful activity, for I was not good at gymnastics or physical games, and was considered a weakling.

The forest was also a favourite haunt. Hesse and I used to go there for the pleasure of being among trees, and we were occasionally sent to pick berries and mushrooms. Chanterelles used to grow in profusion, and Hesse could smell them out from a distance, even under a pile of fir cones and needles. Mother would make a delicious meal with them.

One day workmen arrived and laid railway lines on sleepers directly on top of the ground right across the road and the grass plot, a few yards in front of our house, with no protective barriers on either side. Hesse was terribly frightened by the appearance of the *muzhiks* who looked strange, dressed as they were in sheepskin coats. In no time at all the railway station was also built, and trains began to run twice daily. This made a great difference to the inhabitants of the town, for they no longer felt isolated and cut off from the surrounding country, and it surely hastened its growth — and our removal!

Beyond the pier there rose an embankment, the remains of a defensive buttress, which was now only a grass mound with a broad walk on top of it. I often used to go up the steps leading to this walk, for from there it was possible to see the expanse of water and sometimes a ship or two that were anchored in the estuary. It was on one of these walks that I came across a woman seated on a sketching stool, painting a sailing ship some distance off. Like the boy I was, I stopped to watch her at work from a little distance. When I saw her sketch in the two masts with assurance and ease, I realised that she was a professional artist, yet to me, the masts she had painted were much closer on her sketch than I saw them in reality. Although I had never seen a person painting from nature this needed an explanation and reasoning out. Here was I, a young boy ready to criticise an artist who painted without hesitation

16

and with rich colours. Why then did she paint the masts closer together than I saw them? This incident haunted me for a long time and I had to find the answer. Only years later did the solution dawn upon me. I could not have been as observant as I thought I was. It was natural for the artist to begin her painting with the ship, for this was the central feature of her sketch. The ship's stern must then have been slightly turned towards her. By the time she had finished painting the water, the sky and the foreground, the tide, or the wind, had swung the ship broadside. I saw the masts as they were when I arrived on the scene, and not as they must have been originally, when she began to paint. The masts were naturally the final touches and she had placed them on her ship in their true perspective.

Pärnu had many other attractions. For one thing, it was a health resort and it had a long golden seashore within easy walking distance of the town. The streets to it were in straight lines all the way, and the avenues were bordered with rows of high and stately trees, and in the summer they looked lovely, forming what looked like Gothic arches overhead. During the summer the thunderstorms did not last long, and the rainbows were magnificent. I liked to go out walking in the rain, if it was not too heavy, to feel it on my face. For some reason it gave me the feeling of being enveloped by nature, of being part of it, of enjoying its warmth, or coolness, its haze and friendliness. I would return home refreshed and full of zest.

The climate in summer was wonderful, not too hot, but with plenty of sunshine. During summer the twilight lasted for hours, and for weeks one could read a newspaper at midnight when the moon was up. Often as students we would walk along the shore in the evenings to watch the sunset, to watch the sea and its changing moods, with the moon reflected in it as a wavering and scintillating line of silver. Sometimes we would wait for the sunrise, returning home sleepy, but contented.

Halfway along one of the avenues a nightingale nested for some years in one of the trees. When we went down to the sea for a walk in the evenings, or on our way home, we would stop and listen to its singing. It was a most emotional and educational experience, to listen to the bird learning its song, which develops only gradually. At first it makes but a few experimental notes which nightly become more and more pronounced and intricate, and one would begin to hear some of its theme notes, though not in sequence. Invariably we would stop and listen to its progress until after a week or two it would burst into the most glorious song of any bird.

It must have perched very near us, for its notes were very loud. Its trills, its staccato notes, and its full throated coloratura variations kept us spellbound for long periods. No prima donna could have bettered it, and the wonder of it all was that such a small bird had such power and clarity. It was a lesson I could never forget. When I think back on it, my

17

mind turns to Wagner's opera *Die Meistersinger,* where the final triumphant *Preislied* is now and again heard in little snatches during the opera and is gradually clarified until the final revelation of the victorious song.

During the summer, visitors would come to our town from all over Russia, some for a month, others for longer periods. They used to rent *dachas* near the sea, and there were enough and more to accommodate them. There were bathing huts on a jetty which ran a fair distance into the sea where the water was nearly waist deep. There was also bathing from the shore, men and women having separate parts of the beach.

Above the sands, facing the sea, was a glass fronted *Kurhaus* where one could enjoy refreshments and where there were occasional cabaret acts. Now and again I would accompany my sister Elsa to watch the performance, for its was not seemly for a girl to go there by herself.

Near our house there was a small park with a clearing in the middle, at one end of which there was a bandstand in the shape of a sea shell, where an orchestra would play several times a week. The violinist-conductor was a good-natured and good-looking, slightly-built man, who would acknowledge with a smile and a bow, the applause. He played extracts from classical music, and Strauss waltzes. We loved to stroll about listening to the music, and our musical education began there.

The winters had their own delights to be enjoyed by the local people and the students who came to study in our *Gymnasia.* It was a fascinating time, although the temperature could often fall as low as minus fifteen degrees Centigrade. We would sometimes wager how far we could go before our ears or cheeks would get frostbitten, and then have them rubbed with snow to revive them.

Robin redbreasts would appear, brilliant against the snow, on the branches of the trees. We were fond of birds, and Maxie would try to snare them with a trap cage and a decoy bird. Even now I blush and grow hot at the thought of the apparent cruelty. Yet the incentive was the love for these small creatures and the wish to possess them. We did not think that we did wrong. Elsa had a canary, and we all tried to look after it, sometimes letting it out of its cage for a 'breather'.

It was while skating on our local ice-rink that I became conscious of a girl who began to interest me. She was of medium height and plumpish, but fair to look upon. I began to look out for her when skating, and I believe she began to do the same, for when we passed each other on the ice we would both blush and feel selfconscious. But she was non-Jewish and we were never introduced. Later I heard that she became a high class prostitute.

This was not the first time that I was attracted by beauty. One day, as a small boy, when mother took me to a fair, I saw a wonderful lady;

such a radiant face; such sparkling eyes and such lovely colouring. I was spellbound until I realised that she was not of flesh and blood, but just a dummy to display a dress.

My next emotional experience went very much deeper. Elsa had trained as a milliner in Riga. She had a talent and a flair for it, and when she returned to Pärnu she opened a shop of her own and did well, for there was a great demand for her hats. Because of this she needed an assistant, and engaged a girl from another town. Her name was Clara, and to me she looked beautiful, with a lovely shaped head, dark luminous eyes, regular features, and very thick dark hair. She was a little smaller than I and had a dainty figure. Needless to say, I fell in love with her, but I managed to conceal it, for who was I to fall in love with a mature girl? I was still at *Gymnasium* with a year or two to go.

I remember giving my mother a hug and a kiss when she asked me why I prowled about my room during a nice summer's day, instead of going out into the fresh air. She must have realised that I was upset, perhaps even guessed the reason. We were not a kissing family and she was surprised at my action, but I loved her dearly for her silent understanding, though I was never able to tell her so. Yes, I felt lonely, although I used to go about with friends.

I pined in silence for Clara, and watched her getting involved with an Estonian actor, a handsome fellow beside whom I felt like a boy. Only when I left Pärnu did I write her of my feelings. By then it was too late. Hesse wrote me that after receiving my letter Clara wept the whole day, for she was marrying the actor. When the German Army was approaching Tallinn during the Second World War they committed suicide, rather than end their days in a concentration camp.

My love for Clara was purely platonic, and while I felt that I loved her, I also went about with other girls. Sex was never the reason for our friendship, certainly not mine, for our conversations were usually of a cultural or political nature. It was only some years later, when I was already in Glasgow, that the force and excitement of sex gripped me.

My father had a shop where he sold watches and clocks as well as repairing them. One of its walls was completely covered with clocks of varying sizes and shapes, their pendulums swinging about 'tick tock, tick tock', but never in unison. I tried to get the pendulums to swing like soldiers on a march, not realising as a child that this was an impossibility, the pendulums being of different lengths and the works of different makes. I spent quite a lot of time in my father's workshop learning how to clean and assemble watches, and how to turn and make fine spindles for wheels. I could, if need be, have earned a livelihood as a watchmaker. I became used to handling tools, and this stood me in good stead when I decided to become a sculptor. My training had only one drawback, for having been used to watchmaker's tools, I bought similar ones for my sculpture, to find that they were far too delicate, and I had to buy stronger, heavier and more solid ones for the work I wanted to do.

My father was just above middle height, had sandy hair, with perhaps a touch of ginger, and a neatly trimmed beard. He was well read in Hebrew, Yiddish, and German; he spoke a rich Yiddish, German like a native, and Estonian and Russian well enough to carry on his business and a normal conversation. Between themselves my parents spoke Yiddish. My father knew Biblical Hebrew perfectly — Modern Hebrew had not yet come into being. He knew it so well that he could read us a story in Yiddish, yet when we wanted to read it ourselves, more than once we would discover that the original was in Hebrew. He was an instantaneous translator.

In the evenings, when we were by ourselves, or when the company was congenial, father would read us chapters from Peretz, Sholem Aleichem, Mendele Mocher Sforim, or the other authors who were then becoming great names in Yiddish literature. When father was telling a story he made you see the scene in front of you, and when he was telling something funny his acting would be so astonishing, that we would roll with laughter, tears streaming from our eyes. But many evenings were spent discussing authors and artists. I believe now that it was because of these discussions that my interest in Art grew and flowered.

Father was very religious and wished that his children should also remain observant Jews. He tempered his religion by not forcing it upon us, but hoped that we would follow his example. We had in our living room a whatnot which was stacked with huge books of the *Talmud,* and which were constantly handled as reference books. One was badly fingered from my constant study of it. We also had a beautifully written miniature Scroll of the Law, with ivory handles, in a small case fixed to the wall, which has become an heirloom, being passed down from eldest son to eldest son.

Father was by inclination a poet. He wrote poetry in Hebrew and Yiddish, and wrote plays for children to be performed at our Festivals, but he was never ambitious to have them published. Perhaps, had we lived in a Jewish town, and been in contact with other intellectuals, he might have been encouraged to go in for literature more seriously. But in Pärnu he was isolated and had no one to guide him and no one to talk to about his writing. My own time, except for the vacations, had been fully taken up with my studies to gain a medal in my finals. As it was, I should have taken a greater interest in his literary work, for I was already myself writing verse in Russian, whilst Jeannot and Maxie had different interests. The difficulty was, of course, that I seldom saw his efforts. I was too shy to ask him to let me read them, and he only lived seven years after my last visit to Pärnu. The sorrow over the loss of

Maxie, then the loss of our mother, and in a way me also, may have been too much for him to bear. Nothing remains of his writing, or of my own early poetry.

At the turn of the century, Russia still suffered from terrible illiteracy. Only an estimated five per cent of the population were able to read and write. The Russian intelligentsia began to rumble and bestir themselves. University students began to visit villages in their spare time, and during the vacations, to teach the peasants the 'three R's'. The unrest intensified, but little was done by the Government, for at that time it was preparing for the 1904-5 war with Japan, which was a disaster for Russia.

I remember well the coloured illustrations in newspapers and magazines of the battles, where the Japanese were always represented as defeated and running away. Yet in reality the reverse was the case. I have lived through three major wars, and have seen that wars have unforeseen consequences and side effects.

The Russo-Japanese war was followed by the first Russian Revolution in 1905. It could not succeed because the Russian army, although no match for the Japanese, was powerful enough to quell with great barbarity, the revolutionaries who were unprepared and insufficiently armed to fight the army. Army units and Cossacks even came to Pärnu, and I heard that quite a few local men were marched to a field near the sea and shot. One day I was walking on the pavement of a narrow and quiet street, when suddenly I saw coming towards me a company of mounted Cossacks. My heart leapt into my mouth, for I was afraid that one of them might playfully swipe me with his *knout,* but they passed by and I sighed with relief.

We students had many discussions about the political situation. The Russian intelligentsia were in favour of political reform and gaining some say in the running of the Government. The Jewish intelligentsia sided with them. During the Revolution the Jews mounted the barricades in support of the non-Jews. It was their belief that by helping to free the masses, their own lot would also be improved.

This ideology ran parallel to the growth of Jewish Nationalism which was being fanned to a bright flame through the emergence of Hebrew and Yiddish literature and a Jewish Press. It took a long time for the French Revolution to trickle through to the Jewish Ghettos, and the hope of returning to Palestine was taking root and gaining strength. The pogroms helped to give it direction. History has always affirmed that when the time was ripe for a certain movement, a man would surely appear to lead it. In this case that man was Herzl. In our town my father became the leader of Zionism, the word derived from 'Zion', the name of a hill on which Jerusalem is built. Our home became the gathering place for discussions and talks about Zionism, and I listened with open ears and tried to absorb all I heard. I remember the afternoon

21

when father came home weeping with the news that Herzl had died. Something also died in him that day, but his striving and urge did not diminish. It was sustained by a slow and determined will and a spiritual fire that once kindled can never be extinguished. He was beginning to look old, and the strain of providing for his family was also having its effect. Had he not suffered from heart trouble I am sure he would have wished to emigrate to Palestine.

I don't remember my mother when she was young. She must have been beautiful then, for I remember her sister, who came to us to say goodbye before leaving for South Africa to join her husband, who had emigrated some years earlier. She was much younger than mother, and still looked beautiful, and the likeness was unmistakable.

Mother went about her home quietly doing her work, and never raising her voice. I never heard her shout at us, even when we deserved it, and when we were playing she would run an errand herself instead of asking one of us to stop for her sake. She was the driving force behind our education, for her mind was alert and active, and she lived for her children, to see them well educated and set up in life.

Her life was not an easy one, and she had lost her bloom before I began to take note of people and their looks. Every morning she was the first to get up to go to the market and bring back provisions for the day. She never had a housekeeping allowance as such, but every morning she would take from my father's trouser pocket whatever money she felt she would need. This was an accepted practice in our home, and it seemed to work well enough. I have a suspicion that father left in his pocket just the amount, or perhaps a little more than mother required. The market was a good distance from our home, and she had to carry the heavy load all by herself. When I had my vacations I used to go with her or would go later to help her bring her purchases home. In later life, when it became too difficult for her, she would hire a *droshky* to bring her home.

I was a bit of a dreamer, and it was mother who, when she noticed this, decided to encourage me to read. At first I found it difficult to concentrate, but gradually reading took hold of me, and I was seldom without a book in my hand. Poetry was my favourite subject, then biographies of poets, writers and artists. I was proud of mother, for I realised how observant she was, although she tried not to show it.

My mother's father died from having contracted dysentry while helping the sick during an epidemic. I do not remember him myself, but from the stories I heard about him he was a tall, fine looking and impressive man, and we had a small photograph of him on metal, wearing his prayer shawl. One day an artist came to our town, and hired an empty shop next to father's. When father showed the artist the little photograph of grandfather, he was captivated by it. He asked father's permission to enlarge it, saying that it would bring him many customers. I don't know what method he used for the enlargement, but it looked like a charcoal drawing. It was beautifully executed, true to life, and about life size. As arranged, he displayed it in his window. Mother knew nothing about it, for father wanted to give her this enlargement as a surprise gift. But things don't always work out the way one expects or anticipates.

Some friends who had known grandfather hurried post haste to tell mother of the wonderful portrait they had seen. Hardly believing the story, mother put on her coat and hat, and went to see it for herself. When she reached the window she burst out crying, for true enough, it was her father to the life. A few of her friends had stopped to comfort her, and in no time quite a crowd had gathered round the window. Father looked out, saw the commotion, and went to investigate the reason. Then, and only then, did he see mother standing there weeping. He took her in his arms, and led her into his own shop to comfort her, disappointed that his surprise had miscarried.

Later the portrait was hung in our drawing room. I discovered that grandfather was looking straight at me, no matter where I stood in the room. So long as I could see his face, the eyes followed me. I could not understand it, or how it was achieved, and it fascinated me. This drawing is one of the few things that my sister Hesse brought from home.

I often wonder what happened to a violin that used to hang near it. Instead of the usual scroll it terminated in a lion's head, from whose open jaws protruded a long red tongue curling downwards. I wondered about it, but never asked father how he came by it. It hung as a decoration only, for nobody played it, and I have never seen its like since.

When I was young, there was no compulsory education in Russia. Of course there were some elementary schools, but tuition had to be paid for. My parents, especially my mother, did not believe in sending their children to school too early. Mother felt that a child should be given time to play and develop before being harnessed to school routine. It was also the general practice to send a child to the *Gymnasium* when he was about nine or ten. *The Gymnasium* had eight classes, so it took at least eight years to complete one's studies, and to have two *Gymnasia* in a town of only twenty thousand people was most unusual.

The Russian Government had issued an edict that only five per cent of the total number of students could be Jews. As our town had few Jews — we were only a community of sixty families — and not many took advantage of this wonderful opportunity, there was room for more Jewish students from elsewhere to make up the five per cent of the *numerus clausus*. Quite a few students from different parts of Russia came to study in our *Gymnasia*. Among those were the brothers Steinberg, the elder of whom became a minister in Kerensky's first

23

Cabinet in 1917 between the fall of the Tsar and the Bolshevik Revolution. Jeannot gave them private lessons. My brother was a brilliant student and won the gold medal with his leaving certificate, which made it simple for him to get into the University of Riga. I lacked his memory and did not do so well.

Although our secular education began when we were nine, it was different with our Hebrew and religious education. A child began to learn the Hebrew alphabet at five. Well do I remember the day when I mastered it, and the teacher who used to come to our home called my father in to hear me repeat the letters of the alphabet one by one. Suddenly a coin fell on the book from which I was reading. Surprised, I looked up and asked father where it came from. "From Heaven," he replied. I have heard many stories about Heaven, but I had never heard that it dropped money!

But how could I doubt father's word? He would never tell me a lie; so I looked up to the ceiling, and true enough, there was a crack in it right above me, and the coin *must* have fallen through it. This was my first experience of miracles, and I have good reason to believe in them to this day. In my long life I have witnessed many singular happenings, both to myself and to my people.

I was not a healthy child, and would frequently get a sudden attack of sickness which our doctor could not diagnose. Because the attack would pass as quickly as it came, by the time doctor arrived he could find no symptoms.

One time I was ill for some days. Being alone I fretted and periodically cried. Elsa, returning to her shop after lunch, promised to bring me a peppernickel cake when she would come home. These were small flat brown cakes stamped out in the shape of people or animals, and decorated with lined icing in different colours. They looked ravishing and their taste was cool and refreshing. That afternoon seemed endless and I cried almost all the time waiting for my sister's return. Mother was sympathetic and did not scold me for crying; she was worried, I suppose, for she did not leave me by myself.

When Elsa at last arrived I jumped up in my bed to receive her promised present, but when I looked at the peppernickel and held it in my hand, something strange took hold of me. I was thinking "Is this what I was crying for all afternoon?" I was almost ashamed of myself. It had lost its magic and seemed commonplace and worthless. I lay back in my bed empty and defrauded. I think this was the last time I ever cried when ill for something to take my mind off my illness. It cured me from wishing for things in case they cheated me like the peppernickel cake had done.

I spoke to my parents in German. In Liefland, the name of our region at that time, German was spoken extensively, as many Germans, mostly of noble lineage, had settled there centuries before, living in Pärnu

24

and its environs. To speak German was a sign of a cultured person, of gentility. The signs over the shops were usually in three languages; Russian on the top, since it had become the official language; then below, the sign was in German; and only below the German was the inscription in Estonian, the native language of the country. Even the town was renamed Pernov to sound Russian. Hence the three names of our town, Pernov, Pernau, Pärnu.

When I was nine years old, I realised the incongruity of I, a Jew, speaking to my parents in German! I was suddenly struck by the falseness of the situation. After that I began to speak to them in Yiddish. Strange to say, my parents took it quite naturally and never remarked on the change. They probably accepted it as right and proper. Perhaps they felt that I was beginning to grow up to be a Jew. Of course, it may have had to do with the birth of Zionism that fired us with a new found idealism. I began to read our Yiddish poets and literature that had then started to flourish.

When a circus used to visit the town, and it did so every year, we children used to play at circuses. When a fire occurred in the town we played at being firemen. We devised all kinds of games to keep us busy. When I entered the *Gymnasium* all this ended at a stroke. Classes were from eight a.m. till two in the afternoon, and we had to study hard at home. We also made new friends and developed different interests. We grew away from our former playmates, most of whom were not sent to the *Gymnasium* as we were.

A uniform was compulsory — a black jacket with an upstanding military collar, a broad leather belt, and black trousers. Some sported a white frill which projected a quarter of an inch from the collar and cuffs. The overcoat was of military grey, and at night soldiers would mistake us for officers and salute us when passing on the opposite side of the street, and we would salute back, not to confuse them.

With the Revolution of 1905-7 began the revival of Estonian nationalism and a revival of the Estonian language. I had only a smattering of it, sufficient to talk to our maid, but I began to hear it spoken more openly at school among the Estonian students, and they even started to write poetry in it.

The Germans always behaved as if they were in a class above the rest of the population. The German students always kept themselves apart from the rest, as if they were noblemen — and some were. We, the Jewish students did not count at all. There were only a few in each class, and we fell between the two factions, the Estonians and the Germans.

When I try to recall my school days they seem to be bathed in a hazy mist. I used to study fairly diligently, but my memory would retain little after a month or two. Mathematics was my favourite subject. In later years I realised that my memory was a pictorial one, and if anything made a deep impression on me it remained there forever vividly and clearly etched, and some of my teachers come back to me in my vision, and I even remember some of the lessons they had given because on those occasions the teachers themselves loved their subject and were inspired.

Our history teacher was of middle height and corpulent, slightly bald, and with a ruddy complexion. We suspected that he was fond of vodka, for he was not always sober when he entered our class. Yet, he would hold our attention with stories of heroes and adventures, and having the gift of oratory, kept us spellbound. He was among our favourites.

For some reason, when I think of our Latin teacher, I see first his coat of blue, with two rows of brass buttons. It must have been new, for teachers also had to wear a uniform. I remember him only because on one occasion he tried to explain how great a poet Virgil was, by reciting some lines in which Virgil, in words, simulated the sound of weeping, of sorrow. This I remember because at the time I was already beginning to write poetry.

I had a secret admiration for our Russian teacher. He was younger than the others and had newer ideas. He was tallish, thin, and with auburn hair. A bachelor, he would invite a few of us at a time to his rooms for afternoon tea, to talk to us and to get to know us better.

The one every student disliked was the teacher of German. I still see him walking, his bulky body slightly bent forward, his head heavy and square, and I doubt if a smile ever lit up his face. It seems strange to me, that although mathematics and geometry were my favourite subjects, that teacher is one of the few I cannot recall.

My drawing teacher looked like an artist, but there his teaching ability terminated. He taught us little; squares to draw by hand; cubes; circles and spheres; nothing freehand, and nothing to inspire one. No wonder I was weak in drawing when I finished the *Gymnasium*.

I remember a drawing one German student was showing another after class. I happened to be standing not far away, and saw it clearly. I heard the student say to his pal, "Isn't it strong?" At that time I could not make out what the drawing represented, but true enough, it was strong, and I could not forget it. Years later, when I already knew a great deal about sculpture, and some of the fragments to be seen in an art school, I realised what the student had drawn. It was a plaster cast of a clenched hand holding a rod, seen from the top, the rod represented by a circle. I wonder what became of that boy. Did he become a painter or a sculptor? I must have already then been drawn to art, otherwise this incident would not have made such a deep impression on me. I felt frustrated, even envious, that I could not examine the drawing at close quarters and ask about it. I was too timid, for I am sure the student would have been pleased to show it to me.

We had a nice Synagogue with two rows of octagonal wooden pillars supporting the high roof, which were placed on either side of the wide entrance right up to the steps of a small area, leading to the Ark containing the Bible Scrolls. In the centre of the Synagogue was a *Bima* — a rostrum with a reading desk — which served for the reading of the weekly portion of the *Torah*. There was a rectangular porch to allow worshippers to shake the snow from their garments in the winter, or the rain in the summer, before entering, which formed a recess on either side in the Synagogue itself. The one on the left had a big table with benches around three sides where pious Jews could study the Bible or the *Talmud,* and where a vagabound Jew might find shelter for the night. We all sat on hard benches, the floor being sprinkled with sand, but on High Festivals with straw. There were large brass spittoons at every bench, and in front of each pew was a long reading desk broad enough for one's prayer book.

Pious Jews believe that on the Day of Atonement one is inscribed in the Book of Life or Death. We read it in our prayers and this idea becomes absorbed by us with our mother's milk. The Jewish religion believes in Destiny, not Fate. The word *Fate* falls from peoples' lips without their giving it much thought. Fate is final, unalterable, and irrevocable, but Man can shape his destiny and even change it by 'Penitence, Prayer, and Charity' — at least this is what we read in our prayers. It was Martin Buber, the famous philosopher — he did not believe in organised religion — who corrected me when I used the term Fate instead of Destiny. Perhaps this is why Jewish prayers are so long and repetitive.

It was during one of our prayers of supplication that my father burst out sobbing and weeping. I must still have been very young, for there I was, standing beside him, almost ashamed, wondering what it was all about. I felt that all eyes must be turned towards him, and finally took courage to look out from behind to see. But no, nobody was looking, for everyone was busy with their own prayers, some weeping like father.

When I was a little older and began to understand the meaning of prayer and my father's belief in its sanctity and purification, his weeping became clear to me. As I was then already doing some modelling I said to myself "Were I a sculptor, how I would wish to portray this scene: the father praying and weeping, his small son looking up at him in wonderment and with a questioning gaze."

Now and again, after I became a sculptor, this idea would persist, and on one occasion I was given a huge trunk of oak by Lady Lithgow to carve this subject. Yet each time I shrank from the undertaking, feeling that I was not ready for the task. Ultimately I did model it on a small scale and made two versions in terra cotta, when I was still bound by the classical tradition. I modelled the boy nude in contrast to the completely draped figure of the old man, but I realise that it was not right to model the boy thus, and I believe that I could now produce a better work by dressing him.

How could I dream that perhaps seventy-five years later I would myself shed tears while reciting the same prayer but *my* son, being already a grown man, was no longer beside me.

The Sunday before our Day of Atonement, the Jewish women, or those who were pious, would go to the cemetery to 'measure' it. They would bring with them a ball of thin cotton thread, which they would unwind, measuring the inside of the cemetery fence with it till they had circumscribed the whole area. This thread was then used for the wicks of wax candles, the thread being doubled or trebled depending on the size of the candles to be made. The women rolled softened wax round the wicks by hand, to be sure that the candles were properly made.

This custom of measuring cemeteries may stem from superstition, and may be an appeal to the Almighty that the cemetery should not increase its dead during the coming year.

The days of our calendar are counted from sunset to sunset, and so our holiest of Holy Days, our *Yom Kippur* begins in the evening. In the afternoon, the women would come to the Synagogue and place the candles they had made in trays specially provided for the occasion. There was always room for every candle, and before the service began they would be lit. They made a lovely sight. On one occasion, a candle that was near the centre — it may have been a little taller than the rest — bent over and gutted out. The heat from the other candles may have done it, or it might not have been properly made. Whatever the reason, there it stood, its top half bent over and lifeless. A terrible commotion arose among the women when they noticed this, for to them it meant a death during the year, in the family to whom the candle belonged. As it happened, the father of the house did die that year, but who knows whether he died from a natural illness, or whether the superstition was so great and so deeply rooted in his own heart that he had to die. To the community, the reason for his death did not matter, their superstition was justified and corroborated.

One family was generally disliked. They had two sons who were boorish and coarse, and few people had anything to do with them. For some time they had a store in our yard, and I used to see them cut up large sheets of metal on the ground with chisel and hammer. They may have been second hand metal dealers. A match had been arranged between one of the sons and a girl from Russia, probably by a *Shadchan* — a matchmaker, and I would not have been surprised to learn that they had never met, or seen one another beforehand. She was a beautiful girl, with a charming oval face, dark hair and flashing eyes, elegant and genteel, not the right type of girl for this gross and stupid man. She must have felt very lonely.

28

We began to hear stories about trouble between them, and that he ill treated her. Finally it came to the point where she could no longer stand the life. She had a nervous breakdown, and decided to return to her parents, an unprecedented step in those days, for a divorce among Jews was then rare. I heard that when she was stepping on to the boat to take her to Riga, she cursed her husband and said that dogs would lick his blood from the gutter. A year or two later, the husband had a quarrel with a *moujick* who stabbed him to death. He fell into the gutter and lay there till the police arrived to remove the body.

This episode made the people even more superstitious than they were already, and I shuddered later when I once saw a batch of prisoners march past our home, with shackles at their ankles, their chains loudly clanking.

Once I was standing at my father's shop door, waiting for him to return from an errand. It was winter, and the horses were drawing sledges, for the streets were thick with snow and ice. The snow from the footpaths would be brushed on to the roads as much as possible, but nobody worried about the roads themselves, for they would be tramped down gradually by the hooves of the horses and the sledges. As I was standing there a peasant from the country was driving past on top of his sledge, which was well loaded. He may have seen something in a shop window, for he shouted to his horse to stop. What happened next I did not see, for it took place so quickly. The horse may have stopped too suddenly, or raised its head high, for the man must have pulled at the reins. Perhaps the driver was not sitting securely on top of the load, for he fell backwards, hitting his head sharply on the ice. He continued holding the reins, but within seconds his face became purple and his limbs began to curl up toward his body. In death he resembled the shape of a baby in the womb. It was some time before a policeman arrived grumbling and cursing at the carelessness of the victim, and with the help of others managed to pile him on top of his sledge and drive him away.

In Estonia and in Russia death was commonplace and hardly a day passed without a massacre here or a tragedy there. One's senses were blunted by the constant repetition of violence and murder. A revolution had just been put down with extreme brutality, and we Jews were familiar with death — the pogroms were still fresh in our minds. I mentioned the accident to my father when he returned, but I doubt whether I told anyone else. It was of interest to nobody, because he was a peasant from the country, unknown, and only his family would miss him.

On another occasion a woman had been completely dismembered, and her head was displayed in a window to see if anyone could identify the victim. I saw it accidentally, but by then my reactions were not so intense, for I was already modelling, and had modelled a death mask of

29

our servant who died when a local woman had given her a fateful abortion. This time I looked at the head with an 'anatomical' eye, and studied the face and features, and their formation at close range.

I was present at only one Jewish funeral in Pärnu. The dead person though poor, was well liked, and as many as could went to the cemetery and followed the horse drawn hearse. The grave was shallow, two feet six inches deep, if that much, and a plain board was laid at the bottom. The body, wrapped in a shroud, was carried in by a few men and laid in the grave. An upright board, projecting perhaps two feet above the ground was placed at the head of the grave to mark it, and then, after two shards of pottery were placed over the eyes, the grave was filled in.

When it had been fully covered, the beadle of the Synagogue came forward and knocked on the upright board. He bent low and called out to the buried corpse, "Reb Yossel, I have to tell you that you are now dead. You are no more a member of our Community, and you are no more a member of our *Shool* and of our Congregation. Don't come back to disturb us, and we wish you a long and peaceful sleep till the coming of the Messiah". I could never forget such a trauma.

When Ben Zvi, the second President of Israel died, and was to be buried in a coffin, there arose a great outcry from the ultra religious group in Jerusalem. The controversy was only resolved when holes were drilled in the bottom of the coffin so that earth could come in contact with the body — "From dust to dust". I happened to be in Jerusalem at the time.

Our Minister, Reverend Bassel, and his wife had six children, four girls and two boys. One of the girls had a keen and lively imagination and occasionally she would seat herself on a chair in the middle of their room, with us younger ones crowded round her on the floor. She would then tell us fairy tales. She would look straight ahead, as if she was seeing vividly what she was describing to us. I am sure she made up most of the stories herself, for she never told us the same ones twice. I can still recall the scene in their home as we sat round her, enchanted by her tales, and see the two live lions on either side of the throne on which the king or the prince sat, and the two eagles perched on the back, waiting to do their bidding. I remember little of her stories, but they stimulated my imagination, and fed my constant daydreams.

Their eldest daughter was a cigarette maker. Cigarettes could be bought in shops, but those who wanted a special brand of tobacco had to have them made. She sat in front of her small table, a narrow strip of paper attached at one end to its top, her movements so swift and sure that I cannot recall how she pushed the tobacco into the holders. The cigarettes had a long mouthpiece and a small piece of cotton wool to absorb some of the nicotine. However she had to give up this work, for the inhaling of the tobacco dust injured her lungs. In those days in

Pärnu girls usually stayed at home to help their mother, or waited till a suitor came along to marry them. It was the exception for a girl to take up a profession.

My father smoked about forty cigarettes a day, and would order a box of 500 at a time. When I turned seventeen, father, not wishing that I should smoke surreptitiously, said to me, "Benno, here are my cigarettes, smoke for a week and then decide whether you want to smoke or not". The week was hardly over when I decided not to. I only took up smoking again later on in Glasgow.

Reverend Bassel was of middle height, unassuming, insignificant looking, with dark hair and a fair sized straggling beard. He was of a quiet disposition which belied his knowledge and wisdom. Father soon discovered this, and they became firm friends, for they had a great deal in common and enjoyed discussions of the Bible and the *Talmud.*

Reverend Bassel occasionally went to private houses to kill a fowl, but the usual practice was for the housewife to go to the Reverend's house with the bird, which he killed in his own backyard. I had seen a number of ritual killings, and as I knew this was necessary it did not affect me very much. The Reverend would take the bird under his arm, take hold of its comb and pull its head slightly back, pull some feathers off its neck, and whilst reciting a prayer would cut the neck with the ritual knife, severing its jugular artery and nerve. When released from the Reverend's arm the bird would fall to the ground, usually dead.

One day, when the Reverend's younger son and I were present, the cockerel was dropped to the ground, but it was not dead. Far from it. It rose, and began to run round the yard frantically, its head held high. I looked on with incredulity. It must have run round the perimiter of the yard several times before the loss of blood made it drop to the ground. From that day, nay, from that moment, the minister's small son resolved to become a vegetarian, and so he remained to the great worry, inconvenience, and annoyance of his mother, who had to provide suitable food for his nourishment and health.

It was an echo out of the past, when in 1955 I received a letter from one of the daughters telling me that she was married and that she and her husband had finally settled in Israel. I was then holding a one man show of my sculpture in Jerusalem, but as she was a postmistress in an outlying district she could not come to see me. As my own time was limited, unhappily we never met, though my sister Hesse corresponded with her for some years afterwards.

My brother Maxie was called up to the army when war broke out in 1914, and he was killed on the Austrian front in the winter of 1915. His body was never found. Mother did not get over his death. From the day he left to join the army she had a premonition that she would never see him again and would shed tears most of the time. She died eighteen

31

months later in 1917. There is no doubt in my mind that she died of a broken heart.

It was Jeannot, in London at the time, who received the cable announcing mother's death. It added "Tell Benno". My brother took it literally and arrived in Glasgow to see me. It was only when we were in my room that he gave me the news. He told me that when he read the cable he gave a great shout. My reactions were different. They numbed me but my emotions grew and grew. They did not take hold of me all at once. I felt the loss grow and it lacerated my heart, and even to this day the wound is open and it hurts. I have heard women say when a friend died, "May she be a good pleader for me before the Almighty". Did my mother plead my cause, and did she bless me, just as our father used to bless us children?

I remember well how father used to bless me. I would be called out of the room, and he would lay his hands on my head, pray for a while and then pronounce the benediction. This he would do once a year on the Eve of the Day of Atonement, and because of its rarity it would make a deep impression upon me, for I believed in its power and felt sanctified, thankful and redeemed. And father, laying his hands upon my head, his prayers quietly recited, made me feel in union with him in spirit, in reverence and love. To this day I see him towering above me, his gaze spiritual, for he believed in his blessing, and just as Jacob, our forefather, believed in receiving his father's blessing, so did I.

Father died in 1920, and by that time Reverend Bassel had already left Pärnu. They never lost touch with one another, and used to correspond and meet occasionally. When on his deathbed father expressed a wish to see him, he came without delay, by overnight train, and was in good time to talk to father before he died. I often wondered what they talked about. Did he administer the Last Rites? Every devout Jew knows some of it by heart, for he recites it three times a day, if he says his prayers, but father would have wanted it done properly, and by one he respected and who was a true believer.

When father took his fatal illness it began with a cold. Both Elsa and Hesse begged him not to go to the Synagogue, for it was cold, being early spring, but he insisted, and returned much worse. He developed pneumonia, and told my sisters that Mama would come on the Wednesday to take him with her. Each day he would ask what day it was, and when Wednesday came they tried to cheat him by telling him it was Thursday, but he was not going to be fooled, for in the evening he died.

Not having been at their deathbeds I remember them exactly as I had known them when I left for Glasgow in 1913, never to return. There is a sentimental song that was very popular in my young days, *A Brievele zur Mame* — A Letter to Mother — but for me it was a reproach, for after the War broke out, when it took a few months for a letter to reach its destination, if it did, I hardly ever wrote home. I have more than a guilty conscience over this unaccountable lapse. I would put off writing, although in my mind I lived with my parents most of the time.

I had begun to model before my teens, although I had never seen a real piece of sculpture except in reproductions in magazines or on postcards. Once we had a visitor from Germany, and the talk turned to Art. Father mentioned to him my modelling attempts, and asked me to bring in one of my efforts. Father was pleased with my progress and wanted to impress his visitor. Naturally I brought in my latest work, the head of an old Jew, his beard blown to the side by the wind. I could see the visitor's condescending smile change to a serious expression, and he began to talk to me about symmetry. The face of my Jew might not have been mirror-sided — what person's face is? But he was probably referring to the beard, not realising that I had done this to indicate the blowing of the wind. I stood silent, not wishing to explain or argue, and to this day I dislike to argue, talk, or to explain my work.

I remember well the first head I modelled. It was under life size, and when I had it completed and dried, I placed it on our mantlepiece to study it better. Only then did I begin to look at people and compare them with what I had modelled. The first thing I discovered was that my face was flat, and that the ears were too near the front, just round the corner, as I said to myself, not at all as in reality. This was my first lesson in observation.

In later years, when I began to study sculpture seriously, and came across Zadkine's early Cubistic heads, they were exactly like my first attempt. This made me wonder whether he carved them thus because he knew no better, or that Cubism was an escape from serious study, and from reproducing nature accurately. Later, his work, and the movement he and others had created in sculpture — Cubism, and I am not concerned with the movement in painting which preceded it — developed into a cerebral and theoretical exercise, upon which they were able to invent and superimpose a philosophy to explain their creations.

But I, my aim being to reproduce nature, realised my mistake. I saw that a head was not square, that a face is not flat, and that the ear is fairly far round to the side. So to soften the clay in order to remodel the head I put it into a tub full of rainwater, that stood outside our back door. When I went to retrieve it the next day, there was no head. It had dissolved in the water. This was my second lesson, but this time it was about my material. I discovered that clay disintegrates in water, and that a different method was needed to soften it. I had to learn from experience, and this empirical way has been mine throughout my whole artistic life.

The last house in which I lived in Pärnu was single storied and rambling. It had a common yard with smaller houses which faced ours across it. Next to our house was a monumental sculptor's workshop. All the work was done inside by hand, but in the summer, when weather permitted, the big doors onto the yard were opened, and I could watch the men at work.

I would spend hours watching them cut holes in a block of granite, about four inches apart, with long chisels, and when they had reached near the bottom, drive in long round wooden pegs which they would water. The pegs would gradually absorb the water, swell, and the granite would split in two. I saw them sharpen their chisels, harden and anneal them in a shallow tray of water — what a hissing noise they made — chisel the granite into a fairly smooth surface, then smooth them further with a combination of heavy scraping irons fixed to a long handle, and finally polish them, shape them into tombstones and make them ready for the inscription.

The master mason had a front shop facing the street, with a door for customers, and a window in which to display his work. One day I saw him carve an inscription on a small marble tombstone inside the window in view of passers by. I stood spellbound and could not go away, watching the expert way and the ease and sureness of his touch with which he cut the letters. Little did I think that one day I would be able to emulate him, and keep my students entranced likewise.

I wonder sometimes, whether living beside a sculptor's yard influenced me in my choice of profession. I might have taken up painting, for I used to stand glued to the window of a shop that sold paints and paper, being fascinated by the twirls of the different colours displayed on a white porcelain palette. But the clay I needed for modelling was at hand in the yard, at the end where the ground rose, and only had to be dug up, while colours had to be bought, as well as paper or canvas. I was not a demanding boy, and my frequent illnesses taught me patience. We were really never given pocket money as such, and I never thought of asking father for paint and paper, and so reveal my hidden desires, although I am sure he would have been glad to know that I was interested in painting, and would have bought me all I needed.

As a young boy I was fond of reading the *Talmud* and the Prophets, and I would recite them aloud with their cantillations, and mother, hearing me, would say lovingly, "Benele, you will be a Rabbi". But later when I had begun to model, she soon realised that my bent was in another direction, and accepted that I would not follow the path that she originally thought I would.

When I finished at the *Gymnasium* in 1911, I failed to obtain a silver medal, since I was only given a pass in German in my examination, although it was almost my mother tongue. At the time it seemed a terrible blow, for the whole direction of my life changed. It was therefore obvious that I would have difficulty in obtaining a place in a Russian University. Also, I had not decided what profession to follow. Sculpture, as a profession, had not entered my mind.

As a stop gap I applied to the Mathematical Faculty at Dorpat, later called Tartu. I was fond of mathematics, and thought that as not many Jewish students went in for it, I might have a chance of a place there. I did not realise that as far as the Government was concerned, the faculty did not matter, just the total number of Jewish students.

However, because students entering a university were given seven years deferment from military service, it was destined that I should go abroad to study. Russia was not blind to what was happening in Europe, and could see signs that a war was soon inevitable. She therefore decided to curtail the deferment of students by a year, for she needed to train officers for the army. This meant that many students had to abandon their university studies and join the forces, which lowered the total number of Jewish students who could be admitted. I was number twenty seven, but only twenty five were admitted! This made my going abroad imperative, and so my odyssey began.

Interlude

Interlude

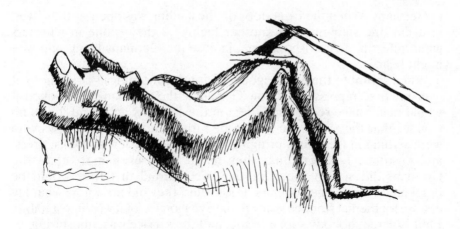

Most of the Jewish students who could not get into a Russian University, went to study in Germany, usually to Heidelberg, for Law or Medicine. Very few went in for Engineering, the faculty I finally decided upon.

My idea was to go to Zurich to study. Switzerland was famous as a centre for manufacturing watches, and having been trained in a watch-maker's workshop I imagined that I might be able to get part time work to augment my allowance from home. On the journey abroad I met a former student from Pärnu *Gymnasium*, Moses Seidelberg, who hailed from Riga, and who was well known to our family. He had been studying in Heidelberg for some years, and was very much aware of what was happening in Europe.

When I explained to him my reason for going to Zurich, he disillusioned me and told me that I would have no chance of finding the work I was anticipating. He advised me to go to Darmstadt in Germany where there was an important Technical College 'Die Grossherzogliche Technische Hochschule', famous for its Engineering Department. I therefore took his advice and changed my plans. I had to do so without consulting my family, as I felt it unwise, because of the expense, to stay in Berlin till I could communicate with home and receive their approval. So I found myself in Darmstadt and not in Zurich. I don't remember what reaction my first letter home created, for they certainly did not expect to receive one from Darmstadt. This was my first exercise in making quick decisions for myself, and it gave me a feeling of independence and courage, and I had many occasions to use it afterwards without regret.

I arrived in Darmstadt in October — I still have my matriculation card dated 27th October 1911, and I found lodgings with an old lady and her daughter who turned out to be Jewish. I discovered this when I lit candles for *Chanucah* — our Festival of Lights — and when they saw it, they revealed themselves. I realised then that anti-semitism was rife

39

in Germany. When the front door on the landing was open — they lived in a flat one stair up with another facing — they spoke in whispers when referring to Jewish matters, in case the Germans living opposite might hear.

When I went to the Synagogue on Saturday mornings I could not get over my first impression of how Germanic the German Jews looked. I would never have recognised them in the street as Jews, and it was no wonder that they were the first to be furious at the Russian Jews who were settling in Germany, bringing with them their Jewish looks, dress, and customs. I believe that they hated them even more than the Germans did at that time, for they were afraid that they would be bracketed with the newcomers. Poor souls, they did not know what lay in store for them. I stopped going to the Synagogue, for it was inhospitable, I felt isolated, nobody spoke to me, and the service was uninspiring.

Although the local German dialect was harder and more gutteral than the one I knew, I was able to follow the lectures without difficulty. As was natural, the German students took pride of place in the classes, and we, foreigners or Jews, had to take what places were left vacant. I considered that this was quite in order, and none of us ever grumbled, but it told me one thing, that my eyesight was not as good as it should be, for my place was usually high up right at the back of the class.

The German students' chief pastime was fencing, and they all belonged to fencing clubs and had rival fencing matches. Many of the students had disfiguring cuts on their faces, but these were considered marks of valour and honour. These students were regarded by the others with great respect almost amounting to veneration, and even the professors spoke to them with deference. They were the heroes in the university whom the others wished to emulate. Their scars made me think of the tribal marks on the faces of primitive peoples. But the German students were anything but primitive, for they were schooled for war, for courage, for efficiency and leadership, and the Government backed the clubs, encouraging them and allowing them various privileges.

In our college there were display cabinets in the corridors along the walls, where all kinds of mechanical instruments were on display. In one of them was a mobile gun, the barrel of which was probably about four inches in diameter. One day the Military came and took it away. You should have heard the language of the professor, who was furious at its removal. But the Military knew what they were doing, for it was already Spring 1912, and they were preparing for the 1914-18 War. They could not know when war might break out, but they had to be prepared well ahead of time, not to arouse suspicion.

One day, while in my bed-sitter studying, everything began to shake. I could not think what was happening, for I had never experienced anything similar. I jumped up and stood in the middle of the room, my hands stretched out, to prevent the wardrobe and the chest of drawers, which faced one another in the narrow room, from toppling over. It lasted only a few moments and then everything became stable again. I resumed my studies and forgot all about it. When I arrived at the Technical College the following morning, the whole place was agog with excitement, for Darmstadt had experienced a mild earth tremor, and the professor later explained to us the seismographic reading it had registered.

My sister Elsa married her childhood sweetheart, Nanu Lewin (the son of our first neighbours in Pärnu) during my stay in Darmstadt. I could not afford the time away from my studies, nor the cash to return home for the wedding, but wrote her a poem in German, which was read out at the celebration, and was received with great delight by all the family.

I grew a beard, untrimmed, wildly all over my face. I was the only student to do so, and this did not endear me to my lecturers or professors. On one occasion when the professor came into an engineering drawing class, I could see that he was ready to ask me to leave, but after exchanging words with the lecturer, or his assistant, I was allowed to remain, for he must have been told about my faultless German and my excellent work. At the time I did not know why I grew a beard, I just let it be. Years later, I began to wonder whether this was an outward expression of the subconscious unhappiness I experienced there. This was the first time I had been away from home, and I was feeling lonely and far away from the girl I had loved and lost. This revelation came to me only when youths in Britain began to grow beards and long hair as a revolt against the prevailing conditions. It dawned on me then that they also must have felt unhappy, frustrated, and disillusioned with life.

In Darmstadt I visited an Art Gallery for the first time in my life. I don't remember what my anticipations and feelings were as I entered the Gallery. It seemed a simple and natural thing to do, although I did not know what to expect.

It was only when I was inside the building that I became excited as I walked around and saw the paintings and sculpture. Then I began to feel at home in the Gallery for I recognised sculpture and paintings with which I was already familiar from reproductions. To see the real thing was a revelation. Stuck's 'Amazon' which I visualised as a life-size sculpture, I found to be small and delicate, in a glass case. In the case were other pieces which I had seen in photographs in magazines and on postcards, but after all these years I have only a dim recollection of them.

It was there that I saw Klinger's monument to Beethoven in variegated marbles. It occupied the centre of a gallery, but as my attention was fully taken up with the carving I don't remember whether there were any paintings on the wall of that room. I doubt it. The carving was large and imposing, but even then I was not impressed by it. It looked artificial and contrived, with too many elements which had little or nothing to do one with the other. The different marbles disturbed my vision and concentration, and when I think of it now, I must have had by then an appreciation of what was true and what was false.

The image that has remained in my memory to this day and affected me greatly was that of a middle aged woman being wheeled in an invalid chair from one painting to another. She was the only other visitor in the gallery at the time. I was studying a sculpture in a case when she stopped for a long time in front of a life-size painting of a young standing woman, and was weeping quietly whilst looking at it. The human element, the emotions of people always gripped me, and this lady in the invalid chair and the way she was moved by that painting I have never forgotten. For all I know it may have been a portrait of herself when young.

I used to think that in that Gallery I saw sculpture in the round for the first time. That is not quite true. During my years in Pärnu several Jewish Ministers had come and gone. One of these must have been very liberal in his outlook. During his stay in our town it so happened that a team of men appeared, carrying on top of their heads large boards on which were displayed half a dozen identical groups of sculpture in white Plaster of Paris. To our community's surprise our Minister bought one of these. One day on a visit to his home with my parents I saw this group at close quarters. It represented a reclining nude female and an angel hovering over her. It might have been about twelve inches long, the composition in the form of a semicircle. I looked at it, but it did not speak to me, it left me cold. Many years later I realised that it must have been 'Cupid and Psyche' by Canova, the famous Italian sculptor, in miniature reproduction. At the time I knew nothing of Greek mythology, and therefore the group had no meaning for me.

Our father used to take Hesse and me for a walk now and again on a Sunday afternoon, surprisingly enough, to the Gentile cemetery. Why, I cannot fathom, but perhaps it was his way of showing us that life is finite, and perhaps in this garden of the dead father found solace and content. It was beautifully laid out, the paths clean and tidy, the grass neatly cut and trimmed. The tombstones of marble or granite were well looked after with here and there a wreath, or a bunch of flowers at the foot. It was here that I used to see carved figures of angels or of Christ, life size, although we never stopped to study or admire them.

I used to see in a main street on my way to the Technische Hochschule a building with tall narrow windows arched at the top. They must have reached near the ceiling inside the hall, for it could only have been a hall. I wondered what building it might be, but never had the courage to ask a stranger about it. Many years later I saw a reproduction of it in a magazine. It was described as the Art Secession Gallery of Darmstadt.

In those years Darmstadt was an important centre of advanced Art, of rebellion against academic tradition. Charles Rennie Mackintosh, the Glasgow architect, and designer of the Glasgow School of Art — the first modern building in Britain — was invited to be a guest in Vienna, and to visit Darmstadt afterwards, but he died before his visit. I did not know then of its importance as a centre of Modern Art, and paid little attention to it.

When Jeannot matriculated from the Gymnasium with the Gold Medal, he was undecided on a profession. A German student with whom he was friendly was keen on Chemistry, and suggested that he should take it up also, hoping that by studying together he would benefit from my brother's brilliance, and this took him to Riga University. One day in 1907, we heard by the grapevine that the police were looking for him and that he was in hiding. His crime? His name had been found in the pocket book of a student who had been arrested. This was still the aftermath of the 1905-7 Revolution, when the Government were conducting mopping up operations, and, had he been found, it might have meant transportation to Siberia, or a long term of imprisonment.

So father got busy and arranged for him to be smuggled over the border into Germany. From Hamburg he sailed to Leith, in Scotland, and from there went to Glasgow, where we had quite a few relatives who had emigrated there some years earlier.

My parents had not seen Jeannot for four years, and feared they might never see him again, for at the time it was out of the question for them to travel to Glasgow. It was therefore decided that the next best thing was for me to visit him during my spring vacation, and later, when I returned home for the summer, to bring back news. My brother, trying to make it easier for me to enter Britain, wrote a letter in which he stated that when I came to Glasgow I would enter the Technical College there to continue my studies in Engineering, but I assumed that this was really his wish, although I had arranged things with my parents differently. This letter he intended to be shown to the Immigration authorities should difficulties arise, although in those days an immigrant only needed to have on him five pounds to be admitted to the country.

Therefore, when I started on my journey to Glasgow, it was with the intention of remaining there as my brother wrote. Hesse and I had worshipped him from childhood, walked on tiptoe when he was about, trusted in his wisdom, and I would never have thought to counter his wishes. Perhaps he also felt lonely in spite of our relatives and wanted a brother to share his student life.

Before catching the train I shaved off my beard and began to look again like my old presentable self. To save every penny I travelled in the cheapest compartment. The carriage had hard wooden benches along its sides. Straphanging in the same carriage were several groups

43

of artistes, and one group were jubilant and gloating over the way they had put the owner of a restaurant on the spot by demanding extra money before they would perform, as he depended on their entertainment for his custom. It appeared from their conversation, and the way they imitated his voice, that the restauranteur was a Jew. Nevertheless I was truly sorry that for them this mode of travel was a distasteful necessity, whilst for me it was an adventure.

Initiation

Have you ever been seasick? In the natural course of events, if you have made a long journey over the North Sea, which is seldom calm, in a ship of small tonnage, and if you are not a seasoned sailor, you will have experienced the feeling. There I was, on a tramp steamer, from Rotterdam to Leith, my bunk in the forecastle, and I the only passenger. The journey seemed interminable. I lay in my bunk almost the whole time, and was afraid to get up in case I would be sick, for I had been sick so often throughout my childhood and adolescence. I have travelled by boat many times since, and more than once wished myself dead. I used to roll about the deck feeling as though my end had come and hoping it would. Yet, as soon as I put my feet on solid ground the sickness would be forgotten, and I would be ready to repeat the voyage, hoping for calmer weather.

I had brought with me on board a bottle of brandy, but I forgot to buy a corkscrew. There I was lying with my bottle in one hand and a penknife in the other, trying painfully to cut away the cork. Needless to say, I failed. I don't remember eating during the whole journey, but when I stepped ashore there was Jeannot to greet me. I stretched out my hand with the bottle, and he was not long in opening it.

The following morning my brother started for the Technical College, but before leaving he handed me a small book dealing with some scientific subject, and a sixpenny Collins Dictionary. I wish I still had this small dictionary, for it was for me a veritable treasure trove, my companion for many years. When Jeannot returned home for lunch I had managed to get through half a page, for my knowledge of Latin helped me to discover the meaning of a word by looking up the alternative explanatory words and cross references.

From this it will have become apparent that when I arrived in Scotland I knew not a single word of English. However, after working hard in this way, and as my brother decided to speak to me only in

English, I was able to start attending classes at the Technical College after only a few weeks. The summer term had begun, and the time I spent in Darmstadt was taken into consideration. Therefore the following session I joined the second year students. But for the language, I had no difficulty with my classes. The Technical College was more practical than theoretical, unlike the Glasgow University Engineering Faculty.

When I had been in Glasgow for a couple of weeks we received a visit from a man we knew from Pärnu, who had settled in Scotland with his family. He came to invite us for a week's holiday. Then I could not yet distinguish single words in the flow of his talk. Later, when we went to his home in Lesmahagow, I was already able to make out his effusive conversation. He had changed his name to Maxwell, and had an ice cream café, and also manufactured lemonade. The bottles have now become antiques, for they had no corks, only glass pebbles. When the bottles had been filled and charged with Carbon Dioxide, the pebbles would remain under pressure in their necks to keep them closed. To open the bottle the pebble had to be pushed down. His lemonade became famous in the district, for it seemed to have a strength the other makes did not possess, and he told us his secret. Whisky was then very cheap, and he added a thimbleful to each bottle. I was surprised that such a small quantity of whisky could single out his lemonade, not that the people who drank it knew what made it better than its rivals.

Mr. Maxwell had a younger brother who joined him later in Scotland, and became a miner. He came to visit us while we were in Lesmahagow, and I could not help noticing the difference between them. Although my vocabulary was very limited, I could sense how more serious the younger brother was, and realised that he was already politically informed. Perhaps because of their life underground, miners think of life in the fresh air, but I have noticed that many miners become thinkers. Keir Hardie, whose name will live forever, sprang from the mine.

As was natural, my brother, whom I will now call Schachno — his Hebrew name which he adopted in Britain — and I were sometimes invited for meals with our relatives, and being 'green' we were being initiated into British habits. One of our uncles invited us for a Sunday dinner. When we sat down at the table it never occurred to me to look at the set of cutlery at each plate. We were rather surprised to be served with small portions of hors d'oeuvre, soup, and meat. My uncle and aunt had to go into the kitchen together and left us by ourselves for a few moments. Schachno whispered, "Benno, fill up with bread".

When our hosts returned to the table, the process of serving started all over again, but with different courses. We were being regaled with a ten course dinner, and I was full of bread!

Schachno could not forgive our Uncle Manny, with whom he had to stay for a time, for taking him to the baths when he arrived in Glasgow, probably thinking he might be dirty, and Schachno spoke to me about it often. He was a fiend for cleanliness and physical culture, and would go daily to the baths in the Gorbals to swim thirty to forty lengths of the pool. He had dumb-bells in our room, and made me use them also to keep fit.

During the weekends he used to take me for long walks, and sometimes we were accompanied by friends. The distance then seemed shorter because of the conversation and arguments on the way. We always had a goal in view, and when we reached our destination our outing was enhanced by a picnic meal and a rest in the sun before setting off for home.

Schachno was a brilliant chess player. I had also learned the game when very young, and had studied it in Pärnu, but I played only occasionally. My brother was a member of the Bohemian Chess Club, who had their rooms in The Eldon, a tearoom at the top of Renfield Street, near Sauchiehall Street. It disappeared long ago. He was placed in a special category, Class A1 all by himself. There was a time when he considered taking it up professionally, but decided that chess was only a game. Naturally, he introduced me to his chess club, where my speech did not matter, only the quality of my play. Let me warn artists against taking up chess. It is a thief of time. I must have wasted years of my life in the chess club. You may find yourself against a slow player, or against one who hates to be loser, and a game which you started just for the fun of it might become a tussle of strength, and I would throw away the game to save an hour for work. I used to play for the Bohemians in competitive matches, but my chess stopped suddenly with the outbreak of war in 1939. I had to give it up, for I had no more time for it. I had taken stock of my priorities.

Our relatives in Glasgow were two uncles and an aunt and their families, my mother's two brothers and a sister. The brothers had tailoring workshops. Not long before I arrived a tragedy had occurred in Uncle Manny's workshop. While one of the workers was machining, a mouse ran up the cloth on to the top of the sewing machine and from there on to the sleeve of the machinist. When he saw the frightened animal run up and down his arm, he called to the others to see the fun, while he held his arm outstretched. He began to laugh heartily, his mouth wide open, and the mouse suddenly seeing a hole in the man's face, jumped in. He died in a few seconds. The mouse had blocked his windpipe.

In the summer of 1912 I did not go home for my summer vacation as originally planned, for Schachno was still doing research at the Technical College during the summer, and I was trying to learn the English language. Foreigners, especially East Europeans, have difficulty in pronouncing the 'th' and the 'w' for these sounds are non-existent in their own languages. Schachno had a Jewish friend, Aaron Cantor, who was a teacher in a secondary school and who also took evening classes in English for immigrants. My brother asked him to give me a dozen private lessons, and specially to concentrate on the two sounds. Mr. Cantor, knowing the difficulty, gave up the effort after a few attempts, and it took me several years to grasp the pronunciation, though in the end I never completely succeeded. I could never forgive him for not having tried harder, for to this day I have an accent, and as soon as I speak to a stranger in Scotland the first question I am usually asked is "Where do you come from?" Sometimes, just for the fun of it, I might look at the enquirer and reply "I have lived here longer than you", knowing that because of his age I had to be right. At the beginning of the last war I was straphanging on an out of town bus beside another Scotsman. We got into conversation and he asked the same question. I simply answered that I was a Jew, for in the final analysis I discovered that this was what they really wanted to know. "Not so good these days, is it?" was his reply. I never expected such a sympathetic answer, and it moved me deeply.

In London it is different. As soon as I begin to speak I am met with the exclamation, "Ah, you come from Scotland!" Lady Epstein said to me once that she had never met a Jewish sculptor with such a Scottish accent!

This double concept of my accent revealed itself at other times. In the early days of the B.B.C., its Glasgow station was situated at the west side of Blythswood Square. My flat and studio was in West Campbell Street, a stone's throw from it. In those days I knew most of the amateur actors and their circle. The B.B.C. were going to put on a dramatisation of John Buchan's *The Thirty Nine Steps* and needed a foreigner to act the character of the German. The producer considered my accent just right for the part, and asked me if I would help them out. We all clustered round the one microphone and each of us spoke his part into it when his turn came. The producer thought that we had done a fine job, and London sent word of its approval, "But why did you not get a real foreigner to act that part?"

I went home during the summer vacation in 1913. The previous autumn Schachno had left for Zurich. For Jewish parents to have a son a doctor was their ultimate dream and aspiration, for a doctor was held in the highest esteem. He was considered not only a healer, but a cultured man to whom all doors were open. Our parents had hoped that Schachno would choose medicine as his profession, and when father suggested it to him he answered, "Father, if you want me to have the title 'Doctor' I will get it, but not in medicine".

I was left by myself, having become used to my new style of life, but was more than glad to return home to bask in the love of my family and to renew former friendships. It was a glorious summer, the last one I ever spent in Pärnu, and the days flew like lighting. I don't remember whether I did any modelling that summer. There was so much to occupy my mind and time, especially to catch up with what had been happening in literature while I was away. Today it all seems very nebulous, except that some daring novels appeared, which dealt with sex much more openly than hitherto, and a new fashion was introduced in some magazines. Poetry was printed in the poet's handwriting. This did not appeal to me, for one had to concentrate on the script, and sometimes decipher it, if it was reduced in the printing. At the same time it made one linger over it, and perhaps for that reason there was something to be said for it.

When the time came for my return to Glasgow, I travelled back in style. We got to know the captain of a steamer that was sailing from Pärnu to Leith. I was again the only passenger, but now the sea was calm, and I was the guest of the captain and his wife, and ate at their table.

By then I knew English fairly well and spent every spare moment reading. I had to make up for lost time. I knew little about the English novelists, and was reading the Classics and the poets. I had read *The Prisoner of Chillon* in a Russian translation, and when I read the original I agreed with the acknowledged opinion that the translation was superior to the original. I wondered what Byron might have thought. He had a great influence on Russian poetry, especially on Pushkin and Lermontov.

Uncle Manny's younger son Harry was not sure what trade or profession to follow on leaving school, but felt he had some talent for Art. By coincidence, I happened to be in his parents' home when he began to talk about wanting to join an evening class in drawing and painting at the Glasgow High School. Perhaps he purposely raised the subject in my prescence. There arose an argument, and to cool the atmosphere I chimed in, "Harry, I will keep you company".

We both joined the class, the only difference being that while Harry registered for drawing and painting, I asked for modelling. My teacher must have been surprised, for this was probably the first time anybody had ever asked him for modelling. He gave me a plaster cast, a mask of a child's head, and asked me to copy it. This took me a long time, but one evening, when Fra H. Newbery, the Director of the Glasgow School of Art, came into the class, the teacher brought him over to show me off, the odd one who was taking modelling.

This coincidence started me off on my life's work. I hate the word 'career' in connection with Art. It is not a career, it is a calling, a passion. It is my firm belief that if one wants something strongly enough, and one has the ability, the willpower and the stamina, one will achieve one's aim. It took me a year after coming to Glasgow to realise that all doors in Britain were open to everybody, irrespective of creed or race, and that it only depended on one's willingness to work. My cousin dropped out fairly soon for want of stamina, or attention, but my teacher urged me to continue at the Glasgow School of Art, and persuaded me to sit the Evening School test. If one was successful one had one's fees paid.

I sat my test in the evening of the day I handed in my Diploma work in the Engineering Faculty of the Technical College. I passed both, and so I started evening classes at the School of Art in the summer term of 1914, a couple of months before the declaration of the Great War.

It is strange how certain things affect one. Rather, it is not strange at all, it must be natural. I described earlier my reactions when I entered for the first time the Art Gallery in Darmstadt. Then I was cool and composed and felt that it was something that had to be there and something to be visited. I do not even remember my first visit to the Kelvingrove Art Gallery, and I must have paid it many visits during the first year of my stay in Glasgow. There were organ recitals in the Gallery in the evenings once or twice a week, and I attended those occasionally. How different was my reaction when I began to ascend the few steps leading to the entrance of the School of Art. I was deeply moved, I was so excited that I was physically trembling, as if I was about to enter a sanctified building. I tried sometimes to analyse the reason for the feeling that came over me. Was it that I felt that by passing through those portals I was entering a new world so far hidden from me, its mysteries to be penetrated and discovered, its art to be revealed?

I have only once had a similar experience which I hardly dare mention in this connection, though in time they were not far removed one from the other. It happened in the Garnethill Synagogue during one of our Festivals when we carry round our Holy Scrolls and the pious Jews dance with them in religious ecstasy after every round. At each round the Scrolls change hands, and suddenly one was thrust into mine. I was not surprised to be given one, but for some reason I became terribly excited and veritably trembled. I thought of all the pogroms we had suffered; of all the slaughters we had been through during our Dispersal; and I said to myself, "Here is the *Torah* for which we have suffered martyrdom, for which we have allowed ourselves to be slain", and yet I hugged it close to me and cherished its possession and said to it in the firm belief that it heard me, "You were worthy of all our sacrifices, of all our blood that we shed in Your Name, for You are our Divine Heritage and Revelation".

Such experiences dare not and do not repeat themselves many times in one's life otherwise they would become commonplace and of no importance. I must have had a somewhat similar experience when I fell in love and proposed to Milly. But in this case it was a feeling of

52

mounting joy which grew stronger with the passing of days and finally flowered in our marriage.

When I received word that I had passed my finals in Engineering I wrote to several firms applying for a post. I was surprised to receive a prompt reply from the world famous shipyard, John Brown and Company, of Clydebank, who engaged me in their Mechanical Drawing office, the office that designed the ships engines and pipes, and generally dealt with everything inside the ships. There was another drawing office that designed the hull of the ship and the superstructure. My wages were, to begin with, twenty five shillings a week, but I was delighted with the offer, considering that until then I had made do with under fifteen shillings a week, my allowance from home.

Only a few weeks later did I realise why they were keen to have me. My knowledge of Russian was the bait. John Brown was building the Russian navy, not in Clydebank, but in Petrograd. The firm had men there to supervise the work, but the material was being sent out from Scotland. At that time there was a Russian Consulate in Glasgow, and a clerkess was translating the specifications. Not knowing the technical terms she made many mistakes, and this resulted in much material being rejected, causing John Brown's the loss of many thousands of pounds. Neither did I know the Russian terminology, but when I was asked to translate the specifications that had been received, I bought a technical dictionary, in five languages, including Russian. This made my work simple, and I was even sent to London to translate gun specifications and the like for the War Office.

I enjoyed my trips to London, for Schachno now lived there after his return from Zurich. On one occasion I experienced the London smog, when flares were set up in the streets to guide the traffic. The barrels of a tarry substance gave light, but produced much extra heavy smoke. It was quite an ordeal to return in the evening to my brother's lodgings, and it was a case of trial and error to arrive at the right door.

Not long after I arrived in Glasgow, Schachno decided to take me to the cinema in the Gorbals. We arrived in good time, took seats in the balcony, and I was watching the people filling the hall. They were peeling oranges and bananas, eating nuts, and throwing everything on the floor. The crowd was noisy, some shouting to friends seats away, and generally making themselves at home. Having never seen a crowd of Scotsmen before, and being used to regimentation, this was surprising and unfamiliar to me. I must have made some derogatory remark about them to my brother. "These are the people who rule the world," was his reply. His remark gave me a start, and I looked at them with a fresh eye. In the war the Scots distinguished themselves with their bravery and fearlessness. The Germans used to call them 'The Ladies from Hell' because of the kilts they wore.

The City of Glasgow appealed to me and seemed a friendly and colourful place. True, it had its drawbacks, its ugly side. Smoke was belching from every chimney, and every building had a forest of them. In the autumn and winter fog would obliterate the town, and movement in the streets and even breathing, would become a hazard. Rickets was then still known as the Glasgow disease, partly for the lack of sunshine.

The brightest time used to be during the Fair Fortnight in July, for the factories were closed and the air became clear, and the sun sparkled. Most Glaswegians missed this, for they went on holiday, usually to the seashore not far away. Steamers plying down the Clyde to the islands and coastal towns did a thriving business. German brass bands used to entertain the trippers and reap a rich reward. As soon as the 1914 war broke out they disappeared never to return.

On a Sunday morning singers would invade the back courts, and when one had a good voice, coins would be showered down from the windows in appreciation. On Saturday afternoons Argyle Street would be so crowded with shoppers as to be almost impassable. One was constantly stopped by shop criers inviting one inside with confidential promises and assurances. Sauchiehall Street was a promenade for the more affluent population, and walks usually included a visit to one of the tearooms of which Glasgow boasted. It was said that Glasgow had more tearooms than any other city in Great Britain. Cranston's Tearoom in Sauchiehall Street, and another in Ingram Street were both designed by Charles Rennie Mackintosh and were the pride of the city.

There was a Glaswegian who used to publish a weekly halfpenny sheet, called *The Clincher*, after which he was nicknamed. He was a tall imposing figure of a man, dressed in a frock coat and top hat. He was the only person I have known who parted his hair also at the back of his head.

Glasgow teemed with street-corner speakers, and on occasion I would find myself drawn in to listen. I remember the Clincher speaking just off Argyle Street, and I heard him warn his audience that our freedom was being taken away from us bit by bit, and that soon we would all have a meter strapped on to our chests, and when we would want to breathe fresh air, we would have to put a coin in the slot. This was before the first world war! He used to declare that he was the only sane person in Glasgow and that he had a certificate to prove it. He had been in an asylum and was discharged cured and sane.

In those days I used to walk with my eyes to the ground. I soon discovered that if Glasgow was not paved with gold, as London was supposed to have been, it was certainly studded with threepenny bits and sixpences. Trouser pockets could not have been made of as strong material as they are today, and I would pick up many of these coins on my walks and strolls.

At that time the tramway system was still in its infancy. There had been horse-drawn trams, but by the time I came they were already electrified, for Glasgow was an advanced city, the second largest in Britain. The tramcars had a top deck open to the elements, for the brave fresh-air fiends. As the trams moved at a leisurely pace, sitting on top was actually refreshing. Later, the main upper deck was covered in, but even then for a time there were seats at either end open to the elements. The Glasgow tramway system became the pride of Britain. No other town could compare with it. To see on a Saturday afternoon the uninterrupted line of trams almost touching one another and stretching from Eglinton Toll on the south side of the river, to Sauchiehall Street on the north side, was something to remember. At Sauchiehall Street some cars turned right, some left, and some carried straight on. It was the cheapest form of transport in Britain. Delegations came from all over the world to see our system, and I for one was sorry that it had to give way to speed. Speed has taken over everything, and on speed now, it seems, depends our survival. Speed and mechanisation. How should an artist feel, whose work does not depend on speed? If we employ speed we use it for a different reason and purpose, not for viability, but for an artistic expression of freshness and spontaneity.

The celebration of Hogmanay in Glasgow was quite an affair. Crowds would congregate at Glasgow Cross late in the evening, many with bottles of whisky in their hands. They would chat with friends, occasionally refreshing themselves from a bottle. In those days there was an equestrian statue of William of Orange at the side of the pavement near the Tron Church. I was told that it was cast in lead and that it was deteriorating. Lead has a habit of 'creeping' if not properly supported. The statue was later removed, repaired and reinforced, and then given a new site on Glasgow Green where it would not be ill treated. At Glasgow Cross it was obstructing the traffic. As the evening progressed the crowds would grow denser — standing room only — so to speak, and there would be community singing to pass the time till midnight. When the clock on the Tron Church began to chime the midnight hour a great cheer would break out from the waiting crowd and empty bottles would be shattered on the statue. The people having brought in the New Year in the time honoured fashion would feel satisfied and begin to disperse. I used to watch their good natured, slightly inebriated jollification, and feel at one with them, and as happy.

I had only been at the School of Art a few weeks, when Fra. Newbery, the Director, himself a painter, passed by my stand. I was copying a head by Donatello, and he must have noticed it, or remembered me from his visit to the High School, for he turned back and began to question me about myself and how long I had been at the School. Right away he offered me a scholarship of fifteen pounds to become a day student. Not so little, when as a college student I had made do with three pounds a month. I was sure that the offer was not made lightly,

55

and it was for me to consider it with due importance. It gave me a mighty uplift and I walked on air.

Thus I was thrown on the horns of a dilemma. It must have been a strain for my family to support me, and I was pleased to have completed my studies and to have secured a job. They were now free from any obligation towards me, and all of a sudden I was being asked to give up my post and begin again as a student, although this time of sculpture. True, I had written home that I was going to change from engineering, and that I would try to become a sculptor. The news was received with gladness, especially by mother. She said she knew that one day I would become a sculptor. When asked how she knew, her reply was that when I used to talk about the different professions I would have liked to follow, and as I spoke a great deal about them, she guessed that they did not mean much to me. She said that I never used to speak about my modelling, I just did it, and this she felt was the real thing. Personally, I don't remember the professions I had in mind. It just proved that mother appeared not to notice anything, but in fact saw and heard all.

I felt sure that my family would have been glad to subsidise me again, but I could not ask them right away to make the sacrifice, and I did not need to give an answer immediately, for the session only started in September. When war broke out in August 1914, all direct contact with Russia was broken and letters had to go via Japan. It took a few months for them to reach their destination if at all. So I could not depend on a regular allowance from home and had regretfully to refuse Fra. Newbery's offer. However it gave me such an impetus that I decided to carry on on my own.

I have often been asked if my parents had artistic leanings. It used to perplex me. Must it be inherited? Somebody had to be the first. My father however, composed poetry. And I remember that when my mother baked bread she used to fashion two little birds from dough, about three inches long, with beak, head, and tail, and with two tiny bits of charcoal for eyes. When they were baked Hesse and I were each given one as a treat. Perhaps this was an embryonic expression of her artistic nature. She was certainly glad to see the love of Art beginning to take root in her son. Perhaps this was why she encouraged me and helped me to dig clay when I was going to model.

The Sculpture department was in the basement of the School, which had been designed by Charles Rennie Mackintosh. The department was partly below street level, with an area between the basement and Renfrew Street protected by a typically decorated Mackintosh stone and iron railing. When the building came into use it must have been discovered that the department was too small for the number of students; so it was extended by cutting away the wall and window of studios 19 and 20, and covering the additional space by a skylight to the street level. Today the two rooms are completely separated, but when I first came one could pass through from one room to the other at the extensions and partly see and hear what was taking place in either. I was working in Room 19, which was the beginners' class where we were copying heads from plaster casts. No 20 was the evening life class studio, and on occasions I tried to get a glimpse of what was being modelled there.

That year, Alfred Drury, a famous London sculptor was invited to adjudicate on the Diplomas and he was invited to look into the evening life class. I was modelling my Donatello head, but I could hear all that was being said in the life class. Heads were being modelled, and I heard Drury remark about one, "This one is quite good, except for the lower part of the face which protrudes a little too much". He explained that in the clay head the mouth and the chin were jutting forward more than in the sitter.

He continued, "We have no time to remodel such defects; when I model a portrait I have an assistant who watches me all the time, and when I want fresh clay I give a knock on my board and the assistant hands me the clay I want. I work with different consistencies of clay, and when I knock once, or twice, or three times I am given the clay I ask for. We are too busy to lose time". He broke off his lecture and became the instructor. "What then would I do with this head to correct the mistake? I take a wire; with this wire I slice off the mouth and the chin from the nose downwards; slice off a thin wedge from the head; roughen the surfaces; wet the two parts and put back the cut-off part, pressing it on well. Usually we paint the two surfaces to be joined with clay slip, and sometimes even push matches in to hold the joined pieces firmly in position. It only takes a few moments to touch up the seams and the head is now corrected." I am sure that it took Alfred Drury less time to make the correction than it has taken me to describe it. He received a big cheer from the students and left the class satisfied. This was a lesson I have never forgotten. Although I did not see how Drury did it, I could easily visualise it. Many a time I have used this method to correct a part, and not only a head. Why waste time, even when you are not in a hurry? Modelling takes long enough, and the piece might be delicate and tricky to remodel. It also gives you a sense of confidence and a satisfaction that you know your craft.

I did not know that when my brother left for Zurich, he had a heart to heart talk with the Director of the Technical College, Dr. Stockdale. He had asked him to keep an eye on me while he was going to be away. I must have written him about my taking up sculpture, although I doubt whether I wrote him that I would be giving up engineering. It must have given him a jolt, for one day I received a letter from him telling me about the futility of my idea, and that I had an 'honest' profession. Why chase after something that might bring me little reward, and might even land me in a garret, and did I have the talent for it?

At the same time he must have written to Dr. Stockdale to ask him to have a word with me, for I was invited to go to see him. I was puzzled, for there seemed to be no reason for such a request. Dr. Stockdale was somewhat embarrassed and told me about his talk with Schachno. He explained that it was not for him to enter into a family dispute, and he did so now with great reservations. Was I really set on this adventure? Did I think that I would make the grade? It was not his desire to lecture me, but having given my brother his word, he wanted to fulfil his promise. We had quite a lengthy conversation about my feelings in the matter, and I finally agreed to give myself five years in which to decide whether I had it in me to become a sculptor. On this note we parted. Schachno on his return from Zurich had to admit that I had made great strides and no longer questioned my resolve. I even modelled a small bust of him, now lost.

Uncle Manny had an empty room in his workshop, and in the summer of 1914, before I started Art School evening classes I asked him to pose for me. I had been reading Albert Toft's book on modelling, read it like a bible, and knew it fairly well by heart. Therefore I was not afraid to model my uncle and produced quite a good likeness. In those days I only thought of likeness. In the style of that day I gave it a big high base. I even cast it in plaster and the mess I made was indescribable. However my uncle tolerated me for he wished me success, and did not throw me out. Later I cut off the head and mounted it on a separate small base. Later still I cut part of the head off and mounted it on a plaster board as a high relief, framed it, and for many years it hung on the wall of my uncle's living room, looking out on us in earnest contemplation.

When the Great War broke out and all able bodied teachers were more or less compelled to join the forces, the teacher who was delegated to teach us modelling in the evenings was appointed Registrar, and acting Head of the School. We hardly ever saw him again all the time I was in the Evening School. I had three evenings modelling, and two evenings drawing. During the three years in the drawing class the teacher who supervised us never once came over to my board to make any criticism or offer me advice. I tried to see how other students were drawing, which was possible during the rest periods for the model. I used to try to imitate the better ones, though I did not find this easy, for my shading was bad, and I would therefore concentrate on the outline and make it definite and strong. On one occasion the Director came in to see what was being done, and when he stopped to look at my drawing the teacher hastily told him that I was a modelling student and liked a strong outline! This lack of attention was my own fault, for I should have asked the teacher to help me. In later life, when I was the Head of the same Sculpture Department I used to tell my students that it should not be for me to run after them, but that they should run after me for advice and help — probably because of this early experience — and this they did.

Quite a number of students used to enroll for modelling, and the class was lively in the early days of the session. Either because no one came to supervise or instruct us, or because of loss of interest, the numbers began to dwindle until there came a time when I was the only student in the class. I needed no encouragement, for my urge came from within, and I was even glad to be left by myself, for the class became a personal studio with a personal model whom I could pose as I wished. On one occasion I had hurt the ball of my thumb, and while it was healing it had a certain roughness to it. This gave my modelling a slightly rough surface, more interesting than the completely smooth one, and I rather liked it. How sorry I was when my thumb healed and my modelling lost this artificial texture which enhanced it.

We felt the impact of the war upon us daily. People hardly spoke of anything else, and seldom a day passed but we heard of this one or that one having been killed. I was exempted from joining the forces as I was doing war work, and I was not yet a British subject.

Important personalities from the war front would come to John Brown's shipyard to give us lunchtime talks to keep up our morale and to inspire us to greater efforts. One of those was General Smuts. He told us about the atrocities the German soldiers perpetrated on the French population, and how they had thrown a French peasant into a river for some slight offence. As he was beginning to drown he called out, "Vive la France, Vive la France!" at which the German captain shouted "Did you hear the fellow? He has to be punished. Pull him out!"

One day a unit of Indian Sikhs marched through the shipyard with fixed bayonets and I was surprised to see that those who wore beards had them spiralling in strands round wires. They resembled the beards of the Assyrian kings as represented in their sculpture. I had always thought that the sculptors had given the kings their decorative beards, but now I realised that the representations must have been realistic.

The year 1915 was a year of revelation, of gaining a glimpse into the supernatural, and one of resolve and affirmation.

My first real shock of seeing profound and inspired sculpture on a grand scale was on one of my visits to London in 1915 in the Victoria and Albert Museum. The assassination of the Grand Duke Ferdinand and the overrunning of Serbia was still a recent outrage. Serbia had a few fine artists, mostly carvers in wood, and the greatest of them was Ivan Mestrovic, who had studied in Vienna, and was carving great marbles for the monument of Kosovo. Britain decided to honour him with a one-man show which had two purposes. It demonstrated that

Mestrovic was a great sculptor, but his work was also a monument to patriotism and a love of one's country. I was overwhelmed with what I saw. Here for the first time I came face to face with mastery and grandeur, depth of expression and meaning. These works opened my eyes to something vital and wonderful. If my mind was not yet ready for the 'sanctification', this vision, this exultation and traumatic experience bound me hand and foot, and if resolve was still needed this was the moment to take the vow, "I must become a sculptor". From that day my mind was made up, for to me Mestrovic was the modern Michaelangelo. In those days he was my idol, and I will always be grateful to him.

After his exhibition in the Victoria and Albert a small collection of his sculpture was brought to the Royal Scottish Academy in Edinburgh, where I was able to study them more intimately. I can see his influence in my bust of Robert Sivell whom I modelled in 1917, but in no others. He taught me how to enter into the spirit of a creation. His style was only its outward manifestation, and I knew that I had to evolve my own. I needed to see the power he was able to inject into his work and to realise that great sculpture did not stop with the Renaissance. I have not seen his work since then and wonder how I would evaluate it now.

That year I became involved in spiritualism. How, I cannot remember, but spiritualism became a talking point because of the thousands of soldiers who were being killed in the war. Living in a world of science people began to distrust faith alone and wanted proof, if that was possible, of a life after death. Spiritualism claimed to be the answer.

At school in Pärnu students were already experimenting with hypnotism. I was always an outsider, and observer, but it made me think of powers in us still latent and of a spiritual world we knew nothing about, certainly not then. It generated a wish to explore what lay 'Beyond'.

It may have been the memory of the experiments I witnessed in my school days that gave me the impulse to go to the spiritualist meetings when I heard about them, or it may have been the scientific experiments in spiritualism then being conducted by Sir Oliver Lodge. At a typical meeting, all seated in a circle, after a hymn or two and a short inspirational address, people from the circle who considered themselves mediums would give 'readings'. From time to time we had visits from London mediums, but the usual practice was for the members of the circle to get up and single out a few people and give them 'messages'.

I must have had psychic gifts myself, for I was soon able to give descriptions of people and situations which the appropriate person was able to recognise and understand, though I myself was innocent of what I was revealing. I used to sit quietly in my room trying to empty my mind completely of conscious thought, for this was the essential requirement for allowing thoughts from the 'other side' to fill the mind.

The ability to make one's mind a blank at will is the prime factor in becoming a medium. Some mediums went into a trance, though others found this unnecessary.

Spiritualism attracted many drifters for whom it was an escape and a diversion. I also disliked intensely it being turned into a religion. When my mother died in 1917 I decided to give up the practice. Perhaps my Jewishness came to my rescue, remembering the story of Saul seeking and bringing up the spirit of Samuel. There was, of course, the reverse of the coin — my intense desire to become a sculptor. That took precedence over everything else. It would have had to be either the one or the other, and I had already dedicated myself to sculpture and it allowed me no compromise.

Although I gave up going to meetings, I have remained a staunch believer in the hereafter. According to the spiritualist dogma every person is supposed to have a spirit guide. Various mediums have told me that mine is a monk in a brown cassock. Perhaps then, it is he who has been the inspiration behind my church works, some of which are considered my best.

Working beside me in John Brown's drawing office was a draughtsman called William Boyd. I want here to affirm his influence on me, and to say that I will always be indebted to him. Being a pacifist, he felt his position in the shipyard was inconsistent with his beliefs. Ultimately he left to start a chicken farm in 1916, but before leaving he presented me with his personal Bible as a memento of our friendship while we worked together. As I have it in front of me now I see that it was presented to him by the Ardeer United Free Church of Stevenson in 1901.

When he discovered that I was a Jew he became greatly interested in me. In the years that I had been away from home my religious fervour had dimmed, and I seldom attended Synagogue. Although I was a staunch Zionist, Mr. Boyd brought me back to Judaism with a jolt.

He told me that he now belonged to a sect initiated by Pastor Russell of America, and explained how the Pastor had worked out the future of the Jews from the Bible prophets. He gave me a small booklet which contained the data, and I am sorely grieved that I lost it during my many changes of lodgings and studios. In it Pastor Russell calculated that:

1. The Jews would come back into God's favour in 1917.
2. One third of their numbers would be annihilated; one third would assimilate; and only one third would return to Israel.
3. That the whole world would rise against them, and only then would God show His Hand and perform the miracle He had promised.

He based his theory principally on Isaiah XL 2:

"Speak ye comfortably to Jerusalem and cry unto her, that her warfare is accomplished, that her iniquity is pardoned: for she has received of the LORD'S hand double for all her sins."

It was on the word 'double' that Pastor Russell made his calculation.

When war broke out in 1914 his adherents considered it the beginning of Armageddon, and that Pastor Russell might have made a slight error in his calculations; but as time passes his predictions are becoming realities. The Balfour Declaration of 1917 formulated the return of the Jews to Palestine. Six million were exterminated by Hitler — then one third of World Jewry: three million have already assimilated, and three million have so far returned to Israel, which it is calculated can support up to double that number.

I will not be here to see the final exultation, though now I have faith that no matter what the enemies of Israel will plan against her, they will not prevail. All I know for certain is the anguish, the heartache and tribulation of my soul over the loss of my kindred, my flesh and blood. Having lived with anti-semitism all his life, now being cloaked as anti-Zionism, having grown up in countries where the Jew is looked upon, if not with hatred, with suspicion, and only seldom with tolerance, it is easy to understand why he is compelled to think a great deal more about his religion than the Gentiles have to about theirs, then compare his with other religions and hold his head high from the comparison.

I am sure Mr. Boyd did not realise the effect of his talks with me. To discover a Christian who took pride in a Jew and who opened a window for him to look into the future, why, such a person was a magician, for he revived my faltering faith, the most powerful weapon in the armoury of Jewish survival. He instilled new hope in me, in our future and our redemption, and lightened my life in the Diaspora.

I deeply regret that after he left John Brown's office I did not keep in touch with him. He did not leave me his address. I did not have the courage to emigrate to Israel myself, which I should have done. This was left to my son Amiel, and I feel now that I have a real stake in that country.

Should some of my readers think that I have expressed my feelings with bitterness, and too vehemently, I need not apologise for the truth. I need only to quote a penitential prayer composed by Pope John XXIII shortly before his death:

"We now acknowledge that for many centuries blindness has covered our eyes, so that we no longer see the beauty of Thy chosen people and no longer recognise in its face the features of our first-born brother. We acknowledge that the mark of Cain is upon our brow. For centuries Abel lay low in blood and tears because we forgot Thy love. Forgive us the curse that we wrongfully pronounced upon the name of the Jews. Forgive us that we crucified Thee in the flesh for the second time. For we knew not what we did. . ."

Every year at the end of the Art School session there was an exhibition of student's work. I had not shown in it before, but having seen the standard of the work exhibited, I decided, in 1917, to show the head of my uncle to the supervisor. He looked at it carefully, asked me when I had done it, and finally passed his judgment. "Mr. Schotz, if this is a head you modelled before you came to the School of Art, then you are forgetting your modelling." This gave me a shock. If I could model better before I came to the School, why should I continue attending? Yet that year I received the Silver Medal for modelling, the highest Evening School award. It must have been for my attendance, if my modelling was as bad as my supervisor said, or because I remained the only student!

I decided not to return to the evening classes the following session, but to find a studio and start to model on my own. I found one without difficulty. It was a tenement flat in a yard in the Gorbals, not far from where I rented a room. I soon gave up this room and moved into the flat which I furnished most economically. Orange boxes in those days were large, at least three foot long, with a solid division in the middle. They could be had for nothing, and I got one, set it up on end, screwed castors to the bottom, and had a ready made modelling stand. The centre division I used for clay and tools. After a time I covered it with jute, and I used it for many years.

In my early days one of my heroes was Tolstoy. There was a bust of him in the Art Gallery which was always on display. I used to study it carefully, and in the end decided to model him myself. I had many photographs of my hero and tried to emulate the bust in the Gallery, which I thought must have been modelled from life. What I did not know was that I was undertaking what is considered in the profession the most difficult of tasks. It was a folly of mine, yet in my ignorance I completed the bust, and even had the temerity to send the plaster cast to the exhibition of the Glasgow Institute of Fine Arts. To my surprise it was accepted, and so I began to exhibit there in 1917, and have shown there nearly every year since.

My Russian passport had my name in three languages, Russian first, then German as I now spell it, and then in French, Chotz. I tremble to think how my name would have been pronounced in Scotland had I adopted the French spelling. Having first studied in Germany, I used the German spelling; it was a natural thing to do, and I think I was wise to continue using it, although for the first three years that I exhibited I used the anglicised spelling of Shotts. Some people had different ideas on the subject. When Frederick Lamond came to live in his native Glasgow in the thirties, after he retired from the concert platform, I decided to pay him a visit as he lived nearby in Woodlands Road. I had met him in the Art Club. He was a famous exponent of Beethoven and strange to say, he had the same massive lionine appearance as the great composer. Had my visit been successful I might have asked to model him — the reason for it. When he heard my name and its spelling he said to me "You are lucky. I was very popular abroad, but could get no engagement in Britain till I changed my name from Lamont to Lamond. Then I had no difficulty. A foreign name works wonders in Britain". Did he really think that my success, or what it amounted to was due to my name? After this conversation I simply could not ask him to pose for me. Perhaps today I might have been able to laugh it off, but by nature I was shy, sensitive, and reticent, and did not want to appear to be pushing myself. Of course I was probably too emotional; he might have been only too glad to have given me sittings. He was later modelled by Alexander Proudfoot.

While still at the School of Art I became friendly with three Jewish day students, the only three then at the Art School. One was the son of a Glasgow Rabbi, and his father must have stretched a point to allow his son to take up painting. He gave me my first lesson in oils, and wishing to demonstrate his virtuosity and easy handling of the paint, made it too fluid. It began to drip down the canvas. How unfortunate for him that this was ahead of his time, or that he did not realise what an important discovery he had made. Had he continued to paint leaving drips of paint on his canvases, he would have preceded Picasso, who used this method occasionally. His name was David Hillman, and he moved to London with his parents when his father received an important appointment there. For a time he was a pupil of Solomon J. Solomon, a Royal Academician and famous as a portrait painter. Hillman was not able however to make an impression on the London scene, and took up stained glass. He died some years ago.

Another student was named Joseph Ancill. When Hillman introduced me to the Ancill menage, Joseph was working in a room given him to use as a studio. He was small and so young that he was still wearing shorts. As is usual with small people he was engaged on a large drawing that almost covered one whole wall. I can still see the composition; a life-size male figure lying as the base of the drawing, and a female figure floating diagonally upwards from it. It was most likely Adam and Eve, though I did not ask. Some years after he finished the School of Art we became very friendly, almost inseparable.

The third was Saul Yaffe who had won a poster competition to be displayed in Glasgow tramcars at the beginning of the 1914-18 war. It represented a woman with her child in her arms, fleeing from a fire behind her. Yaffe later joined the forces, and for a time was stationed in the same unit as Jacob Epstein. He told me, when on leave, how incongruous it was to see Epstein scrubbing the floor of their hut, with a large diamond ring on his finger. When the war was over he returned to Glasgow, but did not stay long. He decided to try his luck in Paris, having spent much time in France.

He introduced me to Robert Sivell, then an aspiring artist with whom I became very friendly. Through Sivell I met a group of artists who were considered rebels by the Establishment, but who later achieved an importance in Art not only in Glasgow but much farther afield.

I soon found my Gorbals flat too inhospitable and left it when Robert Sivell, who had a studio at 65, West Regent Street, pointed out to me that there was an empty studio on the opposite stair of the same building. It belonged to a Mr. Haswell Miller, a teacher in the School of Art, who was then in the army. Some years later he became the Keeper of the National Portrait Gallery in Edinburgh. His wife, Josephine Miller, also a painter, was not using it, so she sublet it to me till her husband would return after the war. I was now able to occupy a real studio for the first time.

I was still working in John Brown's, but on my return to Glasgow from Clydebank I would have a meal in a restaurant and then go upstairs to my studio and work there till all hours of the night.

British people consider that their police force is the finest in the world. In Pärnu nobody liked policemen, that I know, and Jews least of all, for they had good reasons to hate them. There they stood, in the middle of the streets, in their uniforms, a sabre at their side and a revolver in its holster, strapped on to their belts. I had an inbred fear of them, though I tried not to show it when passing one. It took me some years in Glasgow to get over this fear, till I began to learn that in Britain a policeman is your friend, not your enemy, whether you are Jew or Gentile, so long as you keep within the law. My conversion came about in a singular manner.

Studios are usually on the top floor of a building, to get good light from a large window in the roof, or a high window in a wall. I had moved to 79, West Regent Street, and mine had both. Late one night there was a knock at my door, and when I opened it I was confronted by a policeman. He had noticed the light in the window, and had come up to investigate. I got a shock on seeing him, but tried not to show it. Instead, I called him in, and he was surprised to find me alone and working. He stopped for a little chat and a smoke, and then left. After that he would occasionally pay me a visit, and even brought up a friend to show him the 'curiosity'.

Then it dawned on me that he was really glad to have a seat, a heat, and a smoke. This incident not only reconciled me to the police, I began to like them. I discovered that they were not only human, but sensible, observant, and likeable men. I grew to admire them, and when my son obtained his M.A. I toyed with the idea of suggesting to him that there was a useful and rewarding career in the force.

It was probably in 1917 that I became friendly with a girl about my own age, a Miss Ura Collins, who had close relatives in Glasgow. We met often, and the first head I modelled in Haswell Miller's studio was of her. We used to visit Sivell on the other stair, and there she met many of my friends, such as Archibald McGlashan, James Cowie, John Lamont, and Alec Scott, an architect and painter. Another visitor to Sivell's studio was James Arneil who lived in Paisley. He wanted to become an artist, but soon realised that he did not have the talent. He became a heating expert, made money, and helped out his friends in need. The head I modelled of Sivell in 1917 in his own studio is the only one that survives from that period. I later carved Ura's head in mahogany, from the original plaster, now destroyed, and it was acquired by the Kelvingrove Art Gallery, Glasgow.

For some reason I never thought of her sexually. I doubt whether I ever thought of her as a possible partner, just merely as a good friend. In Glasgow she needed a suitable male companion, just as I needed a female one. In the later stages of our friendship she told me that she could easily have made me make love to her, but she did not want to take advantage of an innocent boy, even had I been willing, for she assumed that I was still pure. She did not know, nor could I tell her, that on my last visit to Pärnu friends and students took me more or less forcibly to a brothel, and when I told them I had no money on me, one of them volunteered to pay for me. The incident stands out as one of the most distasteful experiences of my life. I was not yet ready for sex, and when I was about to leave the prostitute's room without paying, and assuring her that a friend would pay for me, she jumped to the door, a powerful figure of a woman, and stood against it with arms stretched out horizontally to prevent my leaving. She made a veritable cross. I was stunned — a cross, a cross, — it filled my eyes and mind. . . Then came a knock on the door; the spell was broken; she opened it, and my friend was there.

Ura Collins seemed to have no roots, and Glasgow was just a pause in her travels. Had I fallen in love with her she might have found an anchor in me, but she was no fool, and knew that I was not ready for marriage, not for many years. She went to Paris where she had some friends, and I never heard from her again.

The Israeli author, Benjamin Tammuz, in his novel *Castle in Spain* makes his hero fall in love with the legs of the woman who is interviewing him for a menial post. You might say "What a ridiculous story". Well it is not. Something similar actually happened to me after Ura left. I became involved with a girl from John Brown's office. What her job was there, I never knew, nor bothered to ask. I used to see her walking to the train that took us back to Glasgow from Clydebank after work, always at some distance ahead of me. What attracted me to begin with was her walk. I had never before seen a girl walk as straight as she did, as if she was walking on a line, her body erect, without the slightest movement. Her legs were beautifully moulded and close together, her figure tapering down to her legs in a line, shapely enough for a Venus. Gradually I began to look out for her, for I was never satiated with looking at her legs and back. What she was like from the front I did not know, nor did I speculate, but I was determined to make her acquaintance. A girl with such legs dare not disappoint me!

We all travelled in set compartments with the same friends and it took some stratagem to change over and take a seat in my lady's compartment. For a woman she was of good height and well proportioned. She had dark hair with a 'cow's lick', a broad forehead, high cheekbones, a sensuous mouth, a well formed chin, and dark, sparkling eyes, somewhat kittenish. I was not disappointed. It was not long before I got to know her well enough to take her to a tearoom and ask her up to my studio. She obsessed me, and my mind was full of her. Round about then, a French sculptor had received the Grand Prix of the Salon, and one of his pieces was a Medusa head rolling after having been severed from its body. This had given me the idea of modelling a Medusa mask using my 'captive' as a model. The hair I though would turn into snakes, which would also peer out of the eyes, project out of the open mouth instead of a tongue, and curl round to the neck, supporting the mask. Why did I want to represent her thus? Was it because she bewitched me, and by modelling her as a Medusa I might break her spell over me and become free again? At that time, however, I did not have the technical skill to carry out this conception, and my infatuation and involvement with her came to a sudden end through an incident involving one of her former beaux or so I thought. In the end, I never modelled her, though earlier I made a mask of her younger sister.

When Jews lived in a prescribed Ghetto, their emotional lives were simple, and marriages were normally arranged by parents, sometimes even when the respective spouses were still children. People married very young and problems did not often arise. It was only when Jews began to break out of the confines of the Ghettos and begin to mix with the Gentile population that the problem of intermarriage began to raise its head. Love is blind, the saying goes, though it is used here in a different context. It can strike as a thunderbolt and asks no questions. Would I have married out? Up to that time I doubt if I seriously thought of marriage. I was introduced to my girl's two sisters, an elder and a younger, but I knew nothing about her parents or her background. I did not enquire. I knew one thing; had I fallen in love with her beyond recall I would have married her. Her past would not have mattered.

But what might have troubled me would have been whether she would have embraced the Jewish religion. That I would have considered the all important linchpin in our lives. I was and am a strong nationalist and a believer in the Jewish faith. Girls when they marry out are usually lost to the Jewish people, and men sometimes also. I would rather see additions to our community though it is well known that Jews do not go in for proselitising. It seems to me that foreign blood strengthens the strain of a people. Jews need not worry about this for throughout the generations our women have been raped on innumerable occasions.

An autobiography is not just a record of one's factual life, and should not be. It should also explain the reasons for one's actions, and in the case of an artist, his motivations, and how his ideas germinated. Had I modelled the Medusa mask no one would have known the reason for its creation. It simply would have been looked at from the aesthetic point of view. It is not the onlooker's duty to ask "Why?" But in an autobiography, the hidden springs that water and feed a work into flower should be revealed, if the author considers it important. Thinking back, perhaps I did not want to work out the idea of making a sculpture of the little boy and his father in the Synagogue on a large scale, because, in the final analysis it tells a story, albeit a personal one. If one does tell a story it should not become obvious, it should withhold something that the artist alone knows. Genre sculpture can look vulgar.

Every artist has a graveyard of ideas and works he has never been able to produce. We all know and need no reminder that he puts part of himself into every work. With some it is more, with others less. It so happens that in my case my sculpture is mostly autobiographical. All the compositions I have done have sprung from within. They had to have a raison d'être. This was why at first I found it difficult to express my ideas in a tangible form, for to translate ideas from one medium into another was most difficult for me. I never wanted to produce genre sculpture, no matter how successful and lucrative they might have been.

What can be described in words should be the sphere of literature. Sculpture should deal with form, real or abstract. Even when I model a portrait I do not set myself up as a judge of my sitters, to tell the story of their lives, and do not concentrate on producing a likeness only. I always used to say, and still do, that if I modelled the features correctly, the likeness and character would appear of its own accord.

The Glasgow Institute of the Fine Arts was the only gallery where one could exhibit free in Glasgow. It was the best 'shop window' for local artists. Quite a few depended for their livelihood on their sales in the exhibition. In those days there was an Art Union lottery in connection with it. The prizes were cash, but one had to buy a picture for the amount won, which later was modified so that the winner could buy more than one work to the total amount, which gave him greater choice. Some artists who knew from past experience the amount of the first three prizes would price their paintings accordingly. This automatically gave them a good chance of selling their paintings, especially when they were friendly with the agent who was in attendance at the Gallery.

The Art Union draw was the mainstay of the exhibition. The British are fond of a flutter, and tickets sold well. This did not help the quality or standard of the show, for many artists produced paintings for the draw which would be most popular with the public. There was a time when I tried to dissociate the lottery from the exhibition, but in the end it died a natural death for lack of support. The Institute had fallen into disrepute because of its reduced standards, and people lost their desire to acquire a painting from it, and stopped buying Art Union tickets. It is now regaining the influence and position it had before, at the turn of the century.

For some reason our group of painters were considered rebels. Why, I could never make out, unless it was that some of them were denigrating the established artists, especially whose who painted for the Art Union, and who were repeating themselves *ad nauseam* by painting subjects that proved saleable. The result was that whenever paintings by the so-called 'rebels' came up before the jury, they were automatically rejected. This naturally infuriated them and they decided to strike back by forming a rival show.

In 1919 the Society of Painters and Sculptors was formed with Robert Sivell as its President — it was his idea. It attracted many members but it proved short lived. The Society was able to hold only two exhibitions before breaking up through internal differences. The stumbling block proved to be one of the rules of the Society. Every work of a member had to pass a jury, and no member had a guarantee that his work would be hung, although he had to pay his subscription. It was a hard rule that was pushed through by Bob Sivell, who wanted to make the Society's exhibition an artistic success. The first exhibition was a trial show to explore the ground, but when it came to the second one it was decided to make a severe pruning with the result that only about half of the members found their works on the walls. Those who were rejected resigned, and the Society could not continue for lack of funds. It never occurred to the Society to double the subscription and carry on. To be fair to Sivell, hardly a single one of those rejected became a professional artist. The exhibitions lasted only for a fortnight, and sales did not materialise.

Robert Sivell did not receive in his lifetime the appreciation he deserved. I hope that a serious study of him and his work will ultimately be made. I met Sivell during the first World War. He was my own height, dark skinned, with dark hair and dark, deepset eyes, a chiselled rugged face, and a Roman nose. He used to say that his forbears must have come from Seville, and that one of them must have been a survivor from the Spanish Armada. It used to annoy him when he was occasionally taken for a Jew.

He married Isobel Sayers, the daughter of a Kirkcudbright boat builder, and later rebuilt a derelict boathouse there into a lovely home

69

and studio. Kirkcudbright was famous for its artists' colony. Hornel had his house and studio there, E. A. Taylor, the painter and art critic, and his wife, Jessie M. King, lived at 'Greengate', Robson and Sassoon, both painters, and quite a number of others whose names I have now forgotten. Later Jeffs took a house there to carry on his sculpture and craft work, and Cecily Walton retired there. Phyllis Bone also settled there to continue to model her animals.

John Lamont, a painter, became Sivell's brother-in-law, and built himself a cottage beside Sivell's. Lamont was the son of a Glasgow doctor, and was gassed in the war of 1914-18. His health deteriorated, and he died young, leaving unfulfilled a promise of fine works to come. I modelled him in 1922, the best bust I had done by then, the chest and shoulders beautifully modelled. Great was my vexation when, having invited it for my Retrospective Exhibition in 1971, I discovered that Lamont, for reasons best known to himself, had decapitated the bust, and only the head remained.

It was quite an effort for Sivell to make ends meet, and as his place in Kirkcudbright was adjacent to a wood, he was able on occasion to poach a hare from his back door. Having been a Territorial he made good use of his shooting skill. I was present when he shot a hare, and he told me that some time earlier a rabbit had begun to nibble their lettuces and other greens in their vegetable garden, and their little daughter, Elspeth became very fond of it, and would hand feed it. Because of this he would not touch a rabbit, and they had the run of the place.

Like myself, Sivell had no art degree, for he had to leave the Art School for lack of funds and was, for a time, a deck hand on a boat. James Cowie was the Head of the Painting School in Gray's College, Aberdeen, one of the few artists who managed to break out from being an art teacher in a secondary school, and when he had to leave he recommended Sivell for the post. By then Sivell was already well known, and he held it till he himself had to retire. It is my opinion that a person's character is not finalised in his early childhood, but continues to develop and change throughout one's life. When Elspeth was born in his parents' home in Paisley they nearly lost her. Isobel was very ill, and Sivell pocketed his pride, for he was sorely in need, and paid a visit to a Mr. James Begg, who was then the President of the Paisley Art Institute. He made him buy a seascape he had painted in Italy, showing the cross currents at Capri. He brought back the notes and showered them on to Isobel's bed. These were still his days of trial and tension, and it may have helped to stimulate his resentment and indignation at life's vagaries, and to set his face into a mould of suffering, with eyes that shone with a brilliant fire, ever ready to defend his artistic stand.

Sivell had little use for the Impressionists. In his opinion they had not produced a single major painting. He placed the Renaissance painters as the highest achievement in art, and confirmed it in his mind by a visit to Italy. Uccello, Raphael, Leonardo and Michaelangelo were his idols, and art stopped with them for him. We would often argue about his attitude, but we could not shift his point of view. This coloured his opinion of the paintings of other artists, and in the Society of Painters and Sculptors, where he held such a great sway, he made his influence felt by the ruthless rejection of artists of whose work he did not approve.

Bob Sivell was born in Paisley. For its size Paisley held a remarkable record for the artists she had reared. Noel Paton, R.A. the Pre-Raphaelite, hailed from there. The friezes from the Parthenon and from the Temple of Apollo were engraved in miniature by a Paisley sculptor, John Henning, a monumental achievement. The original engravings in slate are now in the British Museum. Paisley also claims the two brothers Fillans who attained some fame as sculptors. Archibald McGlashan was born and spent his youth there. Kenneth Clark, now Lord Clark, belongs to the family of the famous Paisley thread mills.

In Sivell's formative years as an artist Augustus John was the idol of the rebels, and his influence can easily be seen in some of his paintings as well as in those of John Lamont, his devotee. The Spanish painter, El Greco, became their model for colour and drawing. Normally Sivell produced only drawing-room sized paintings, yet he considered that the acme of an artist's creation was mural painting.

He spent a good many years of his life in Aberdeen, painting two murals for the Students' Union. He had great difficulty with composition, and he therefore worked hard to make sure that every work of his was faultless. Otherwise he might have produced more, but he expended himself on those two murals, trying to make them perfect in composition. I have only a faint recollection of them now, but in the first one he had tried to embody man's life cycle and to introduce in a modern guise some Greek myths. The other dealt with student life. Sir W. O. Hutchison, in his introduction to the catalogue of Sivell's Memorial Exhibition in 1960 wrote:

"It would require a visit to the Students' Union in Aberdeen to savour the full stature of Sivell the artist. For the decoration of that hall is without doubt the greatest mural painting carried out in Scotland during this century, and perhaps any other. . ."

Sivell himself feared that they might be destroyed with the Union, so he transferred them onto canvas.

Bob Sivell could be a great friend, and once this had been cemented, he would stand up and defend you without fear. When some of his colleagues wanted to put him up for the Royal Scottish Academy he would not allow his name to go forward for Associateship until Archibald McGlashan, his close friend, for whom he had a great admiration, had first been elected.

At the same time, if he did not agree with a work you had produced, he would tear it to pieces, even in public, hoping he touched you to the deep. He once did that to me. In the latter years of his life we did not see much of each other except at meetings in the Royal Scottish Academy, and although we at times had differences, deep within us we loved and respected one another. When he was cremated, a part of my past died with him.

1920 stands out as an important milestone in my life. That year I was elected an artist member of the Glasgow Art Club, although still not a full-time sculptor. This created a bit of a stir among my artist friends, for they disliked the idea. The Club was saddled with the running of the Glasgow Institute of the Fine Arts, a responsibility it could not refute, for all the Art members on the Council of the Institute were also members of the Club. What was worse, these artists were responsible for the annual rejection of our group.

In those days the Art Club was a powerful institution, although I knew little about it, except for the gossip that was flying around. I was told that it was due to the influence of the Glasgow artists, which meant the Glasgow Art Club, that the City was made to buy Whistler's 'Carlyle', now one of its most precious possessions. A story went around shortly afterwards that our City Fathers wanted to have their Lord Provost painted by Whistler. They did not know that when Whistler accepted a commission the size and composition was for him to decide, and the price did not depend upon it. The Councillors did not want to spend much, so they sent Whistler a wire asking him what he would charge for a half length portrait, and by return they received a wire back, "Which half?" That, of course, closed the matter. Whistler could enjoy a jibe, even at the cost of a commission.

I allowed my name to go forward for membership of the Art Club because another sculptor friend asked me. There were hardly any sculptors in the Club. I knew that it had a prestige value, nothing more. Yet my critics put sinister reasons forward for my joining, even suggesting commercial motives, though I never made use of its opportunities in that sphere throughout my life. However, a month or two later, Sivell confessed to me privately that had he as many finished works as I he would also have liked to join. The Club gave me a certain standing, not yet being a professional sculptor.

In spite of the fact that the inner circle of the Society of Painters and Sculptors considered me somewhat a traitor, I was elected its President in 1920 to lead the Society to what happened to be its final exhibition. I was already being invited to important group shows in Edinburgh, and galleries were opening their doors to me. I was working hard trying to tread my own path till it would become broad and hard worn, and known as mine.

That year Jacob Kramer came on a visit to Glasgow, and I was introduced to him. Kramer had studied painting at the Slade School of

Art in London, and was beginning to make a name for himself with his provocative paintings in search of a personal style. He told me that he had posed for the feet of Epstein's first Christ of 1919. The figure was covered up and he did not ask, nor was he told what the figure represented. Epstein promised to pose for him, but all he finally managed to obtain was a black and white sketch of his wife. Kramer seemed rather sore about this, yet the following year he posed for Epstein for a bust that created quite a stir with its power of nervous tension and intimate characterisation. Kramer has this bust to thank for becoming known throughout the world.

I took him up to Sivell's studio where he met the inner circle of the Society of Painters and Sculptors. He was invited to join our Society and he exhibited with us in 1920. Sivell had paid a visit to Dublin, and had met there Jack Yeats, who also exhibited with us that year.

By joining the Art Club I got to know other artists who were not members of our coterie, including my former evening class drawing teacher. I discovered that he himself was a fine draughtsman. There was another advantage in being a member of the Club. The artist members — the Club had more lay members than artists — held an Art class once a week in the evenings, and for years I never failed to attend it. I would be surprised if these classes did not do more to improve my drawing than my attempts in the Art School.

After our father died, Schachno and I had been asking Hesse to come to Britain. Hesse loved Schachno very much, and he being very persuasive, she finally agreed. She was arriving by boat at Hull, and we both met her there. I left Glasgow early, so that I could stop for a few hours in Leeds, to see the Art Gallery and to meet Jacob Kramer, who lived there, for a chat. It was good to be in his home surroundings, to talk to his mother, a homely 'Yiddishe Mama', something I should easily have deducted from his own behaviour when I first met him in Glasgow.

After meeting Hesse, I returned to Glasgow, while she went to London to stay with my brother. Although at home she had been employed as a governess, or as a tutor for backward pupils, here she began to take shorthand and typing lessons to prepare herself for a new life. Shortly afterwards Schachno married, and Hesse felt that she could not remain in London.

She became my housekeeper, for I was still working in John Brown's, and in the evenings she would stay with me in the studio, or go with me visiting friends. I did not realise that she was just drifting along without a set purpose, while I was busy working away and oblivious to everything around me. She could easily have pursued a trade or profession but this did not enter my mind. Perhaps I hoped she might marry, for she had refused four proposals whilst still at home, the last one being a German soldier who was ready to convert to Judaism for her sake, but luckily she refused him. What an escape she had!

Hesse believed in dreams and had a book interpreting them. Of course straight away I began to remember my dreams. I had studied handwriting somewhat seriously, and was able to delineate character fairly accurately. Being psychic, I was popular at parties because I read teacups, and also I had made a study of Chiromancy. Yet all these I took lightheartedly for they were only entertainment and did nothing for me and my art. I began to desert my friends for work, and when they got annoyed with me for neglecting them, my reply was, that if I continued to socialise, I would have no time for work, and I wanted to immerse myself to master my craft.

My sister realised in 1923 that she was aimless, and decided to return to Pärnu to help Elsa to look after her two children while she and her husband carried on their own businesses. I was sad to let her go, but we felt it was for the best.

The person who first put me on the map, and drew the attention of the public to my work, was Frank Rinder, the London art historian and critic. In 1920 I exhibited, in the Institute of Fine Arts, a mask I then called 'Herostratus', but which I later renamed 'Mask of an Artist', for an artist friend had posed for it. In those days Art criticism in Scotland was considered a serious and important function of the Press, and *Glasgow Herald,* the chief local newspaper, used to invite a well known London critic to 'do' the Institute. That year they had invited Rinder, and he gave me a heading and a fine write-up. I met him later and we became quite friendly.

He was the first man I had seen wearing the very heavy eyeglass frames which became so fashionable all over Britain. It hid part of his face. In addition he always wore a bowler hat which was another hindrance to seeing his head. In 1921 we met in the Gallery, and while walking round he suddenly asked me, "Would you like to model me?" I was taken by surprise, for I had no chance to study his features. I asked him to take off his hat. Then I received a real surprise; he was bald; he only had a little hair round the edge of his bowler. This worried me, for I had never modelled a bald man and I did not know whether I would succeed in making a fine head. So I asked him to replace his hat and said that I would think it over. I did not refer to the matter again.

Some time later, on one of my visits to London, he invited me to his house for an evening. I was received warmly, and he invited two other Scottish artists to meet me, both well known painters and etchers. One was D. Y. Cameron R.A. and the other William Strang, also a Royal Academician. Frank Rinder prefaced his introduction with the words "Here is the fellow who refused to model me!"

In those days I brimmed over with enthusiasm when I saw a sculpture that touched me deeply. I had not seen many fine pieces. That evening in Rinder's home I saw for the first time a group by Eric Gill, at most five to six inches high, a little Madonna and Child, in bronze, which at the time I thought so beautiful, so delicate and chaste, that I could find no words to adequately express my admiration for it. This Madonna and Child had a flowing line, and elegance and a plasticity which one misses in his stone carvings, which I find stiff and formal. In his letter-cutting Eric Gill revealed his true mastery. I could not understand why I failed to see his carvings in exhibitions, until one day, whilst travelling about Britain collecting works for a Glasgow Festival of Jewish Art, as part of the 1951 Festival of Britain, I paid a visit in Liverpool to a Mr. S. S. Samuel, who was a great patron of Jacob Epstein, and also had an important collection of paintings. I discovered that Mr. Samuel had most of Eric Gill's carvings, and a high bookcase full of books which Gill had illustrated. He was an ardent collector of Gill.

That same evening in Rinder's home I also saw for the first time a bronze figure of a youth by Jacob Epstein on a slab of green marble, about twelve to fifteen inches square. The youth was seated on the slab and the pose was so arranged that the elongated limbs filled the square base. The figure was modelled in the style of Lehmbruck's elongated figures, which later created a period style in sculpture.

Rinder also showed me a large volume of the works of William Blake with his illustrations in them. He was one of the first art historians to rehabilitate Blake to the unique position he now occupies in the Literature and Fine Art of this country. Then I knew little of Blake, but this triggered off my interest in him.

I used to go and see every exhibition that was mounted in Glasgow. I regularly visited the Reid Gallery in West George Street, and got to know Alexander Reid and his son McNeill fairly well. McNeill Reid had wanted to become an engineer, but his father made him come into the business. Alexander Reid would go to Paris and bring back some paintings to Glasgow. He would then call up a client and tell him that he had brought him back a painting. When the client would object, he would say, "I brought this painting for you, and if you won't buy it from me I will never sell you another as long as I live". He was in a position to talk to his clients in this manner because he had become the famous dealer in Impressionist paintings. In his early days it was different. Then, he told me, he could not sell two Van Goghs he had brought from Paris for five pounds a piece. When Reid went to Paris to learn to paint he shared lodgings with Van Gogh, but soon discovered that he lacked the talent, though he loved the Art. He told me that at one time he went in fear of his life, because Van Gogh, imagining that he, Reid, was pursuing his sister, threatened him with a knife, so he had to make himself scarce.

The centre of art dealing was then Paris for the French considered art an export business, and McNeill Reid would have to go to Paris once a month with their French partner Lefevre, to a meeting of the dealers, who would decide whom to 'run' that month. They would then watch the public response, and if it was favourable, they would continue to promote the artist, otherwise they would drop him and concentrate on somebody else. Only then did I realise the power of the dealers. This did not endear me to them. I found it difficult, and sometimes even humiliating to approach them.

About the same time a young art dealer, Duncan Macdonald, an assistant in the Scottish Art Gallery of Aitken Dott in Edinburgh 'ferreted' me out and befriended me. He used to come to Glasgow once a week to deal with clients by appointment, in a photographic studio in Sauchiehall Street, and we used to meet there, or in my studio, and in due course he invited me to his home in Edinburgh.

Duncan Macdonald's wife, Lily, was a fair, lovely, gentle girl to whom I became deeply attached. She was the type of girl I thought I would have loved to marry. I could certainly have fallen in love with her, perhaps I did, but she was married, and I would never have dreamt of coming between husband and wife. I believe that to some extent she reciprocated my feelings, and the three of us remained good friends all our lives.

Mrs. Macdonald's mother, Mrs. Sinclair, also lived in Edinburgh, in what is called the Watch Tower, and we had to climb seventy steps to her place. She was a remarkable person in many ways, cultured and sociable, and I used to visit her frequently. She had a great circle of friends, and her home hummed with visitors.

I was still a hero worshipper, and that year I carved a larger than life stone bust of Herzl, the founder of political Zionism. I knew nothing about carving, not even the tools to use. I knew only what I had seen in the monumental workshop next to our home, when I was a boy. They only worked with heavy points, and I bought one of those. When it came to proper carving, I had to broaden the point. When I think back on it now, I marvel at my audacity in attempting to carve stone not even knowing how to hold carving tools. There is a right and a wrong way. Holding a tool the right way does not hurt the hand or arm. It has to be held so that the tool 'bites' the stone. I did not know this and held the chisel at a more acute angle to the stone. This necessitated exerting a certain pressure on the chisel for it to bite, and this in turn began to cause me considerable pain in my arm. It became like an electric battery, and I had finally to go to a Swedish masseur to have my arm cured. After I learned the craft of carving, it gave me no more trouble.

In spite of this I produced a work of some significance. My Herzl is a simple but dignified work, and what I then considered an innovation for me was the way I treated the eyes. The upper lids are the only feature of their existence, yet one does not notice this, or miss the eyes, for the top eyelids seem to represent them and give them vision and expression.

I was in London in 1921 and met Mr. S. S. Levin, then a young man, who was the secretary of the Jewish National Fund. When he heard about my carving of Herzl he tried to find a buyer for it. He approached a Mr. Joseph Cowen, who was the President of the Fund, and I was invited to his home one evening. It so happened that that evening I suffered from a bad migraine, and could not have made a good impression on my hosts, for I was hardly able to utter a word. Later in the evening a young man arrived and Mr. Cowen introduced him to me as Mr. Herzl. He was a handsome person, tall, fair haired, and blue eyed. He must have come on some errand, for they both excused themselves and went into another room. Nothing transpired of this visit, and I hardly expected more, for I did not help my case. Of course, this young man, who later committed suicide, was the son of my hero.

Mr. Levin however managed to find another private individual who bought my carving and presented it to the Tel Aviv Museum who accepted it for 'permanent' display. In those days the Directors were glad to get gifts for their Israeli Museums, but now its 'permanency' is in the basement, and it is difficult to have a work accepted unless it bears an international name.

My membership of the Glasgow Art Club had an all important consequence for me. An architect, John Keppie, began to take an interest in me. He was a partner in the firm that had employed Charles Rennie Mackintosh. What made him take to me I cannot say, except that he was a bachelor, and so was I, and I was young enough for him to take me under his wing. We remained close friends until his death. He began to find commissions for me, and among the early works I executed for him were the two bronze groups over the Bath Street entrances of the Pettigrew and Stephens building, now demolished. The two groups are now in the United States of America.

John Keppie was a fairly big and heavily built man. He told me he had been in love with a girl who preferred E. A. Walton, the well known Edinburgh painter. Perhaps this was the reason he never married. He had two sisters living with him, a Mrs. Henderson, a widow, and the younger, Miss Jessie Keppie, a watercolour artist. She had been in love with Charles Rennie Mackintosh, but he married Margaret Macdonald, and she also remained unmarried.

Through him I received the commission to model the first Lord Weir. I was alloted a room in his factory and would arrive in the morning, not knowing when Lord Weir would have time to pose for me. I might get two fifteen minute sessions from him in the morning, but I would be invited to have lunch with the members of his Board, at which he presided. During lunchtime I would study him, for then he revealed his true character. He would be relaxed and alive, and would constantly ask questions from those present about matters of which it seemed to me he knew more himself. He would look at the person with a quizzical eye and an enquiring smile, and this was to me the real Lord Weir.

The bust I modelled I called the 'official' one, while in my own studio I also modelled another head of him, giving it the expression which I felt was typical of the man. Lord Weir did not hide the fact that he was descended from Robert Burns, albeit on the wrong side of the blanket. On the contrary, he seemed rather proud of it, and the likeness can easily be seen in the 'unofficial' head. Years later, when I saw Charlie Chaplin's film *The Great Dictator,* I was struck by how similar my own position was in the Weir factory when modelling Lord Weir, to the situation in the film, where a painter and a sculptor were waiting for the Dictator's appearance for a few moments, when they worked as if possessed.

I carried out several architectural commissions for John Keppie, but they had to be as Keppie wanted them. He was a classical architect, and his figures had to be pseudo-Greek. I was surprised that even in those days architects had to hide the cost of the sculpture in the brick or woodwork, otherwise the clients would have cut them out, and this was a time when there was no scarcity of money. They simply had no time for the ornamentation of their buildings. Yet, once they saw it, they asked no questions. They were even pleased to have it, and took pride in it.

The Head of the Sculpture Department in the Glasgow School of Art, when I first started to attend the evening classes was Alexander Proudfoot, who had to join the army when war broke out in 1914. I had left the School before he returned to take up his duties again. By that time I was getting to be fairly well known by the artistic fraternity. Proudfoot helped me to make a wax replica of a mask I wanted to cast locally. We made two waxes, and one of the bronzes I presented to him in appreciation of his assistance.

In the meantime my friendship with Duncan Macdonald had ripened, and in 1921 I decided to ask Lily to pose for me. She made pottery, working in a little outhouse in the courtyard of their home in George Square, Edinburgh. It had all the materials I needed, and I modelled her head at the open door of her workshop. I still consider it one of my best, although even then I completed it in one day. At the time I did not know that her closest friend, Maria Waddell, a Glasgow bookbinder, had a wager with her that I would ask her to pose, and that Lily had said she would refuse to sit for me. She lost her bet, but I am sure she did not regret it, for the head is now the property of the City of Edinburgh, and when their Art Gallery is built, as one day it will have to be, it will be exhibited there. A little blob under one eye I have always said was Lily's tear. Did I place it there to remind me of my attachment to her?

Duncan himself I modelled in 1923, and when I exhibited it in my first show in the Reid and Lefevre Gallery, London, the sculptor Maurice Lambert told Duncan that he would have given his left hand to have modelled it. Yet this work had an unhappy sequel. Macdonald was trying to promote me and approached a well known Edinburgh couple on my behalf. They were wealthy and influential people. I was still working in John Brown's and Duncan suggested that they advance me some money to allow me to give up my post at the shipyard, and later take a work in lieu. I would never have accepted such an arrangement. When he discovered that they were also not willing to do so, he tried to sell them my bronze of his own head. When he told me about it I said, "Duncan, don't push my work on people". I may even have said "Your head". I simply had a distaste of people being pressurised to buy my sculpture, not realising that a dealer who wants to promote an artist must push his work on to clients, otherwise he is no dealer. However Duncan assumed that I did not consider his head good enough to sell.

I have always suffered from an awkward way of expressing my thoughts, which often gives them a meaning other than that which I intend to convey. This misunderstanding became clear to me only when it was too late and useless to set the matter straight.

When Alexander Reid was retiring from his business through ill health, they needed an addition to their staff. I told McNeill Reid about Duncan, and how highly I regarded him, and he was invited to become a Director of the firm. Duncan afterwards built it up, although I heard that the clients nevertheless, had great confidence in McNeill's judgement.

Hugh Walpole, the novelist, used to visit Edinburgh periodically, as his father was a minister in one of the Edinburgh churches. Walpole was already an author with a considerable reputation and his visits to Edinburgh gave Duncan Macdonald the opportunity to get to know him better, and at the same time find me a well known personality to model. Walpole readily agreed to pose, and I modelled him also at the door of Lily's outhouse. Just as with Lily's head, I took only one day to model him. At that time, being heavily built, he had an intimation of a double chin, and would hold is head erect, almost stretched. I modelled him as a visionary, his lips ready to part and speak, his face lit up in anticipation of what might be revealed to him.

I don't know what Walpole thought of my effort, but Duncan did not sell it to him. I exhibited the portrait again in my second one-man show in London, and he came into the Gallery when I happened to be there. He seemed surprised and embarrassed when he saw me, and sent me a letter afterwards hoping that I had caught a 'big fish' with his head. He probably felt uncomfortable as he had given Epstein a commission to model him, though I did not know it at the time. Later Sir Alexander

Walker of Troon presented the head to the Scottish National Portrait Gallery.

It was interesting to read in Epstein's autobiography published in 1940, his remarks about him. He writes that when he began to model Sir Hugh he could see from the very beginning that it was going to be a failure, the reason being that Walpole sat "with head held high and chin stuck out". Epstein apparently did not realise that Walpole did not want to be represented with a double chin. For some reason commissioned portraits always intimidated Epstein. He took measurements and tried to satisfy his sitters. They wanted to be modelled by Epstein, because they wanted an Epstein, not a mediocre, though possibly well modelled head, bearing Epstein's signature. Epstein himself admits that he had to satisfy his sitter, or the sitter's wife, or relatives, and he did not do himself justice, because then he compromised.

In this respect I have always been more fortunate. My clients seem to accept what I produce, and are satisfied with my representation of them. They seldom ask me to change something. Private galleries are not keen to recommend an artist to paint or model a client in case the result is not satisfactory. Disagreements and quarrels can arise, have arisen, and the Gallery can lose a valuable client. If I have a weak spot, it is that I happen to be a great optimist. My life is centred round my sculpture, and when modelling I could not be happier. Perhaps this is the reason why my portraits usually have a certain light strain, for I see my sitters in their better aspects. On the other hand, if I also try to compromise, then I know beforehand that the result will be a failure.

About the same time that Macdonald introduced me to Hugh Walpole, he also introduced me to James McBey. McBey started as a bank clerk in Aberdeen, turned to etching, and became one of the three best known etchers in Great Britain, the other two being Sir D. Y. Cameron, and Muirhead Bone. In the Macdonald home in Edinburgh there used to hang a Zorn etching. One day I missed it from the wall. Then I began to hear that the bottom had fallen out of the etching business. I was told that it became known that Zorn was steel-facing his plates and was making albums for different countries and they were not limited in numbers, as they were supposed to be. Each country had an edition, and this multiplied the prints many times over. This affected the whole market, and it seemed to prove that etchings were bought for their investment value, not for their artistic content. A sad reflection, but true.

James McBey had also been painting watercolours, rather like tinted pen and ink drawings. Then he began to paint with oils. He had a good eye and was soon a fairly accomplished portrait painter. Macdonald was selling his watercolours, and also began to find him portrait commissions. Because his sitters were mostly Glasgow people, or living on the outskirts, I used to meet him occasionally. He was a handsome well built man with a lion's mane of hair, an ideal subject for a sculptor. It was natural that I should want to model him, and Duncan encouraged the idea. One day, about noon, McBey came up to my studio, and said that his sitter wanted a rest for the day, so he was free, and would I model him now. I was always ready for such surprises, and was able to start without much delay. After an hour and a half we stopped for a bite in some restaurant, and when we returned to my studio I was able to complete the head in the course of another hour.

McBey went to live in London, and some time later emigrated to the United States, where he married a wealthy girl. He also bought a home in Morocco. I only saw him once again, many years later in the Chelsea Art Club. He did not recognise me, but I could not mistake him. I asked him to visit me in Glasgow, as he was coming up to Scotland, but he told me that his time was strictly limited, as he could only stay his ninety days in Britain. I later heard members saying that he was smart to live in three countries, avoiding taxation in each.

I sent the head of McBey along with that of Hugh Walpole as my first exhibit in the Royal Academy, in 1924.

Some time earlier, Alexander Proudfoot received a commission to execute a memorial for Bearsden, a few miles from Glasgow. He had asked an assistant in his Department, Archibald Dawson, to build up the group for him. This he did. He did not build it up to last a lifetime, for Proudfoot assured him he would complete it quickly. He did not. Being Head of the Sculpture Department, and a bachelor, he was fond of socialising. He took a long time over it, perhaps hoping for other commissions to follow, while showing this one in the studio. He did in fact receive another.

It was still not finished when one morning as he opened his studio door, he found that the whole group had collapsed, and was lying in pieces on the floor. A year's work must have gone into it, if not more, and I can well imagine how he felt. He told me that he did not even enter his studio, but sat down on the front step of the door, not knowing what to do. On the whole, sculptors are long suffering individuals. Dawson refused to take the blame, for he had done what he was asked to do. Had he known that Proudfoot would take as long to complete the group, he would have made the armature stronger.

It was then that Proudfoot turned to me and asked me if I would build up the group for him again. When I pointed out that I was working in John Brown's office, he said, "Chuck it. It is time you did".

I had reached the crossroads of my life, and I was waiting for the day and the opportunity to leave the Drawing Office. Was this the sign? I was standing looking at the signpost. John Brown's was only a transitional stage in my life, and were I to accept Proudfoot's offer, it would mean that I would have to leave the shipyard and become a professional sculptor. It was an irrevocable step. Yet I felt that I was being given a singular opportunity to start as a sculptor, for a few months which I would spend in Proudfoot's studio would give me a chance to adjust myself to the change from amateur to professional status.

However, I did not want to take this important step without asking advice. And who was better fitted to give me this friendly advice than John Keppie, with whom I had become very friendly indeed? By now he was for me in *loco parentis*. When I put the proposition to him, he replied, "Benno, the longer you wait, the more difficult it will become for you to make the break. This is a good opportunity, take it, but give me one promise. Should you be hard up, don't go to a moneylender, come to me". This was a wonderful piece of advice on his part. I knew about moneylenders, for their sign of three golden balls was prominently displayed on many Glasgow streets in those days. It never dawned upon me that an occasion might arise for me to avail myself of their help, for I possessed nothing of any value. But John Keppie was far sighted, and he was thinking of the years to come. He had seen many artists sorely pressed for their daily needs, and he did not want this to happen to me — and he was right. On more than one occasion in later years I had to go to him to help me out with the rent, but he was always business like. I had to sign an I.O.U. for every pound I borrowed, and when I came to repay what I owed him, his invariable question would be, "Can you afford it?"

I had asked for advice and I took it. So I decided to leave John Brown's office. This opened before me a new vista whose horizon was still hidden from me. I did not look far ahead. For the present I was satisfied to enter Proudfoot's studio and begin work as his assistant.

I spent almost six months there, building up his group of a soldier being held up by an angel. He must have had great trust in my ability, for he let me carry on without assisting me, or making suggestions. There came a time when I felt that I had done as much as I could, and that it was ready for Proudfoot to take over. We then said goodbye to one another.

Roots and Response

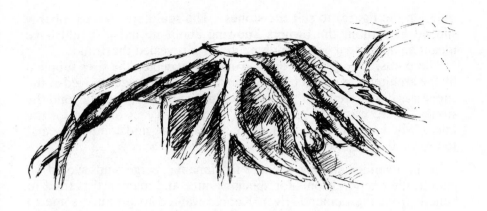

Was I going to measure up to the challenge when I left Proudfoot's studio to work on my own? I had been preparing myself for this step for many years, yet when my dream became a reality I was not actually ready. I did not know how sculptors dealt with their work, or sold it. I would just go to my studio in the morning, and work away till it was time to go to bed, though that is rather too simple. For a time I was fortunate. As I started my professional life with forty pounds in the bank, I considered myself rich, and John Keppie was finding me commissions. Already in 1922 I had modelled him in appreciation of our friendship. He must have liked the bronze, for he in turn made me a member of the Glasgow Institute of the Fine Arts.

When John Keppie was building a new warehouse at Glasgow Cross he included three groups of sculpture on the three facades, and he decided to share the work between Alexander Proudfoot, Archibald Dawson and myself, to avoid being accused of favouritism. The building was wedge shaped and each of the three sides were to have two figures. They had to be seated or crouching figures because of the design. The architects had sent us the dimensions of the stones they had ordered, but knowing builders I felt it safer to measure out the stones that were placed in position. I had already designed the two figures, and after my visit to the site I discovered that the stones which the builders had provided had a smaller projection than the architects had specified.

Just then John Keppie brought in Sir William Reid Dick, the London Scot, already a distinguished sculptor, to show him my designs, which represented Painting and Sculpture. They were to be on the most important facade, facing Trongate, a kind of peace offering in case I might be offended at not being given the whole commission.

When I told him what I had found out, Sir William turned to Keppie and asked him if he would get the builders to change the stones, as would have been the case in London. "Oh no, Benno will slightly redesign the figures to suit the stones." The sculptures were probably slipped in without the owners knowing about it, and it would have meant an additional cost, which might have revealed the 'fraud'.

There was, of course, a sequel. Proudfoot accepted the sizes supplied by the architects as correct, and when his full scale model arrived at the site it was discovered that the knees of his figures projected beyond the stones. There was only one solution — to add pieces of stone for the knees. My figures I redesigned, more solid looking and compact — and to my mind a better composition.

In the twenties etching became fashionable. Large sums would be paid in the auction rooms for special prints, and many artists tried to benefit from the demand. Even Keppie wanted to produce some to prove that he could master the medium. For this he had to draw, and he was really keen. Every Saturday afternoon we would both go out to sketch. We would walk along the Forth and Clyde Canal, or we would take a tramcar to the outskirts of the city and walk from there. When we found something which Keppie considered suitable, we would sit down, make ourselves comfortable, and draw.

For me, the outings were of immense importance. Usually I had to draw what Keppie chose, but this did not worry me, so long as I drew. It helped me to loosen my hand and my line. On the way back to town we would stop for a cup of tea, and it became an unwritten rule that he would pay one Saturday, and I the next. He kept good accounting, and if I was not quick enough he would say, "Benno, it is your turn". We continued these outings for years, even for some time after I married, until my wife began to protest that it was not fair to leave her alone on Saturday afternoons, considering that she herself was busy all week in her dressmaking shop. She was right, but Keppie, being a bachelor, remained unconvinced.

All this time I was trying to learn my craft. I could find no one then in Glasgow, who could inspire, or even guide me. It was like working in no man's land, or in a vacuum. I got friends to pose for me. I studied the masters, Donatello and Michaelangelo, and tried to understand how they achieved their results.

Having had an academic education, my tastes naturally leaned towards the academic. Michaelangelo was the giant, the supreme master of carving marble, and his figures evoked the majesty of mankind. His mind, I always felt, was above the human concept, and the feelings he aroused in me when looking at his figures were not of the figures themselves, because they were so majestic, but of the sculptor who created them. Only in the unfinished slaves can one feel a certain human contact with them because of their suffering, but all in all, although we admire, even venerate Michaelangelo, his figures, great though they are, lack the touch of humanity.

86

This humanity is the touchstone of Donatello's sculpture. His prophets are people one can meet and pass in the street, for they are people of flesh and blood, people one can talk or argue with. Although Donatello carved almost all his larger figures in marble, he also worked a good deal in bronze, especially his church reliefs, and mainly from these, as well as from Rodin and Epstein I learned how to model for bronze.

When I began to model, Rodin's name was on everyone's lips. He was the hero who had rescued sculpture from the abyss into which it had fallen, and who had regenerated it from the outmoded and outworn creed of repetitive, dull classicism.

In my student days in Glasgow I used to haunt the second hand bookshops and buy whatever old art magazines I could find. It satisfied my urge to learn about, if only in reproduction, the works I was unable to see in reality. From all those magazines I remember most clearly a criticism of a sculpture by Alphonse Legros 'Death and the Woodcutter'. Legros was a fellow student of Rodin's in Paris, and they remained life-long friends. He spent most of his life in London, having received a teaching post there. Although he occasionally produced some sculpture, he was by profession an engraver. 'Death and the Woodcutter' represents the woodcutter hurrying home with a bundle of faggots heavy on his shoulder, being surprised by Death hovering over him from behind. This work was full of rugged strength, lumpy and sketchy, of shuddering appeal.

The critic in the magazine deplored its apparently unfinished state, for, whilst painting might be left sketchy, because the inspiration of the artist may have been of short duration, sculpture, because of the nature of its material and the labour of its creation, could not stand sketchiness. It must be properly executed. This truly summed up the attitude that prevailed before Rodin came on the scene. Since his advent, sculptors have fought to free their Art from the shades of misunderstood tradition and misapplied conventions.

Sculpture had not yet abandoned its neo-classical tradition, and Carrara marble was still considered the ideal medium for its execution. It is surprising to realise that even Rodin found marble alluring, although his marbles were greatly inferior to his bronzes. He was a modeller par excellence, unequalled before or since, and it was with his modelling that he created the revolution that made him world famous and enshrined his name alongside Donatello and Michaelangelo. He telescoped four hundred years into forty.

One of Rodin's earliest busts, that of Father Eymard, was modelled in 1863. It is important to keep dates in one's mind, for it can tell us which work inspired which. When we look at this bust, we notice that Rodin was still following the accepted tradition of his day. His surfaces are smooth, the treatment of the hair hard and decorative, in the style of carved hair as then practised. But even here we see an innovation, at least, this is how it strikes me. The prominences are strong and the hollows are deep. Whether this was true to life, or intentional, it is impossible to say, for Rodin was plagued for his whole life with bad eyesight. However, later, when he was working in Belgium as an assistant to another sculptor, he saw how light acted on his figures on buildings, how important the shadows became. From this he learned to accentuate the prominences and deepen the hollows. Father Eymard could have been copied in marble without losing anything of the intensity of life it portrays in the bronze.

When we study the 'Man with the Broken Nose' we can already see a slight change, and it was modelled only a year later. The surface has softened, so has the hair: when we look at the 'Walking Man' of 1877 — a study for his 'St. John' — which is intended for bronze, we can see its modelling, and the flow of his undulating surface, with its lumps and 'unfinished' muscles which could not be translated into marble. Its surface has a life of its own, and in marble this would look artificial. His completed 'John the Baptist' of a year later is definitely modelled for bronze. One need only look at the hair and the beard to realise that to copy these in marble would be a thankless task. In any case it would have needed an additional support for strength. The modelling of the face has become fluid and sensitive, and the hands explain what the open mouth is proclaiming.

Rodin himself says in his talks with Paul Gsell that "Sculpture is the art of the hole and the lump. . . In sculpture the projection of the muscles must be accentuated, the shortenings heightened, the holes made deeper". Herein lies the secret of Rodin's modelling. The aesthetic side, the idea of beauty, of character, of expression, is not for me to discuss here. Here my aim is only to show Rodin's development as a modeller — his technique.

The two busts, the one of Jean-Paul Laurens, and the other of Alphonse Legros, both modelled in 1881, seem deceptive at first glance. Their smooth surfaces are really not so smooth, they are modelled surfaces, and the hair and beards are not artificial, they are alive and don't detract from the expressions of the faces. On the contrary, they augment and accentuate their subjects. They unite the rhythm of the rest of the modelling, except that they are more complex and express the virtuosity of the master.

When we look at one of the heads of Balzac — a study for the monument — which was modelled in 1893, thirty years since Father Eymard, the surface modelling has been broken up to take on the quality of a many-faceted diamond, the hair being treated as a sculptural mass, though also broken up. It is in this head that we see in Rodin the sculptor of the Impressionist School. It seems as though he wanted to imprison sunlight in his work, and one must agree that he has achieved his aim.

Rodin had a good deal to say about the 'finish' of a piece of sculpture. "The ignorant say 'That is not finished' but there is no notion more false than that of finish. The public which has been perverted by academical prejudices, confound art with neatness and spruceness."

He demonstrates it in the torso of his 'Walking Man' and in some of his heads, the famous one being the lump on the nose of his Balzac. I doubt whether it got there accidentally. Rodin took too long on a work to make such a mistake. I always try to find a logical explanation. Balzac had a riot of unruly hair, and Rodin probably let one strand fall between the eyes. Then he found that it destroyed the massive forehead and took it away, leaving a bit on the nose to remove later, but which he discovered helped to focus attention on the eyes. These 'lumps' can be seen in some of his portraits, but they only emphasize the fact that he modelled the heads for casting in bronze.

We now come to the portrait of the sculptor, Eugene Guillaume, modelled in 1903. Forty years had passed since he modelled Father Eymard. This head contains all the characteristics which are to be found separately in the preceding works. It has a unity of line, it is composed of lumps and hollows, every part having a sculptural significance, as if the bronze has congealed on the surface of the portrait without a hand ever touching it. In addition, it has not only a lump on its nose, it also has one on its forehead! Talk about 'finish'? A work is finished when the sculptor considers he has put all he can, or needs, into it. Polishing only results in loss of vitality and truth of vision. One feels that this head of Guillaume was created in a frenzy, that is has gone through the 'crucible of fire'. He started on his pilgrimage with the head of Father Eymard, and it took him forty years of researching in the sculptural labyrinth to reach fulfilment, his pilgrimage completed.

At the time I was attending evening classes at the School of Art, French was a language I could read fluently, though I spoke it only haltingly. I had bought a book in French in 1916, *L'Art Entretiens Réunis* by Paul Gsell, about his conversations with Rodin. It made such an impression on me that I never forgot it. Rodin was obsessed with movement, and what remained most vividly in my memory was his discussion of Rude's statue of Marshal Ney.

Rodin explains how the sculptor has portrayed in the figure a sequence of movements, or a progression of acts. From this I learned that a figure in movement should express not just one moment in time — a photograph does this — but that a figure should not be static, it should move and live in time. A whole chapter is devoted to Rodin's exposition of the figure in movement and emotion, yet he forgets to mention that this means an added dimension — the time element — in sculpture.

"A few minutes ago you mentioned the Marshal Ney, done by Rude.

Do you remember the figure well?" asked Rodin.

"Yes," I replied, "the hero has raised his sword and is shouting 'Forward' to his troops."

"That's true! You must take a better look next time you go by the statue. Then you'll notice that both the Marshal's legs, and the hand holding the scabbard are in the same position as when he drew the sabre: The left leg is drawn back so the weapon is better grasped by the right hand, which has drawn it. The left hand is up as though still presenting the scabbard.

Now, take a look at the torso. It must have been slightly turned to the left when he made the gesture I have just described, but now it's straightening up again and the chest is expanding. The head is turning to roar at his soldiers to attack. Then at last, you see the right arm being raised to brandish the sabre.

So, there's the proof of what I've been saying. This statue's movement is changing over from the Marshal's original position, when drawing his sword, to the one of hurling himself at the enemy with raised weapon. There you have the whole secret of the way in which art interprets gestures. The sculptor forces the onlooker, so to speak, to follow the development of action through the individual. In the example we have chosen, you are obliged to move your eyes upward from the legs to the raised arm. On the way up you find the various parts of the statue represented at successive moments. This gives you the illusion of having seen a movement carried out."

Rodin praises Rude for having invented this illusion of movement — the fourth dimension in sculpture.

He discusses his 'Burghers of Calais' at length, in which he expresses the plethora of movements and feelings of its various characters. But this is not my story. Mine was to give you the source of my inspiration, and to explain how I developed it to include it in portraiture.

Living flesh is mobile and soft to the touch. The head can be likened to a flower, and like a flower it opens up and yields its beauty, and often its fragrance — its character. When one looks at an Egyptian mummy, one notices that the skin is stretched tightly over the skull. In a living person the bony structure can still be seen; some parts are prominent, some have to be discovered in one's search for the form. But the skin and flesh can move on the skull, they do not recede. I try to model the fleshy tissue as if it projects towards me, vibrating with life, not receding from me as in death. The face has to feel free from the skull, yet to be seen as supported by it, giving it personal shape, even deciding its characteristics.

In literature, time is optional. Music cannot exist without time. It registers time. Sculpture, on the other hand, deals with mass and volume, and one moment in the expression of a person's face in sculpture is timeless and can extend to eternity. The Greeks, when carving a head, gave its features idealistic form only, with seldom any expression, save that of serenity, in a goddess. The Roman sculptors developed character in their portraits, and they left us a gallery of character studies, the like of which has never been equalled. But even they represented in one portrait just one expression, just one moment in time.

What I have been trying to introduce into my portraits is this element of time. If I have done something that other sculptors did not attempt, or did not think of, it was this broadening of the sphere of portrait sculpture by introducing the time element.

We all know that the human face is seldom symmetrical, and sculptors have used this asymmetry to accentuate character and even gain a stronger likeness. True, it helps, but does not go far enough. What I have tried to do in addition, is to give both sides of the face a slightly different expression, a slightly different touch not easily noticeable, yet sufficient to give my portrait a more lively and evanescent quality. In other words, I try to model a head in motion, not giving it a static look, but rather a fleeting one.

I don't claim originality for this. I learned it from Rude, as explained by Rodin, but even Rodin did not, or failed to apply it to his portraiture.

Yet the freshness of his outlook, the vitality he was able to infuse into his work, made me his disciple, for I felt a kinship with his ideas in the freedom of his modelling. In Donatello I found my grandfather and in Rodin my father. I wish to state specifically the source of my artistic inspiration, because art critics with a superficial acquaintance of sculpture used to call me the 'Scottish Epstein', or were happy to place me in Epstein's camp. He preceded me by twenty years. His character studies were unmistakeably individual and he dominated the art stage throughout his lifetime. Because, before me, Scotland had not produced an original sculptor, the critics were looking for my affiliation. They had to pigeon-hole me, and they found it in Epstein. During the early stages of my acquaintance with him I mentioned what the critics said about me, and he burst out, "Rubbish! You are a sculptor in your own right". Both being Jewish we must have inherited some national traits that singled us out, but in different ways. In another context, when asked this question, my reply was that I considered Epstein as my elder brother.

Although I met Jacob Epstein in the early twenties, I visited him very seldom. I was not often in London on a Sunday when he was receiving, and I did not like to go and interrupt him at his work. I know how I detest people dropping in just to say "hello", and keep me from working for an hour or more. What is worse, one's concentration is shattered and is not easily recaptured.

At one meeting I was telling him about Frank Dobson who had visited the Glasgow School of Art to deliver an address, when he had told us during his lecture that he had gone to see an exhibition in London and had missed a Maillol that was on show there. This took place when Dobson was a young man. "The bastard did not know his father," was Epstein's sarcastic outburst.

On another occasion there were quite a few people in his sittingroom — I dislike calling it a drawing room; he would have disliked it himself. On a sideboard were a few of his busts, and I stood spellbound in front of them. They were really magnificent. I just stood there, silent. Duncan Macdonald, who was with me, feeling that Epstein might misinterpret my silence, assured him that I was one of his great admirers. And so I was. When I got to know him better I told him, "I teach and preach Epstein". He got quite excited and turned to the company in the room "Have you heard what he has just said? Have you heard?"

Although we had two bronze foundries in Edinburgh, after a while I decided to have my bronzes cast in London. It so turned out that the foundry I was recommended to was the foundry that cast all of Epstein's work. He used to visit the foundry every week to see the progress of his bronzes, or to touch up the waxes if necessary. So naturally he was able to see all my works as they were being cast, while I, visiting London only periodically, would only see a few of his before they went on exhibition. When he would notice a head he liked he would say to Mr. Gaskin, the founder, "Tell Schotz it is a jolly good head", and another time, "Tell Schotz he has made a corner in Scotland", to which my reply was, "Tell Epstein he has made a corner in the world".

On the other hand he could be quite jealous of his proprietorial rights, if one can put it this way, for if he modelled a negro he considered it wrong for anyone else to model one. He felt he was being copied. He has modelled a number of negresses, but I have only seen one male negro he modelled, Paul Robeson. I had modelled Berto Pasuka, the creator of the first Negro Ballet. He was a West Indian, and he had a magnificent head. When he brought his ballet to Glasgow I asked him to pose for me and had two sittings. When Epstein saw it in the foundry he exclaimed, "Everybody is now doing negroes!", so Gaskin told me. In my long life I have only modelled three negroes, of which only two saw the light of day. The other is a carving in lignum vitae.

In Epstein's sittingroom there stood on a small low table the draped bust of his wife, between two candlesticks. "This bronze should be in a cathedral or a church!" he exclaimed once. In the Glasgow Art Club we have an early mask of his wife. It was a gift from Sir D. Y. Cameron who could not live with it any longer, or so he told us. That, of course, is a personal viewpoint. In it Mrs. Epstein looks young and attractive. In the bust which was modelled between 1917 and 1920, she already looks aged. In a way, it is a tribute to Donatello, who must have inspired this work. While in Donatello's bust the drapery is simple, Epstein expended himself in making the most of the mantilla.

When I used to visit their home on a Sunday, Mrs. Epstein presided over tea which she poured out endlessly. I never saw her stand up and move about; I was told that she was a mountain of a woman. Epstein was always very gentle towards her. I have seen a number of letters she wrote to a Glasgow friend, Joe Levy, mostly about their finances, and having to dine at clients' homes when they would have preferred not to. They had to do it to stay solvent. This was during the war years when Epstein was sorely hit by lack of commissions and sales. He would be merciless when attacked, but at the same time he was kind to his friends and would not tolerate one being humbled in his presence, as was the case when Peggy Jean, then already well in her teens, began to laugh at the way I pronounced Maillol. He turned round to her and his look was enough to silence her. S. S. Samuel of Liverpool told me that he received a wire one day from Peggy Jean, "Epstein needs a thousand pounds immediately". Seemingly she always addressed her father as Epstein. So Mr. Samuel took the train to London, rounded up a few of his friends, bought the life size Madonna himself, and Epstein received more than he needed.

There has been a great song made about the 'Churchill'. Somebody discovered that there were twelve bronzes of it instead of the stipulated ten. In my opinion it did not matter a hoot about the extra two. Mr. Samuel told me that after Epstein had modelled Einstein and it was going to be exhibited in the Leicester Gallery in London, he was phoned up and told what a fine portrait it was, and that there would be only six bronzes cast from it, and if he wanted one he would have to reserve it. He was being given the chance because he was a collector of Epstein's work. Mr. Samuel had to pay a special price for his, because he was assured there would only be six, but among his own friends he can count eighteen! He was not annoyed or angry about it, but was rather amused. It is not as if Epstein died a rich man. Far from it. There was a demand for this head and Epstein cast them to stay alive. He probably did not even realise how he had overcast, or he may not have been told by the Gallery how many were to be cast.

In 1937 I had to give an address on Jewish Art to a Jewish audience and I proclaimed Epstein as the first really modern Jewish sculptor. In my lecture I referred to a bust of his I saw in the Tate Gallery. I was greatly moved by it.

"I stand and look at a bust of a young woman. Her face is turned upwards, her wide open eyes are straining forward, and the expression on her face — a joy of some approaching revelation, yet in that joy there lurks a feeling of forlornness, a toy in the hands of fate. You feel that she is oblivious to the world around her, that her whole soul is straining towards the fulfilment of an inner fervour — to be lost in its realisation."

93

I read it correctly, but my deductions were wrong. I only discovered that years afterwards. I took this work to express the Jewish consent to fate, or be it destiny, but I was completely wrong. Epstein expresses in this work his personal love for this girl, and hers for him. This was Kathleen, whose love life with Epstein lasted till his death, and whom he ultimately married when his first wife died suddenly after a fall on ice.

Frank Dobson, who was at one time considered the most advanced British sculptor, complained to me that Epstein stressed his 'racial' protest in his works, and by racial he probably meant Jewish. It must have made him feel uncomfortable. This point was never mentioned by critics who vilified him. Did they see it also in his busts, but did not dare to mention it in the Press? English sculptors made portraiture stale and impersonal. Epstein's portraits expressed powerful characters, and at times gave even Gentiles Jewish features.

I, myself, read into his Jacob Kramer the Jewish suffering; in his Robert Graham the nobility and pride of the Jewish race; in Rabindranath Tagore the maturity and wisdom of our Jewish sages; in Einstein's eyes the light of our genius; in Paul Robeson our hope and inspiration; in Lord Fisher our fierce determination, and in his Pinager our ageless humility. I could go on in this strain, for in Epstein's portraits are expressed the whole gamut of Jewish experience. I have not touched on his female portraits, full of beauty, reverence, delicacy, tenderness and love. He is our Shakespeare in portraiture.

The news of his death was withheld for twenty-four hours. Could it have been for pressing financial reasons? Was the large group he was working on for the Bowater building, Hyde Park, not yet assembled, and for the contract to be fulfilled had it to be done by himself in his lifetime? I could be entirely wrong, but at the time it was quite a talking point.

When his death was announced, *The Scotsman,* Edinburgh's national newspaper telephoned me in the evening and asked me to write a short obituary on the spot. As it was required for their morning edition, I had to give it to them on the phone within a matter of minutes. I was greatly shocked, for I did not know of his death until the phone call, and wrote under great strain.

"The news of Jacob Epstein's death comes with stark suddenness. No lingering for him; no waning of his creative genius. He kept working to the very end, just when public commissions began to crowd in upon him.

English good breeding and reserve were outraged when Epstein first burst upon the scene with his carved groups on the British Medical Association building and his uncompromising portraits, character studies in bronze.

He was no respecter of personalities. And his studies were forthright and revealing. Epstein became the centre of a storm of British art and a legitimate target for abuse and vilification, which lost its motivation only with the advent of our post war group of near abstract sculptors.

Yet it was he who made their acceptance possible, but he himself stood in the background, aloof from all isms and movements, remaining true to himself from his first portrait to his last.

It is regrettable that few public commissions came his way when he was in full vigour. Epstein was a traditionalist in the sense that he followed on after Rodin in a logical sequence. He was a supreme master of modelling, using it not as an end in itself but to interpret character and emotion.

Epstein made sculpture a household word in Britain, and one would have said of him, changing the words of T. S. Eliot:

"In the room the women come and go,
Talking of Michaelangelo".

His output was large, and a list of his portraits might read like a catalogue from a Hall of Fame. But as he himself has said, he tried to make each portrait into a work of art, and seldom failed.

His latest and largest work, a group for the new entrance to Hyde Park at Knightsbridge is now being completed — a monument to a giant of British art.

The Scotsman 22nd August 1959.

One afternoon Duncan Macdonald and McNeill Reid climbed up to my studio to see what I might have for a one-man exhibition. I was lifting a heavy clay bust from the floor when suddenly I had to put it down and rush to my washbasin where I vomited blood. Duncan knew what had happened to me, for he had had a burst duodenum. He decided to stay with me while McNeill went downstairs for help. As he was walking along West Regent Street he suddenly noticed an ambulance. Their base happened to be at the corner of Blythswood Square, and within half an hour I was safely in a cot in the Royal Infirmary. I remember the date, as it took place on 25th January 1925, Robert Burns's birthday. I needed no operation, but I was kept in hospital for seven weeks before I was considered fit to leave.

When the Chief of the ward arrived to go round the patients and saw a new face, the first question he asked the nurses was whether they had washed me. "He needed no washing, he was very clean," was their comment. I had to smile, but inwardly was sad that the chief might think me dirty. John Keppie got to know about my collapse and came to visit me the next day. He knew the Chief of the ward, and within a day I was moved to a side room, where I had peace and quietness, except that the nurses would come in and tickle my toes. What a fine bunch of girls!

I had many visitors, and they wanted to know which of the girls who came to visit me was 'the real one'. When Milly Stelmach came in I nodded to the nurse who happened to bring her in to let her know that she was 'it'.

Milly took my affairs in hand. She gave notice to my landlady and removed all my belongings to the studio. She and her younger sister Dora discovered a sea chest full of holed socks, which I used to dump into the chest hoping to have time one day to darn them. Before I left home I was taught to sew, to darn, to mend, all the things that are essential for a clean and tidy way of living. The one thing I lacked was time, therefore little mending was done, as it was easier to buy new articles of clothing and save the time for something more important. I used to dress well. I usually had a rose in the buttonhole of my lapel, wore spats and gloves, and sported a silver topped cane. I was proud of my appearance, and for many years was considered the best dressed artist in town. Dora told me afterwards that Milly had tried to darn some of the socks, and that she must have been really smitten to attempt the impossible.

I had met Milly and Dora in the home of Nathan and Annie Morris. He was a Hebrew teacher who came to Glasgow from Poland, via Liverpool, and we had been friends for some years. They were young, well read, and loved music. Nathan's hours in the Hebrew school were in the evening, and this confined their socialising, with the result that they were satisfied with a few friends. They had three sons, of whom the eldest, Jeremiah became a professor, Max a headmaster, and the youngest, Isaiah, a doctor, killed in Israel during the War of Liberation.

Milly's mother had died leaving four children, three girls and a boy. Mrs. Morris, having no daughters decided more or less to 'adopt' the two elder girls who used to visit her often. Milly, the eldest, was born in London, her parents having emigrated from Russia, but moved to Edinburgh, and from there to Glasgow. Milly, from the age of sixteen had to take over the running of the home, do the cooking, and was also made to come into her father's business to learn tailoring.

I began to see her more often, for I was fascinated by her features and figure. She had a Mongolian type of face, almond shaped eyes, high cheekbones, a sensuous full mouth, dark sleek hair, smooth skin, her face narrowing from the broad cheekbones to the chin. She was of medium height, well shaped, and had high placed breasts, the kind I began to think of as the ideal for a woman, as portrayed in Greek sculpture.

When I began to take Milly out, Annie Morris warned her against me, saying that being a sculptor, I saw a woman as a butcher saw a side of beef. She did not want Milly to fall in love with me and then get the

96

shock of being dropped. I visited her often, and when I would fail to appear for a few days, I would find a note put through my studio door by Dora asking me why they had not seen me for some time. Milly always had a bevy of young men around her, but they began to drop off when they saw me there so often, till the two of us got a better chance to know one another. Joe Ancill became our chaperone, and for some time the three of us would walk out together, not because I wanted additional company, but he visited me so frequently, that he almost became my other half.

Joe had one good quality; he spoke little and was a good listener. When I was working on a composition and had difficulty getting into my clay the idea I was trying to express, I used to talk to him, explaining what I wanted to do, and, strangely enough, while I was talking, and telling him where I seemed to have gone wrong, the problem would often solve itself. Joe could have become a fine artist had he received greater encouragement from his parents, or had he greater willpower. I had hoped that he would receive an impetus from seeing me work, as did some other artists, who used to call me 'the match', for I used to fire them with a new enthusiasm when they visited me and saw me at work. I could not tell him to go home and paint. One can only inspire by example. But Joe was a docile man, not daring to ask for a proper room in which to work, which is why he spent so much time in my place, and why we used to visit the Stelmach home together. Later he also decided to let me go by myself, and so my courtship began.

Milly and Dora I have already introduced to you. Then followed Asher, the only son, and Margaret, the youngest. Max Stelmach was among the finest ladies' tailors in Glasgow, but as so often happens, the man who has the talent lacks business acumen and is incapable of exploiting his talent for gain. He had a fine clientele who came to him from all parts of Scotland, but he made no capital out of his business. Dora won the Gold Medal at the Athenaeum, and she was determined to, and did go, to the University. Asher was also made to come into his father's business. Margaret was still at school, but later took up shorthand typing. When the family began to grow up, Milly opened a dressmaking business to become independent of her father and to speed our marriage. She realised that I did not yet earn enough to support us both.

When I came out of hospital I climbed the three flights of stairs just to see my studio, but then hardly went up again till September. Yet, my first exhibition in the Reid Gallery took place the following year. I still remember my feelings that day when I entered the gallery and saw my sculptures beautifully arranged. Duncan Macdonald was in the gallery with some others, and I only looked, smiled, and said nothing. When Duncan went up to their office I joined him, and when we were alone I embraced him. We were both happy. "I thought you were already blasé about it all when I saw you in the gallery," he said.

The exhibition was a success. Duncan, to my great surprise, had asked Hugh Walpole to write the introduction to the catalogue, although we had met only on the one occasion when I had modelled him.

"Benno Schotz's work is authentic. That is no light thing to say in these days when it is so easy to pick up the externals of an art and pretend that it is the real thing.

I imagine that the sculptor of this post-war world has a difficult task in front of him and especially in Great Britain, because the inroads of the Philistine who is sure that he knows as much about art as anyone else, and who is also certain that anyone who disagrees with him is only posing for effect have been, of late, remarkably vicious. Modern sculpture in this country is tempted therefore on both sides to falsify; it can be on the one hand extravagantly extreme in order to prove its sincerity, and then becomes more intent upon its truth, or in its desire to protest its normality it may be a great deal more insipid than its talent deserves.

Benno Schotz is, I think, one of the sincerest artists I have ever encountered. You feel as you watch him at work that he is conscious of nothing but the capture of the truth. Everyone knows that the truth is the most elusive thing alive, but I think it would be impossible for anyone to study these sculptures of Mr. Schotz and deny that, criticise him as you may, they are finely and even magnificently veracious. They are beautiful too and they promise still more beauty to come. What is to me interesting in this exhibition is the personal individual capture of a truthful beauty that is Benno Schotz's alone, but that is also common to all the beauty in the world. This it is to be a fine artist and by sacrificing anything and everything to an unswerving rectitude the artist here has captured, I fancy, greater splendours than he knows.

Finally his work is, I think, in spite of its strength remarkably tender. Tenderness and delicacy are dangerous words to use about an artist these days. We are, I am certain, far too apprehensive of them, but the tenderness in Benno Schotz's work informs the strength; he is so kindly as a true artist dares to be. That is not to say that he is sentimental; he refuses to give you an inch more of feeling than he knows to be there, but on the other hand no fear of the modern cynic restrains him from showing his feelings.

And in these days how many artists are seeking exactly this compromise and failing to find it!"

Hugh Walpole

I sold well and received commissions. One of them was to model Brigadier General J. B. Walker, the only Territorial officer to reach such a high rank in the army during the 1914-18 war. He told me a rather interesting story, one that convinced him of the truth of the Exodus from Egypt, when the waters of the Red Sea divided to let the Children of Israel pass across. He was present at the Nile or one of its delta branches when suddenly a storm blew up and literally drove the waters of the river back, lifting them like a wall. He was amazed at the spectacle, for the bed of the river became dry, just mud, sufficient for people to pass across it. Did this natural phenomenon take place when the Israelites were leaving Egypt? There are references to such happenings in some histories, but here was a person who had actually witnessed it.

One incident which occurred during my exhibition deserves mention. Mr. John Blyth, a well known art collector from Kirkcaldy had come into the gallery while I was there, and McNeill Reid engaged him in conversation. To me it appeared that he was interested in my 'Reverie', but after a little time Mr. Reid took him upstairs to their private office. When Mr. Blyth left, my 'Reverie' remained unsold. When I asked why, McNeill replied, "If you could sell a man something worth a few hundred pounds, would you prefer to sell him something worth only forty?" From this I realised that one-man shows are 'front window' displays to tempt buyers in, but that the galleries could not survive from their exhibitions alone. They have to sell valuable works on the side.

One day, Mr. Proudfoot of the Scottish Gallery in Edinburgh, (not to be confused with the sculptor) had come in to see my show. I already knew him fairly well, and also that he considered Mr. Blyth his preserve. I mentioned Mr. Blyth's visit, and his interest in my piece. On the spot Mr. Proudfoot asked me how many copies were available. I usually only cast ten bronzes of each work and told him that I still had three available. "I will take the three" was his decision. The show was just about finished and I did not think there was a chance of an additional sale, so I agreed to let him have them. Mr. Proudfoot must have thought that he would sell one copy to Mr. Blyth, and at the same time prevent him buying the work from Reid's.

I found out later that Mr Blyth did not buy a 'Reverie' from Aitken Dott, the owners of the Scottish Gallery, and Mr. Proudfoot was not able to dispose of them for a long time. Every time I went into that gallery, he would greet me with the question, "Can I sell you a 'Reverie'?" It became an embarrassment.

In 1928 the Royal Scottish Academy, in its annual exhibition included a few pieces by Henri Gaudier-Brzeshka, the young French sculptor who worked in London, and who had been killed in 1917. At the private view the galleries were crowded, including the Sculpture Hall. I had been looking at a small marble of a dog by Gaudier and had stepped back a little to study its design. It had been placed on a pedestal against a pillar at the narrow passage between it and the wall. A lady trying to pass someone in the passage came in contact with the pedestal. It gave a slight lurch, and down slid the marble dog and broke. It happened so quickly that I had no time to save it.

I was deeply shocked for I admired the work of Gaudier-Brzeshka, and here was one that could not be replaced. When I visited the gallery a week or two later, there, to my surprise and annoyance, in its place sat my 'Reverie'.

As a result, I did not want to approach Mr. Proudfoot for a one-man show. However, when he died and his French born widow took over, I did not hesitate to ask her for one, in 1945. I did not realise that she would take little interest in it. I had already learned from Duncan Macdonald that sculpture has to be urged onto people. I had a friend in Glasgow who spoke of a certain dealer as one who could not sell a glass of water in the Sahara desert. Mrs. Proudfoot may have been good at selling paintings when she had a client, but even when important people came into the gallery, she would not appear.

During one of my visits to my show, in came Mr. Blyth, and he and Mrs. Proudfoot closetted themselves together, and only later, as a mark of condescension, came back into the gallery where my sculpture was on display, to exchange greetings with me. I asked him if he would buy a piece for the Kirkcaldy Gallery, one of the few that had no work of mine, but he said to me, "There has been a great deal of wire pulling to get paintings into our Gallery, so we decided not to buy paintings of living artists". This made me see red. I just could not contain myself and burst out, "In that case, the sooner it burns down the better". He got a terrible shock. "Oh, don't say that, don't say that." "I do, and I mean it," was my reply. We parted, and when he had left the gallery Mrs. Proudfoot told me that he had bought 'Sleeping Boy', priced at the magnificent sum of twenty-five pounds, for his own collection.

In Kirkcaldy John Blyth was a tin God, and had everything in the Gallery his own way, for it was hoped that he would leave his own collection of paintings to it. Great was their disappointment when he left them nothing. Later the Gallery purchased part of his collection. The Gallery still has no Benno Schotz.

The show was a failure. I could not, nor would I ask for another show from Mrs. Proudfoot. Edinburgh has not been my strong suit, and if I sell there it is to Americans, or to Canadians, or even to South Africans.

While on the subject of Glasgow and Edinburgh, the rivalry between the two cities is no fiction, but solid fact. Edinburgh considers itself the cultural centre of Scotland, while they charge Glasgow with holding the purse, that it is packed with wealthy merchants without culture or education. This seems to extend itself even to art, especially now that the International Festival of Arts is the preserve of Edinburgh. 'The Glasgow School of Painters' at the turn of the century did not remain in Glasgow. Some settled in London, others even moved to Edinburgh to give point to the rivalry, one of the reasons being that the Royal Scottish Academy is based there.

By the time my 1926 exhibition took place Alexander Reid had retired from the business, and in 1927 McNeill Reid asked me to model his father. He lived in Blanefield, near Glasgow, and when I arrived to arrange for sittings I found him in his garden trimming bushes and giving them lovely round shapes. "This is sculpture!" I exclaimed, and he replied, "Yes, it is. Were I to live my life over again as an art dealer, I would pay more attention to sculpture".

McNeill joined us shortly afterwards, probably to make his father more at ease with me, but the chief subject of their conversation was Van Gogh's portrait of him. McNeill told his father that he now knew where it was. The firm wanted £1,400 for it, and should he buy it? Alexander Reid said that it was too much, and in any case it was not very good! Some years ago the City of Glasgow paid £172,000 for it!

After two sittings in his attic I realised that I could not produce my best work in the cramped conditions and the restricted lighting, and I received two more sittings in my own studio. Mr. Reid was failing rapidly, for after sitting for ten to fifteen minutes he would become pale and needed a rest and a stimulant to revive him.

McNeill did not like the head I modelled of his father, because he saw in it a dying man. Indeed, he died six months later. The son then realised that my bronze expressed truth, in addition to a likeness, and ordered a second bronze which he presented to the Kelvingrove Art Gallery. It was interesting to see the Van Gogh portrait and my bronze side by side after the former was hung in the Gallery. Probably fifty years separated the execution of the two, yet the likeness between them is unmistakeable. Milly was always very fond of this work, and considered it one of my best.

After the war in 1918 Messrs. MacDonald and Creswick opened a bronze foundry in Edinburgh and for many years they cast my bronzes. Although their work was quite good, and became excellent when they secured an Italian caster, they knew little about patination and their greens were unsatisfactory. This compelled me to study the toning of bronzes, and after my 1926 exhibition I did little else for two years. Foundries consider their work a secret, especially toning. Sir William Reid Dick also toned his own bronzes, and on one occasion while examining one of them in his studio I surprised him by exclaiming, "I see you've been using iron in this green!" One gradually learns which chemicals to use to obtain certain effects.

It has been my rule, if at all possible, never to model what I have not seen myself. To give one example. The two main doors of the Pettigrew and Stephens building for which I modelled groups, had at their ends rams' heads to represent their trade in woollen goods. To model these I ordered from a butcher a freshly killed ram's head, and it remained in my studio until my visitors began to protest at the smell.

Since I was very friendly with Cecily Walton, the artist, and daughter of the well known Edinburgh painter E. A. Walton, she suggested that I model her. I decided on a large bust including her arms and hands. She wanted me to model her with a bunch of Arum lilies in her arms. I disliked the idea, for I did not see how Arum lilies came into the picture; but I compromised. At that time quite a few of my sculptures had a vertical line somewhere in their compositions, like an exclamation mark. I therefore decided to make of the flower the vertical exclamation mark. My trouble was that I had never seen a real lily. I had seen some artificial ones, and they had for a stem a thin wire covered with a green winding ribbon. I realised that I could not make her hold the lily upright by this thin stem for this would have been artistically wrong, and therefore I placed the flower itself touching the tips of her closed fingers.

Had I seen the real flower and its thick stem I would have raised it up a good deal to produce a better and truer work. For some reason I never corrected my mistake, it was never cast in bronze, and was finally destroyed when I moved to Ruskin Terrace Lane. I regret that I don't even have a photograph of it, but this taught me the important lesson never to model anything that I have not studied closely at first hand. The trouble about modelling a bust with arms and hands seems to be that sculptors and their sitters feel they need to give the hands a reason for being there. Jacob Epstein never bothered about this aspect of his busts. His arms and hands speak with their movement like an oriental dancer. Franta Belsky, the London sculptor, modelled the Queen Mother a number of years ago, and placed Arum lilies in her arms exactly as Cecily Walton wanted me to model her.

In the summer of 1926, Milly and I decided to go on a walking tour of the Highlands. By then we were already engaged. For the past two to three years we had been doing a lot of walking in the outskirts of Glasgow, and were fit to undertake a major hike. We started from Connel Ferry near Oban, our objective, Skye, planning a journey of three hundred miles. We packed a gale rider tent, a light, single pole affair, haversacks of a primitive type for a change of clothes and our food, and we were set for the road. We used to cover fifteen to twenty miles a day, and when possible tried to avoid the highways, choosing tracks among the hills, although in those days car traffic was slight. Almost every day or night we had some rain, but when the sun was strong and the heat tired us, we would rest among the hills, pitch our tent, and feel at peace with the world. We loved the Highlands, their quietness, sometimes serene, sometimes threatening, the drama of the landscape and the majesty of the mountains. Having heard and read the story of the Campbells and the MacDonalds we walked into the Glencoe valley with a certain feeling of fear and unease.

Although the afternoon was clear, the mountain on our left cast a shadow over my thoughts and we retraced our steps to Ballachulish. I used to see Horatio McCulloch's 'Glencoe' in the Kelvingrove Art Gallery, and its dramatic representation was awesome. Our unease lingered on and we decided to spend that night in a house, not in our tent. We would pass low built cottages, their thatched roofs held down by ropes with stones tied to their ends near to the ground to prevent them blowing off in a gale.

At one point we came to a well built, modern, double storied house, and decided to find out what it might be. We knocked, and out came an elderly lady surprised to see strangers at her door. She was the local schoolteacher, and this was the schoolhouse for the children of the surrounding countryside. She was full of anger and indignation at the people living round about but she did not mention why. She offered us tea, apologised for having to give us condensed milk, amidst a farming community, for she would not even be beholden to them for fresh milk. She looked at the schoolhouse, and called it 'this eagle's eyrie' because it towered above all the other buildings, and her quarters being on the top floor, the storms and gales in the winter would strike it with fury. We were not then far from Fort William, which we had hoped to make that evening, but the poor soul did not want to let us go, for we were the first people she had spoken to for some time.

Later, when we erected our tent, luckily on a slope, it began to rain, and then to pour. We were washed out, but as fortune would have it, there was a farm nearby, and we were invited in for the night. They already had some strangers in, a group of hikers with a doctor as their leader. The doctor, I have now forgotten his name, turned out to be the owner of a Nature Cure Clinic in Musselburgh. Some years later I stayed at his place. Next morning the sun was shining and we were able to dry out our belongings and go into Fort William to a hotel to rest and recover from our experience. We had arrived in the afternoon and spent the rest of the day exploring the town.

The following morning was again a grand day; the sun was shining; the air was clear and fresh; and one could see the peak of Ben Nevis. As we were lounging about the town we met the doctor and his party of hikers. "This is a good day to climb Ben Nevis. One seldom gets such a day and such an opportunity to climb it; its head is clear and inviting; join us, for we are going to climb it." Being always ready for adventure we accepted the invitation. It was a long and hard trek.

At that time the little bridges that spanned the streams were in bad repair, or hardly existed. A few boards were thrown over and one had to cross as best one could. I wonder whether they are better now. Although the Ben appeared clear from the town, when we reached halfway up we became shrouded in mist, and we had difficulty in seeing one another. When we arrived at the decaying bothy we knew we had reached the top, although the mist was still about us. Our vision was almost nil.

However this did not dampen our spirit, for we were sustained by the thought that we had climbed the great Ben. We lingered there, ate our frugal meal, and were ready for the downward journey, but by this time we were somewhat tired, especially Milly. Her knees had begun to shake and knock together, and she found it difficult to manoeuvre the bridges, and at times we had to go down to a spot where she could cross the stream on stepping stones. Our inspiration was a sixty-nine year old man who was in the party. We dared not disgrace ourselves.

The Highlands were not at all geared for tourist traffic, and we never knew when and where we might land up at the end of the day. One evening we hoped to find shelter in an inn, but it was already crowded, and some hopefuls had already made themselves comfortable for the night in their cars. Such an avalanche of tourists was exceptional. They were seeing the country the easy way by driving, not like us who knew every stone we had trodden on. The only thing the inn keeper could suggest was that we put up our tent within his grounds near the side of the road. We were disappointed as there were times when Milly felt the cold of the nights very much and could not sleep.

This time the night was fine and warm, but Milly was as usual the first to get up. When she looked out of the flap door she was confronted by a huge hairy horned cow staring at her just a foot away. Naturally she got a fright, but crept out from the back to call for help. When I looked out I was met with the same stare, for Highland cattle are very inquisitive creatures. I also made myself scarce by creeping out from the side. The leader of the herd pushed its nose against the tent pole and snapped it. The collapse of the tent frightened the cattle, and they galloped off. Milly turned round to see what was happening. She believed that I was lying trampled under the collapsed tent, and terrified, screamed for help. The inn keepers's boy jumped on his bike, ringing his bell to drive the cattle away, but they had already vanished. Little damage was done. Only the centre section of the pole was broken and this I replaced with a branch of a tree.

We all know rain. We know that when it rains it does not rain everywhere. It begins and stops with the rain clouds, and we take it for granted. It is however an amazing experience to see rain driving towards you like a curtain of shining, sparkling, transparent tinsel. Looking ahead of us one day we saw this curtain of rain, sweeping towards us. One minute we were dry, the next we were drenched in a torrent. The experience did not annoy us; it was part of our adventure, and walking beside the loch with a mountain rising on our right made us feel a part of nature, as I used to in the days of my youth. The rain soon swept past us, the sun began to shine again, dried our clothes, and we were glad to have witnessed the phenomenon.

At last we arrived at Kyle of Lochalsh. I saw that the village boasted a barber shop, and decided on the luxury of a proper shave. The hut, for it was a hut, was closed. On inquiry I was told that it might open in the afternoon. We explored the village, as our hike was really finished. Eventually the barber opened his shop. When I suggested a shave he told me it would take some time as he would have to heat the water. He had to return home to have this done, which took quite a while. Finally he returned with the water, and the business of shaving began. My first surprise was that he used a safety razor, the kind that I carried with me, but as he began to shave me I realised that this was the only method he could use, for when he moved about the floor shook with every step. Imagine him using a 'cut throat' razor, with people coming in, heavily booted.

Milly had come in with me and was sitting at the door watching the proceedings. He must have been very nervous, for he admonished her, "Don't watch me with your eagle eyes". He was afraid to cut me, even with the safety razor. I suppose that the young people left the village early, and the older ones grew beards. At long last the shaving was done, and I was free from my 'luxurious' experience.

From Kyle of Lochalsh we took the ferry to Skye and carried on to Portree. We had rain or showers every day of our walk. "You call this rain" we had been warned, "wait till you get to Skye, then you will know what rain is really like." The four days we spent on the island were the finest of our whole journey. They were bright, sunny and warm, and we were happy to see the harbour and the sea; to laze and talk with the friendly people, get to know them and what they expected from life. We ourselves were pleased to have accomplished what we had set out to do, and the days we spent in Portree gave us a good rest. Then we returned by boat and train to Glasgow.

In those days the seasons were quite different from what they are now. The winters used to be severe, and snow fell frequently and lay on the ground for weeks on end. Many a day I would arrive at my West Regent Street studio and find the water in my wash-hand basin frozen — there was no water laid on in the studios, and it had to be brought in from the common closet. I would light up the fire, heat up the room, and defrost my clay sculpture with great care to prevent pieces sliding off and so ruining a work of many days or weeks.

When I began to go about with Milly we roamed the centre of Glasgow and the West End to see if I could find a studio suitable for a sculptor. On one of our searches we went into a lane facing the home of John Keppie, then called St. James's Terrace Lane (now called Ruskin Terrace Lane), and there I happened to see a building that looked like a studio. The sloping roof had a large skylight, and the wall facing the lane also had a large high window. I managed to climb up and look into the room, and saw a number of small tables with chairs round them. Climbing down, I told Milly it must be the dining room of a guest house. Most of the houses in the West End were large, but their selling price was almost nil. On the other hand their rentals were high, and so were their rates. At the time it never occured to me to buy one and divide it into several self-contained flats, as property dealers began to do twenty years later.

John Keppie told me that he knew the ladies who owned the place in the lane. One day he came to see me and told me that it was to be had, as they had decided to give up keeping boarders. At one time the house belonged to Sir D. Y. Cameron who had built the studio in the back green, and so it was reverting to its original use. There was even a small rectangular window below the large one, designed for etching. I was delighted to get it, for my West Regent Street studio was three flights up, and to do large work in it was out of the question. Not long afterwards Henry Paulin migrated to London, and his studio was taken over by a business concern, while later Proudfoot had also to vacate his studio, and therefore mine became the only sculptor's studio in Glasgow.

When I moved I decided to take on an apprentice. I needed someone in the studio with me, for I was still frequently ailing, one who could help me in various ways and whom I would at the same time teach the craft of the sculptor. I received a number of replies to my advertisement, and I examined the handwriting of the applicants. This was the only time that I had used my knowledge of graphology for myself. I asked one to come and see me. It turned out that he had not even told his parents that he had answered the advertisement. He was a boy of fifteen called James Barr, whose handwriting was meticulous, clear and accurate. I did not want a genius for an assistant, only one who would follow my instructions and carry out my wishes. I decided that I would treat him like an apprentice in any trade, and began to pay him a small weekly wage. I must have been the only sculptor in Britain to have taken on a boy of fifteen in such a way. I was told that people would have paid a premium to have their son given such an opportunity.

I did not want to have fixed obligations towards my apprentice, yet I allowed him time off to attend classes in the School of Art and encouraged him so that in due course he took the Diploma of the School. Later, when I became the Head of the Sculpture Department, he became one of my assistants. He was promising enough to be elected an Associate of the Royal Scottish Academy, but tragically he died suddenly while still a young man.

Milly and I were married on the 4th January 1927. Our wedding took place in my studio, and Nathan Morris made the only speech on the occasion, unbidden and unrehearsed. Ours was a very quiet wedding, both of us hating ostentation, and I invited only my Glasgow relatives to make a quorum for the religious service. We had already been married by Scots law some weeks earlier. On this hangs a tale.

I had a problem, for we wanted to visit Italy on our honeymoon. I had then what was known as a Nansen passport, which was really only an identity certificate, and had no other value. Milly could have got a British passport, but in those days she would have become a foreigner as soon as we married, and we wanted to travel as husband and wife. As usual, when I came up against a nationality problem I went to the Aliens' department in the Glasgow Police Office. I knew a Lieut. McCaskill there with whom I was on good terms, and I put my problem to him. "Do you really intend to get married?" was his question. Milly was with me, and we assured him that the date of our religious ceremony was already arranged. "Well" he said, "we can marry you here, but this is no joke. Should you decide not to get married, you will have to get a proper divorce."

We assured him again that we *were* getting married. So he called two constables into the room, we declared one another as man and wife, handed over a coin, and we were married. "Now you can apply for a passport as Mr. and Mrs. Benno Schotz."

To Mussolini I must have been a dangerous individual, for we were not granted visas as we had hoped. Weeks later I met the lieutenant in the street, and he asked me how we enjoyed our honeymoon in Italy. When I told him the story he was very angry. "You came to us for a passport. Why did you not come to us for a visa? They would not have refused us." Of course the idea had not occurred to us.

We had a French visa, but unaccountably it never entered our heads to cross the Channel and spend our honeymoon in Paris. I suppose we were too much in love to think. So we finally spent our honeymoon in Torquay, and instead of spending our time in museums we saw only invalids in wheelchairs!

As I was living in my studio, and was actually casting a plaster the day before the ceremony, Dr. and Mrs. Honeyman, with whom I had become very friendly, decided that I must not sleep there the night before my wedding and insisted that I spend the night in their home, which was not far from my studio. That was most kind and thoughtful of them, and this is why I say that I was married out of the Honeyman home in Lynedoch Crescent.

I first met Dr. Honeyman when I was incarcerated in the Royal Infirmary with my burst duodenum. Duncan Macdonald and Tommy Honeyman grew up in the same street near one another and were friends from their schooldays. When I was rushed to the hospital Duncan asked Tommy to come and visit me.

His father was the secretary of the Temperance movement in Scotland,

and was well known. Tommy followed his father in the Temperance crusade, had developed a fine speaking technique, and could be quite amusing on the platform. He had been an amateur actor and had a good voice. Because of his friendship with Duncan he became interested in art. Both Duncan and McNeill Reid were frequently ill, and Tommy Honeyman would drop hints that it was time they had a doctor in the business. He had ambitions to leave the medical profession and start on an Art career, and he was hoping that through his friendship with Duncan he might achieve it. Finally, they began to take him seriously and appointed him a member of their firm.

Our friendship grew, and in 1927 I modelled him. My head, I hope, shows the briskness of his character, his robustness and his diagnostic look. He was not ashamed of the district where he had lived as a boy, and when Duncan put on airs, it would give Tommy pleasure to remind him of their past games in West Graham Street, which by then had become a slum.

When Tommy Honeyman joined the Reid Gallery the first exhibition he arranged was of the paintings of Leslie Hunter, and he later published a biography of his life and work in *Three Colourists*. This was a gesture not only of friendship, but drew attention to an artist who was not sufficiently recognised in his lifetime. Alexander Reid had faith in him, for they had subsidised him, and in the course of time they proved right, although in his lifetime he sold poorly. He was influenced by the Impressionists, and painted mostly in the south of France. I saw him only occasionally until in his last few years he came back to Glasgow, and I got to know him better, when he began to paint Loch Lomond, its boathouses and scenery.

When Hunter died somewhat suddenly, Fred Crow, an assistant at Reid and Lefevre asked me to come up to Hunter's studio and pick what paintings I wanted. He told me that the paintings were really the firm's and that they did not expect to recover their losses. I was rather shocked at the idea and replied, "I would feel as if I was on a battlefield robbing the dead. I will buy one of his paintings when I can afford it". And this is actually what I did.

The Leslie Hunter exhibition was followed by one of my sculpture in November 1929. The foreward to the catalogue was written by Sir James L. Caw, then the Director of the National Gallery of Scotland. I had met him through Duncan Macdonald and as he had a very interesting head I asked him to pose for me. In this way we became friends. He was the son-in-law of William MacTaggart, the famous Scottish painter who, in the opinion of many, was the forerunner of the Impressionists along with Constable.

While I was modelling him, we were discussing various artists, and naturally, Epstein came into the conversation. I decided to describe to him how, in my opinion, Epstein modelled. He was quite surprised to hear my analysis, for he told me he had been present when Epstein modelled a friend of his. "How did you know all this?" was his question. My reply was that modelling is like a form of writing. All you need to do is to study the finished work and it will speak to you. It must reveal itself without reserve, even the technique. Some time later during the sitting he exclaimed, "Ah, I see how you model". When I asked him what he meant, he replied, "You make your tool tremble". He meant that I use my tool as a violinist might produce a vibrato. If I did this, it was quite intuitive, I was not aware of the action. Very recently I caught myself doing the same thing.

I cast two bronzes of this bust, one which Sir James Caw wanted for himself, and one for myself. When an artist is elected to full membership of the Academy he is requested to deposit with the Academy a mature work as an example of his mastery. I chose this bust to represent me. It still looks good to me. His own was presented to the Scottish National Portrait Gallery after he died.

My Glasgow exhibition was a failure. I had good press notices — the Press has always been kind to me. It appeared to the critics that I was holding the torch of sculpture high in Scotland, so it was considered an artistic success. When you hear the term 'artistic success' you can be sure that it means financial disaster. I dare not blame Dr. Honeyman for the lack of patronage, but considering what happened later with his venture in London, perhaps the Glasgow art fraternity also considered him a good doctor, but a novice in art, and did not have confidence in his judgement. There was another potent reason for the failure of my exhibition. It took place at the wrong time, just after the Wall Street crash, which had unhappy repercussions in Glasgow, for steel had been hit badly, and Glasgow depended on steel.

When I married, my friends waited to see how it would affect my sculpture. It took me eighteen months to find my feet again, and then I began on a series of female figures representing a girl or a woman in her actions and moods throughout the day. Some of these I already had in my show, and I was in the gallery when a young man came in.

When he finished his viewing an assistant asked him what he thought of the show. "Marvellous. These figures must be the work of a person in love, or of a man newly wed." The assistant smiled, then we were introduced. He was Graham Murray, an artist who had just finished his studies in the Glasgow School of Art, and who was beginning to make a name for himself as a painter. We became friends.

This exhibition was the beginning of a low ebb in my financial affairs. Being very innocent in business affairs I sat in my studio, hoping for sales and commissions to come my way like manna from Heaven. I used to say, "*I* decided to become a sculptor, and nobody has any obligations towards me".

However, London did not yet feel the shock of the recession, for as I already mentioned, I had my first one-man show there in the Reid and Lefevre Gallery in King Street, in February 1930, and for a sculptor who was showing in London for the first time, I did not do badly at all. The success of the exhibition was also due to the fact that Duncan Macdonald was a fine art dealer.

Reid and Lefevre decided to close their Glasgow branch, as it had become a subsidiary to the London gallery. Had Tommy had the courage to retain it as his own, he might have done well. In Glasgow private galleries were closing one after another, because the owners were retiring or dying off. Dr. Honeyman decided to go to London with the firm, but for some reason he was not a success there. Perhaps his Scottish accent did not appeal to the London art public, certainly he was labelled an amateur, although a gifted one. Art dealers were not free from besmirching one another.

When Milly and I married it was not easy to find flats to let, so we took a bedsitter in Park Road, a few doors away from where Archibald McGlashan lived. Archie was becoming well known as a painter, although his work was not selling in Glasgow. His commissions came from London.

Archibald McGlashan was Bob Sivell's closest friend, but in character an artist completely different from Sivell. McGlashan was a brilliant student, and when he completed his studies at the Glasgow School of Art, he went to Spain on a scholarship to study the paintings of Velasquez at the Prado. He brought back a full size copy of the 'Gentleman in Black', the painting which inspired Lavery when he painted Robert Graham.

Unlike Sivell, McGlashan learned his craft in the years he spent in the Art School. Then he was able to forget it, for it had become a part of himself, and he could paint, so to speak, automatically. For a time he and Sivell shared a studio at 65, West Regent Street. Sivell considered McGlashan the finer painter, yet he could not help having a little fun on his account, and would indulge in boyish pranks. He realised that McGlashan was a natural painter and would paint what was in front of his eyes. Just to play a trick on him Sivell said to a few of us one day when Archie was out, "You see what Archie is painting just now? You see the background?" It happened to be a piece of drapery that hung on the draught screen. "I will hang another piece over the screen and you will see that Archie will repaint the background." He was right!

For years McGlashan sold little, but one year he sent a painting of a child to an exhibition and it sold, so his wife advised him to send paintings of children to exhibitions, and he began to sell. He became known for his paintings of children, mostly his own. I was able to put a commission his way, and in return he painted a small portrait of my son Amiel, then about five years old. In his early days he was interested chiefly in compositions, but later began to concentrate on portraits.

On the whole, McGlashan was the silent member of our group. I admired him greatly for his art, but could not penetrate his mind, for he seldom expressed an opinion, though he always seemed alive to the discussions going on around him. One day I met him near the Pettigrew and Stephens' building where my bronze groups sat over the two entrances. It was not long after they had been erected. We stopped to have a chat. He told me that he had just left a young painter who had come to ask his advice, for he considered this an important function of the artist. "Keep on painting" was what he told him. No one had ever given him even this piece of advice. We then turned to the two groups whose compositions were inspired by Michaelangelo's groups to the Medici. They were not just plagiarised versions, but happened to suit the shape and composition of the pediments. I intended to tell McGlashan something I expected he did not know, for it took me some time to worry it out for myself, and began, "Do you know why Michaelangelo did not finish the head of his 'Day'?" and he answered without hesitation, "Because the head would have been too small for the figure". He surprised me, for this was exactly what I had discovered. I realised then that he knew and understood a great deal although he seldom took part in our discussions. He believed in doing the work and not talking. From that day, my regard for him greatly increased.

One evening I decided to introduce Milly to the McGlashans as they had never met. Archie's wife Theresa had been a most attractive girl. She was of Italian extraction, and her brother had studied in the Glasgow School of Art and become a sculptor before emigrating to the United States. To live with Archie could not have been easy, for he had a one track mind, and he was oblivious to everything beyond his canvas and his paints. I could see it in others, though not in myself.

When we were in the kitchen having a cup of tea on their worm eaten table, Theresa turned to Milly and said, "I asked Archie to paint the kitchen a nice bright yellow, and see what he has done". The dirty shade of yellow might have looked well on a canvas but not on a kitchen wall. Archie could transform the cheapest cloth into the richest silk or velvet, the shoddiest piece of furniture into the finest antique, but when it came to living he was blind and completely unaware of his surroundings.

When we left, Milly was most upset and disturbed. She felt the poverty she saw very acutely and it upset her. "Benno, you must buy something from McGlashan." She did not realise that, poor or rich, his style of living would not change. Yet, the next morning I went to see Archie and asked him if he still had a self portrait I had seen in his show the year before in the Reid Gallery. I had been greatly impressed by that painting, and happened to be there when Alexander Reid had said to McGlashan "You must have painted this portrait when you had your

111

sackcloth and ashes on". He could not have said a truer word, although he did not know McGlashan's financial position. And so it looked to me also, a Christ-like head and a grey painting smock. The head is minutely observed and the drawing is full of perspective; when I asked Archie about the expression his reply was "Oh, it was just because I was near the mirror and had to turn my head". He was trying to copy faithfully and did not realise that by careful drawing he transferred on to his board the chagrin that filled his being at that time. Perhaps he did not even realise it was there.

I could not forget that painting, and he still had it, so I told him that I would buy it. At that time I also had no money but I was waiting on a cheque that was overdue. It must have been about a week before the cheque arrived, and every morning Archie would pay me a visit to enquire if it had come. His place was only a few minutes from Ruskin Terrace, and he enjoyed walking. One morning when he came in I was able to wave the cheque in front of him, and we happily took the tram to my bank.

This self portrait hung in my sitting room until lately, and it was an inspiration to me. When I was low in spirit and depressed I would turn to it for solace and courage. That painting has now become the property of the Kelvingrove Art Gallery to which I presented it in memory of Milly, because she was responsible for its purchase, and because of its calming effect on me in my own days of sorrow and frustration.

In 1970 McGlashan exhibited in the Royal Scottish Academy a painting of his wife. Theresa was looking out at us with sadness and resignation, almost with a smile, but the anguish of her soul was speaking to us, asking for no sympathy. Just as he had painted his own self portrait McGlashan, the true artist, was able to transpose on to his canvas what he saw, but did not realise what he put into it. Forty years separated the two portraits, yet the approach is the same, without compromise and without excuses.

He used to go back to a painting again and again, and must have spent a lot of time on this one, for it is a meticulous character study, and was a very colourful painting. I saw it again in his Memorial Exhibition in the Royal Scottish Academy, and he must have continued to work on it, for he took out all the bright colour from it, yet the spirit of Theresa still survived in it.

Among the coterie of Robert Sivell's friends was Alec Scott, the architect, who hailed from Paisley. He was keen on painting, and exhibited in the Paisley Art Institute. As a young man he won a competition for a new factory for the Templeton Carpet Company, near Glasgow Green, which became quite a landmark. When I met him in 1916, he already had built the Gourock railway station, distinguished beside the other local stations, although because of his youth he had no office or staff. In 1917 he was instrumental in having me elected to the Paisley Art Institute, and we gradually became friendly.

His wife was a very sympathetic person, tall, good looking, slim and straight. Mrs. Scott was a teacher of French in a girls' secondary school, but her health began to deteriorate, and the doctors diagnosed that she had a floating kidney, which gave her a great deal of pain. Ultimately she had to give up teaching.

On more than one occasion I had taken my holiday at the same time as the Scotts, and stayed at the same hotel as they, for they were good company. Mr. Scott would often rise at five in the morning, to paint in the early morning light, when few people were about, and I would join him with my painting kit. He was indeed an enthusiast. He came home one day in 1928 complaining of not feeling well, and Mrs. Scott suggested that he get into bed while she made him a cup of tea. When she came back with the tea, poor Alec was lying on the bed, dead.

The shock was almost unbearable to Mrs. Scott, as Alec had never suffered a single day's illness. She was left without any means of livelihood, as Alec had earned little, and seemed to spend any spare money he had on books. She sold to Aitken Dott's as many of his books as they would take.

I approached McNeill Reid, and asked him if he would give Alec Scott a posthumous exhibition, hoping that this would not only boost Mrs. Scott's morale by making her feel that her husband was getting some recognition, but also bring in some much needed cash. The exhibition was very quickly arranged, and was a great success. Their friends and ours rallied round, and the show was almost sold out. I still have the painting we bought.

Mrs. Scott never forgot my part in arranging the exhibition, which helped her to face the future with a new determination and confidence. She knew that she would have to work to support herself, which she was unable to do in her present state of health, but it was then that she heard of the Kingston Clinic in Edinburgh. As a last resort she went there for advice. Mr. Thomson, the founder, told her she could be cured, and she was. She was far too thin, and she only needed to add some flesh and fat for the kidney to place itself. She returned to Glasgow fit and well, and to her profession, and taught for nearly twenty years, till retirement age.

It so happened that I received a commission in 1930 to model Sir Arbuthnot Lane, the eminent London surgeon, who became a follower of Nature Cure. It was natural that in our conversations he should tell me about his discoveries, and I about my own medical history. "Schotz, you need not tell me what is wrong with you, I can see it in your face. If orthodox medicine cannot help you, try unorthodox, otherwise you will finish with a good going cancer." That was straight talking and it made me think.

When I came home and told Milly of the conversation, we decided to find out more about it. It was then that Mrs. Scott told us about the Kingston Clinic, and advised us to see a nature cure practitioner in Glasgow, a Miss Elizabeth Donnachie. She was a medical student who had changed over to nature cure because Mr. Thomson was able to cure her mother when the doctors could not.

After three months treatment from Miss Donnachie I never had such good health as I had for years afterwards. After my coronary thrombosis in 1960 I began to have a weekly massage from Mr. Alec Milne of the Kingston Clinic, and he told me that had I come to him sooner, I would have avoided the coronary. I feel almost convinced. I have great faith in Alec Milne, and in nature cure, and he on his part considers me his best advert.

From Park Road, we moved to a service flat in Park Terrace, and then to a proper flat in Vinicombe Street, near the Botanic Gardens. Twice we holidayed in the Lake District before our daughter Cherna was born, the first time taking a tent with us, for we did not know that the Lake District was a tourist centre, and the local people were geared for visitors. We enjoyed our walks along the dales, sunbathing when the sun was high, and knowing that when the evening came we were sure to find a hotel for the night. Milly was very orthodox in her upbringing, and would not eat meat which was not 'kosher', so when we went in to dinner and did not take the meat course, only fish, the bill was almost halved! We got to know the Lake District well, and while it lacked the grandeur of the Highlands, it was friendlier, with people turning up unexpectedly at the brow of a hill.

Milly continued her business, and we felt that it would be a good idea to ask my sister Hesse to come back to Glasgow to help her, so that when the time came for Milly to give up work, Hesse could take over and carry on. Things don't always turn out as one hopes or plans. Hesse returned, but she felt unhappy working with Milly, and so she rented a flat of her own, and started dressmaking on her own account.

It was when she returned to Glasgow that Hesse told us about the celebrations in Estonia to mark the tenth anniversary of its Independence in 1927, and the many ways in which the population expressed its joy in its freedom. Shops vied with one another in decorating their windows. Elsa, my eldest sister, decided on the simplest display. She hung dark purple velvet curtains round the backs and sides of her two windows, and in the centre of each she placed a candelabrum of five branches lit with tall candles — ten candles to represent the ten years of freedom. Hers was adjudged the most effective display. I remember the candelabra well, for they had decorated the mantlepiece in our sitting room. They were of ormolu, with delicate round tapering green marble centres, typical of their period — late nineteenth century — with four branches

114

surrounding the taller central branch.

When Milly was expecting our first child, she would have liked a boy, but I hoped for a girl, I was waiting in the hall for the delivery, when suddenly I heard a very lusty cry. "It must be a boy" I said to myself, glad that Milly had her wish. When I was told that Milly was delivered of a lovely girl, my face must have shown some disappointment. The doctor, misunderstanding the reason, told me that we must accept what we get. For myself, I was not disappointed, for I was given my wish. I was sorry for Milly.

When the baby was brought to be shown to me she held her head stretched out, her large eyes staring unseeingly, her face smooth and oval, and her profile very Egyptian, resembling that of Nefertiti, the Egyptian queen. Dr. Agnes Cameron said that if I wanted to preserve that shape I had better model her very quickly, for it would disappear very soon. This is why I modelled Cherna when she was two days old. I have often wondered when looking at the tiny head whether it reveals her ancestry, or was simply elongated during birth, as doctors have informed me.

It is questioned whether babies dream or not. We have proof that they do. One day Cherna's nanny took her to the Botanic Gardens railway station where they saw a train arrive and depart. Cherna was only a few months old, but she had a way of demonstrating her wishes which became demands. From that day her nanny had to take her daily to the station to watch the trains.

The first time we were left alone with our baby for a whole afternoon it was an anxious time for us. When she was quietly sleeping we wondered whether she was breathing or not. I bent low over her basket to watch and listen, when suddenly I heard the mite pipe out "Ch. . . ch. . .chacha. . ., te. . .teeeee". Cherna was dreaming about a train!

One Sunday morning I was asked to go and see John Keppie on an urgent matter. He told me that a studio had become vacant in West Campbell Street. It had been occupied by the three brothers Henderson, all painters, one of whom had been for a time the Director of the Glasgow School of Art. The studio had been offered to David Gauld, the animal painter, who, after a week's indecision, had decided against renting it.

"Go tomorrow and rent it" were Keppie's words. He was afraid that somebody else would steal a march on me. Although the cost was double what I was then paying in Ruskin Terrace Lane, the West Campbell Street place had many advantages. I returned home and discussed the proposal with Milly. I knew the studio, but she had never seen it, so it being Sunday, I decided to take her and look at it at least from the outside.

Strangely enough, on our way home John Keppie boarded the same tram. When I told him of our visit he exclaimed "Had you to do even that?" Being a bachelor he seemed incapable of appreciating that marriage is a partnership.

The studio was in the centre of the town, and very accessible. I wondered if the fact that Keppie's office was just round the corner was one of the reasons for him wishing me to rent it, but the idea appealed to me also. We were glad to have it, as things turned out later. This move took place in 1931.

207, West Campbell Street was a little building which stood on what was at one time the back green of a three story block fronting West George Street. It consisted of one large and one smaller studio, both with top lighting, a side room with a window, looking out on to West Campbell Street, and a large basement which spanned almost the whole floor. I discovered that it was originally converted into studios by Pittendrigh McGillivray, the sculptor, who himself used the large studio while his wife, a painter, used the smaller. I had met him earlier through John Keppie, and modelled him in 1923 shortly after I became professional.

Milly was very busy in her dressmaking business, but my affairs were at a standstill. When Cherna was two, I modelled her again. Her nanny brought her daily to my studio for sittings and I was happy with the result. Milly then concluded that we could not afford to keep up two establishments. She was aware that the studio had to take priority over the home, and that it would take a long time for my financial position to improve.

As the studios were large, she decided that we should give up our flat and move in there. She was always ready to sacrifice every personal comfort so long as I could carry on with my sculpture and make a success of it. I arranged some sort of kitchen in the basement, putting up partitions to screen it from the rest of the place where I stored my casts and material, and where I also carved. It was very rudimentary, and only a person of strong will and character would have undertaken to live under such conditions. Milly was a nest builder, and when people came to visit us they would be very surprised (so they used to say) that in the midst of office buildings there was such an oasis full of beauty and comfort. To them it seemed to exude a feeling of peace and serenity. Little did our friends know the cost of my self restraint and pride, for in two and a half years I had only earned ten pounds.

De Profundis

Bob Sivell arrived at our home late on Thursday evening when we had quite a few visitors. He looked disturbed and distressed, but held himself in check. He told me that his mother had died, and would I come and take a death mask of her. The only sign of anguish was his perspiring face. I had never done one before, but how could I refuse a friend in his hour of need?

I got together my material, and both of us started for Paisley on the tram. I remember how quiet the streets were at that time of night, and the clanking noise the trams were making on the rails in the stillness around us. As we were entering the darkly lit close of their tenement dwelling the Abbey chimed out its twelve notes. It was midnight.

Sivell showed me into their sitting room, and there on a table lay the coffin. He lit a gas burner, the original type that burned as a flat disc. It gave very little light, and cast deep shadows. When he took the lid off the coffin, I saw his mother already dressed in her best for burial. The pillow under her head must have been a little too thick, for the lid had pressed on her nose and it was slightly depressed.

I started to press the sides of her nose a little to bring it back to its original shape. Then we heard a little whimpering from a concealed bed in the room, and Sivell went over to hush a young girl, telling her that we had an important job to do, and that she should not be frightened. Our movements must have wakened her, although all the time we were in the room we spoke in whispers, and walked on tiptoe. The semi-darkness, the coffin, and the general feeling of being in the presence of death hushed us, for it was a room full of sadness. Yet, I came to do a certain job. I felt no fear of death beside whom I was standing, but of deep sympathy for my friend.

I tied a 'kerchief round the head, vaselined the features all round, including the nostrils, and made the mould. It was a most eerie experience, and when we both returned to West Campbell Street, there, with Milly's foresight, was hot coffee waiting for us. I think Sivell was glad of the company, and grateful that I did not shrink from doing this for him.

It took me weeks to feel my hands clean. I would wash them and wash them, and for days on end I was loathe to touch food with my hands. This happened on every succeeding occasion I took a death mask. Is this the origin of the Jewish custom of washing one's hands before leaving a cemetery after a burial? Our people consider themselves unclean till they cleanse themselves with running water. To me it became a reality.

The mask was beautiful. I left part of the kerchief round her head, which made it look like a halo, or laurels. It was cast in bronze, but it hung in my studio for some years, for Sivell's wife Bell was afraid to have it in her home until she got used to it from seeing it on our wall.

We had friends in Glasgow by the name of Michaelson. He was an eye specialist, doing research, and I had modelled their daughter Edna when she was barely six months old. Shortly after the Second World War broke out he joined the forces, while his wife Ora returned with their daughter to live in Haifa with her parents, where she had been born and brought up. Life tries out her jokes on us mortals, sometimes tragic, but sometimes also beneficial. Dr. Michaelson was sent abroad, and he found himself stationed within a few miles of Ora's home, and had more or less a home life for some time.

Well, one day he came to see me to tell me that his father was dying, could barely last more than a few hours, and that he wanted me to make a mask of him. I knew the father fairly well and he was a fine person, who had done a lot of good on behalf of the community. Mike, as we called him, came early to ask this of me, for we Jews bury our dead within a day of their death, and so it had to be done very quickly. Milly and I were just leaving for a function in the Plaza, a fairly new ballroom. It must have been important, for I had to don my dinner jacket. Yet we arranged that as soon as I got word from him to come, I would be ready.

When I saw his father's face I realised that it would not make a good mask, as the upper lip had a scab on it, and I knew the family would not like it. Yet I took the mould and cast the mask to the ears. Then, when Mike saw it he also agreed that it could not be left as it was. So I suggested that I model from the death mask a living mask, and it gives them great satisfaction for it is modelled just as I model living people. It hangs in their home in Jerusalem to this day.

When Mike returned from active service after the war, he found his place filled at the Eye Infirmary, and this talented young doctor was looked upon as an outsider. So he decided to emigrate to Israel, where his skill was needed and where he would feel at home. He became world famous for his work; he was responsible for eradicating Glaucoma from Israel; was consulted by Haille Selassie and Arab Royalty, and by more than one National President. He held the post of Professor of Opthalmology at the Hebrew University of Jerusalem until his retiral.

In 1956 Holland staged a huge Rembrandt exhibition. I had just received an unexpected windfall in the shape of a cheque for my post-war credits, and as Rembrandt was my favourite painter we decided to visit it. It was a feast for the eye as much as for the soul. One could feel that in his later paintings, when fortune deserted him, all because he wanted to remain true to his art, the canvases spoke of his agony and of the forgetfulness he could achieve only when he was painting.

Mike decided to visit the exhibition en route to Britain. He went round the show three times. The first time to get acquainted with his works. The second time he began to study the paintings in greater detail, and the third time only looking at the eyes. When he was finished, he told me, he could now recognise a Rembrandt by the eyes, and that he had a special way of painting them. They were always the same, and he could not be fooled by a fake. He could tell that Rembrandt had an astigmatism, which revealed itself in his painting of eyes.

The taking of my third and last death mask would have made a good short story for Chekhov. Late one afternoon I received a telephone call at the Art School which sounded as if it was from a long distance away. I was right, though I forget from which town up North it was. The undertaker, for such he was, had phoned all over Scotland and to all the local Art Schools, but could not find anyone to take a mask. Then someone suggested that he get in touch with me. I was ready to refuse, but he was very insistent, "Do not refuse, for the sake of the widow" was the plea.

As you will have realised, taking death masks is not a pleasant job, and to put him off I mentioned what seemed to me a stiff fee, but his reply was that money was no object. I then explained that I could not come right away, but that I would come the following evening. Could they preserve the head in a proper condition? Seemingly this offered no serious problem. Then we arranged the time of my arrival, and that a car would be waiting for me at the station.

Late the following afternoon, after my classes finished in the Art School, I started my journey. It must have taken two to three hours to reach my destination. Because of the war, the carriage had poor light, the station was dark and miserable, and my own mood was full of foreboding. When I arrived a car drove me through unlit streets for quite a distance.

When we finally reached the house I was led through a darkened hall into a bedroom where the undertaker took charge of me and indicated the corpse lying on the bed. The first thing I noticed was that to keep the face firm a block of Carbon Dioxide was pressed under the dead man's chin, but in such a way that it pushed the chin up and distorted the lower part of his face. I removed the block, but the features were so frozen that they did not come back to their original shape. I had to apply a warm towel to the chin gently and gradually. The room was in semi-darkness, and here was I standing glued to the side of the bed watching how my efforts were gradually softening the flesh and bringing it back to shape. While I was patiently restoring the features, the undertaker was working at a brisk rate at what he had to do.

My thoughts were with death and the dead, and my mind began to think consciously and purposefully. I have often wondered how rabbis and Christian ministers feel about their congregants when they die, and the memorial addresses they have to deliver. I have never had the courage to ask them privately what they think of life and death, for at times this must weigh heavily on their minds. Do they get used to death like doctors, who learn early that when the springs of life run down the works must stop?

As these and many other thoughts were occupying my mind, I heard the sound of weeping in the distance, not loud, as it must have come from the other end of the building. But that sound went through me and I felt terribly sad for the widow, newly bereaved, for whom the loss of her husband was like a blighted tree in the wilderness of life.

When footsteps would be heard nearing the door, the undertaker would suddenly change into another personality, and would work at a very slow reverential pace I had not seen in him before. The door would open and a lady would come in and ask how we were getting on. We answered as best we could. At long last I managed to get the head sufficiently softened and shaped to be able to take the mask. This operation does not take very long, and when I was finished I was driven to the station to catch the last train to Glasgow. For many days my mood was disturbed, and I heard in my imagination the distant moaning and weeping of the young widow.

When the mask was ready and I delivered it to her, she was composed and able to talk to me about her husband. Upon my asking the reason she wanted the mask, she told me that she came from Norway, where she used to attend modelling classes, and the students would take masks of one another, putting straws in their nostrils to allow them to breathe during the process. She was pleased with what I had done, but I am sure she did not realise the cost to my nerves and emotions. I left her more at peace within myself than when I arrived.

These three death masks left a deep impression on my mind, yet when death came into my own home, and I knew what to expect, I was not really prepared for my personal loss. It never occurred to me to take a death mask of Milly. Would I have wanted one?

New Horizons

From 1933 onwards quite a number of Jewish doctors and other professionals began to arrive in Glasgow to escape Hitler's persecution in Germany. It was well known in Glasgow in non-Jewish circles that I was a Jew, and all the refugees were directed to us, and our house became like a railway station. Doctors had to go through a year's training at the University before they were allowed to practice in Britain, and when they passed their finals they would usually disappear, and, excepting one family in the Midlands, we would seldom hear from them again, although our hospitality to them was lavish. Nevertheless, this did not affect our attitude.

Ernst Cassirer was a famous German Jewish professor of philosophy. They came to Britain, and his son, Heinrich, with whom we became very friendly, told us that one day his father had called his family together and said, "Hitler is on the warpath against the Jews, and in my opinion it will get worse, not better. We are completely assimilated, and know nothing about the Jewish religion, or the Jewish people and their life. But my thinking is completely different to the way the Germans think. I know I think as a Jew, and therefore I am still a Jew. So let us leave Germany while it is still possible."

Cambridge offered him a professorship but as he did not know English he could not accept it, and was given one in Sweden. Heinrich had a Ph.D. in philosophy, and as he used to say himself, was lucky to get a post in the Glasgow University.

Mostly the German Jews still believed in the culture and humanity of the German people. They hoped and prayed that nothing would happen to them and that the wave of atrocities would pass, and that soon they would be restored to their former status. Many of them stayed on in Germany instead of clearing out, even empty handed, but most would not leave their property behind, while some had no means wherewith to escape. My heart was bleeding for them, but there was little I could

125

do, and I tried to concentrate on my work.

Hitler considered himself an artist, but he became a dictator even in art. He believed in natural descriptive art only, and everything outside this was anathema and forbidden. He called such art decadent, and the artists could not show their paintings in Germany. In 1938 an exhibition was arranged in London of 'decadent' German art, under the title '20th Century German Art'. A selected portion of it was going to be sent over to the United States.

Milly and I decided that this section would *have* to be brought to Glasgow for the Scottish people to see before it left for the States. As a Jew, and a hater of Hitler, I did not want my name to appear as the one who brought it to Glasgow, as it would lose its impact. I therefore approached the Saltire Society of which Milly was a founder member. The trouble then, as now, has always been that exhibitions show a loss, and I had foreseen the question "Who will foot the bill?" I had a close friend, Fred Nettler, a furrier, who on his own initiative suggested that he would underwrite the exhibition.

Not only did we not make a loss, but we were able to send a sizeable cheque to the Refugee Artists' Fund. How did we manage such a triumph? We decided that the entrance to the private view would be by ticket only, and a fair charge was made for it. It was going to be a social occasion. Milly got together a number of hostesses who were responsible for providing tea, and there arose such a terrific clamour for tickets that it was a huge success. Then, of course, the Press helped greatly, and we had visitors from all over Scotland. In that show there were artists who are now household names, but who were seen in Scotland for the first time.

Our daughter Cherna used to suffer from fevers and temperatures, but our doctor could not diagnose what was wrong with her. So she asked a friend of ours, Professor Noah Morris to examine her. He could find nothing diagnostically wrong, and after some deliberation made a pronouncement of great wisdom; her ailment was being an only child of Jewish parents.

We did not scoff at his diagnosis, on the contrary, we decided against the odds to venture on another child, and our son Amiel was born in 1936. On 2nd April we all had our 'high tea' together, and I was packed off to the cinema. On my return I found Dr. Agnes Cameron putting on her gloves. "We keep Elders' hours here," was her remark. When I could not follow her meaning I was sent into the bedroom where "I would get a surprise" and what a surprise it was, for there in a basket lay a newly born boy with a wrinkled, wizened face. He looked the image of Milly's father. Milly had made sure he was not born on April Fool's day.

My brother Maxie, who had been killed in 1915 had not yet had anybody named after him, so we decided that one of his names should be Moses, or as in Hebrew, Moshé. We disliked anglicising names. For some reason it never occurred to us also to give him my father's name *Yaacov,* Jacob. In his first name I wanted to reflect my hopes for the future. My tension and tribulation over German Jewry, the mounting anxiety and strain within me and my home, which was always turbulent, never quiet, yet my belief in our destiny, in our ultimate victory over our struggles, personal as well as national, made me seek out a name which would be compatible with my mood of assiduity and purposefulness. In Hebrew 'Amiel' is composed of two words — *Ami El* — which can be translated in two ways; My people are strong, or, My people are with the Lord. It did not fully express what was in my mind, but it was the closest we could approach it, and it was also euphonious.

I had become friendly with Jack Coia, an architect of Italian extraction, though he himself was born here. The Empire Exhibition was going to take place in Glasgow in 1938, and he had designed the Roman Catholic church for it. I received a commission to model the Four Evangelists for it. It was a large panel depicting the four symbols of the Saints. One afternoon I came down from the steps to write a note by way of a rest. Suddenly I heard "One more stab at the lion", and looking round, there was Amiel right on top of my six foot ladder with a tool in his hand. He was only two then, but luckily I managed to get him down safely.

A year later, for his third birthday he was given a present of a cardboard tray with all kinds of tools stapled on to it. Amiel just looked at the tools and threw them away. "These are just toys" he said. He was used to handling real tools, hammering away at my casts when I was not about, having seen me chip out a plaster from its mould.

For the same exhibition Archibald Dawson, then the Head of the Sculpture Department in the School of Art, was asked to design and model a huge St. Andrew. I saw the armature, and was sorry to see it being covered up with clay, for it was in itself a work of art. Dawson died suddenly, in the spring of 1938, before the figure was cast in plaster.

I was friendly with the Director of the School, Mr. W. O. Hutchison, later to become the President of the Royal Scottish Academy, and also with Hugh Crawford, who was then the Head of the Painting Department. I was invited to see the students through their diplomas. This meant joining the staff for the summer term of six weeks, to perform the duties of a Head of Department. I found it stimulating, and I enjoyed being in contact with youth and their problems, and trying to smooth out their difficulties.

When I presented the students for their diplomas, and they all passed, I was invited to take on the post permanently. I had the whole summer to think it over, and Crawford was very keen that I should accept. He must have felt that with me in the School he would gain a friend and an ally. Milly was against it, for she considered that I would lower my status by becoming a teacher, for this was what the post really implied. Yet, I could see that the war was coming, and I knew that the first casualty in a war has always been Art. What I could not tell her was that I had had enough of having to depend on her earnings.

It took Milly some years to become reconciled to my action, but having realised the wisdom of it eventually she was able to give up her dressmaking business. As far as I was concerned, I loved every moment of being with my students, and my teaching was not a task but a pleasure. I expected to be there five, or at the most ten years, and when the question of superannuation arose, both the Director and the Treasurer thought that I was too old to benefit from it, and so I was not superannuated. No one could have been more ill advised, for instead of staying for five or ten years, I remained there until I was seventy!

I arranged my teaching time so that I would be able to attend the Academy meetings, so Wednesday became my free day, for I tried to take an active part in the Academy's deliberations.

I was elected an Associate of the Royal Scottish Academy in 1933, and to full membership in 1937. While I was an Associate I had the opportunity to invite a Henry Moore to the Academy. I believe that this was the first time that Henry Moore exhibited in Scotland. The year was 1935.

Scotland had many fine women artists, but none were members of our Academy. I knew that the Royal Academy in London already had some women among its members. Therefore, shortly after I was elected an Associate I raised the question of their admission, and put forward Miss Phyllis Bone, a fine animal sculptress. She become our first woman Associate and later the first female full Academician. Before long Anne Redpath, Mary Armour, and others were elected.

Were it not for my intervention, Mary Armour might have unhappily missed election. The election in the Spring of 1941 had many names put forward, and a number were eliminated for lack of support. Although I had left the Royal Technical College well over twenty years before, I was still quite good at figures. After the first ballot when the figures went up on the board, some instinct made me compare the number of votes on the board with the original number before the voting began. I realised there was a discrepancy which I pointed out to the President, and asked for an explanation.

Naturally, this caused a stir, but finally the President rose to apologise. Mary Armour's name had inadvertently been omitted in the first instance. As she had considerably more votes than the minimum required, her name had to be included in the voting. Whether the Assembly had been alerted or her name was thus singled out, Mrs. Armour began to gain support, and finally triumphed, being

128

mother, Cherna Tisha Abramovitch.

My father, Jacob (Yaacov) Schotz.

My eldest brother, Schachno Pesach.

My second brother, Moses (Maxie).

Elsa, Maxie, Hesse and me with Mopsi our dog.

My elder sister Elsa 1919 .

My younger sister Hesse 1914.

Myself, 1920.

III

Milly on our tenth wedding anniversary.

IV

With my son Amiel.

My daughter Cherna.

Milly's sister Dora with her children Simone and David, with Milly, Amiel, Cherna and myself.

Leo Tolstoy, my first exhibited work in the
Glasgow Institute of the Fine Arts, 1917.

Mask of an Artist, bronze 1920. C
Museum and Art Gallery, Stoke-on-Tre

Theodore Herzl, my first stone carving
1920. Tel Aviv Museum.

Lily, one of my early bronzes 19
Edinburgh Corporation Collection.

Left to right: Robert Sivell, James Cowie, Archibald McGlashan and I at a fancy dress ball of the Society of Painters and Sculptors in the McLellan Galleries, Glasgow, during our first exhibition 1919.

tendrigh MacGillivray, sculptor, bronze 23. The Scottish National Portrait Gallery, Edinburgh.

The first Lord Weir, bronze 1924.

Ghetto Jew, bronze 1925.

VIII

'Reverie' my first female figure cast in bronze 1925.

'Malka' (Milly Schotz), carving in oak 1927.

'Thank Offering' red sandstone 1938. Aberdeen Art Gallery.

XI

'The Call' Hoptonwood stone 1938. Kelvingrove Art Gallery.

XII

Keir Hardie M.P., bronze 1939. Commissioned for the town of Old Cumnock. One of the bronzes cast can be seen in the House of Commons, London.

XIII

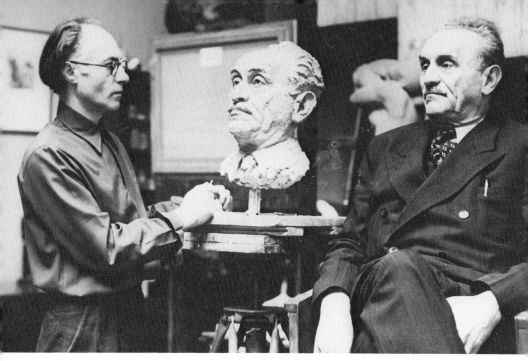

Modelling Leib Yaffe, bronze 1941. Jewish Agency, Jerusalem. (*Photo: The Bulletin*).

Working on a child portrait commission (Jim Ball, aged 5) 1945.

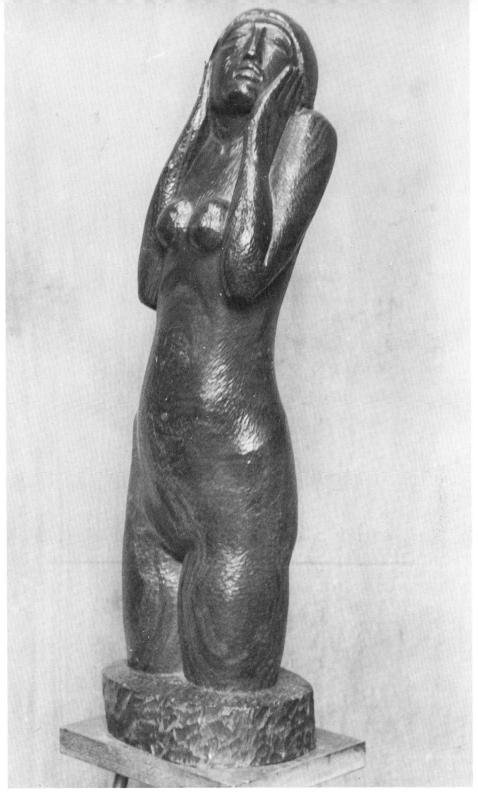

'The Lament' carving in Lignum Vitae 1943. Gallery of Modern Art, Edinburgh.

'Unto the Hills. . .' Wood carving, mahogany 1944.

XVI

Though in the years to come you will
doubtless learn a
lot, and of money and esteem thereby
earn a
lot, my best wish is that you may
always discern a
chief value in the unlearned unearned
gift of still being just Cherna.
" Hugh MacDiarmid "
(Christopher Grieve) Glasgow.
13/2/44

A poem by Hugh MacDiarmid written in Cherna's autograph album 1944.

Milly and I greeting Ambassador Eliash, the first Ambassador of Israel after a dinner at the McLellan Galleries, Glasgow, when my wood carving 'The Blessing' was presented to the Embassy 1948.

Duncan Macrae as Harry MacGog, bronze 1949. Kelvingrove Art Gallery, Glasgow.

XVIII

'St. Matthew' a clay panel for casting in concrete, portraying all the incidents in St. Matthew's Gospel which do not appear in the other Gospels. 1949. St. Matthew's Church, Glasgow.

XIX

Professor Carl Browning, bronze 1950.
Glasgow University Hunterian Museum.

Sholem Asch, novelist, bronze 1954. T
Hebrew University of Jerusalem.

Mrs. L. Robinson and daughter, terra cotta
1957.

Jacqueline and Madeleine Coia, bron
1952.

XX

My wife Milly, terra cotta 1953.

XXI

Francis George Scott, composer, bronze 1947.

William Soutar, poet, (posthumous) bron 1959. Art Gallery and Museum, Perth

Hugh MacDiarmid, poet, bronze 1958.

Ronald Stevenson, pianist and compos bronze 1968.

e Rt. Hon. Walter Elliot M.P., bronze
57. The Students Union, Glasgow
University.

James Maxton M.P., bronze 1938.
Kelvingrove Art Gallery, Glasgow.

Paul and Esta Henry of Edinburgh, bronze 1953.

XXIII

Alan Fletcher, life size terra cotta 1957.

XXIV

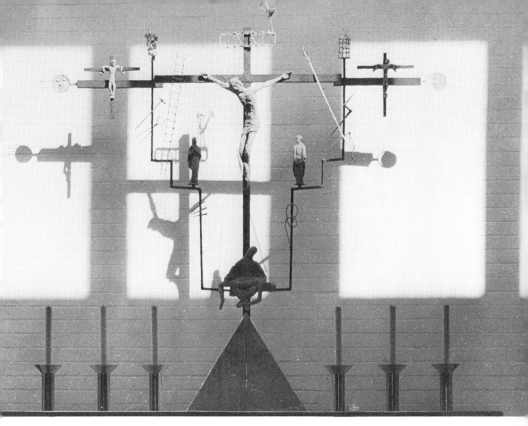

The Altar Cross in St. Paul's R.C. Church, Glenrothes, 1958.

Adam Mendelov, Prof. of English, University of Jerusalem and I after the unveiling of my bronze of Ben Gurion in the grounds of the Israel Museum, Jerusalem, 1963.

With 'The Phoenix', a welded bronze 1963. (*Photo: Geo Outram & Co.*).

My favourite photo of Milly and me, 1965. (*Photo: Dr. Maurice Gaba*).

A view from my sculpture garden. Left to right: 'The Mourners', life size welded bronze 1966. 'The Acrobats', welded bronze 1965. 'Ezekiel's Vision', plastic metal 1961. (*Photo: Scottish Field*).

XXVII

One of a series of pen and ink drawings made in the Garden of Gethsemane in 1963 which inspired the sculpture on the opposite page.

XXVIII

'Mary and Elizabeth' (The Visitation) 1976.

Golda Meir, Prime Minister of Israel, bronze 1968.

XXX

Receiving a presentation from Dr. Gerald Jesner, President of the Jewish Representative Council at the A.G.M. on 1st June 1981 in recognition of my receiving the Freedom of the City of Glasgow. (*Photo: Lewis Segal*).

Sir Samuel Curran, retired Principal of Strathclyde University and I on the occasion of us receiving the Freedom of the City of Glasgow, 15th June 1981. (*Photo: The Glasgow Herald*).

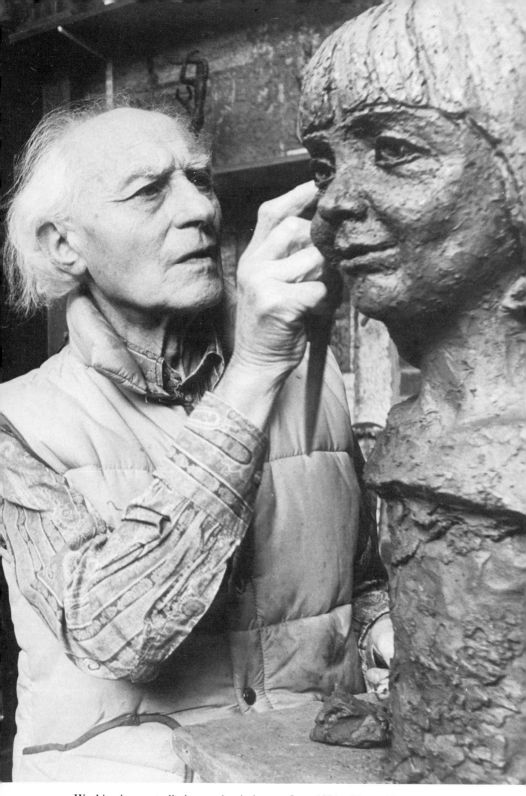

Working in my studio in my ninetieth year, June 1981. (*Photo: The Glasgow Herald*).

elected an Associate. After the meeting everybody crowded round me to ask how I noticed the discrepancy in the numbers, but I could not enlighten them, for it was entirely intuitive. Mary Armour is now among our finest artists, her paintings of still lives and flowers greatly prized.

My second one-man show in London took place in the Reid Gallery in March 1938. A few weeks earlier Duncan Macdonald sprang upon me the news that he had to go to New York, and would be away for my show. He asked me whether I would like to postpone my exhibition till his return. Did he suggest this because he had already taken Dr. Honeyman's measure as a dealer? I considered Dr. Honeyman a friend and did not know his standing was being questioned. To postpone the show might have appeared as if I had no faith in him, and I certainly expected him to do his best for me.

Can you imagine my surprise when Dr. Honeyman debarred me from the gallery during the Press View, to prevent me meeting the critics? It was in his interest that my show should be a success, and notices in the National press could help this. I was a stranger to London, and it was important that the critics meet me face to face so that we could talk about my sculpture. Here I was in London specially to meet them and not allowed into the gallery! I blame myself for being meek and modest, and not insisting on being there.

There was another exhibition on at the same time as mine, that of William Roberts, of tubular paintings of figures. He was a Londoner, and had a teaching appointment, and so could not be in the gallery for the Press View. Dr. Honeyman might have wished to be even handed to us both, but the bias was against me, coming from Glasgow. Needless to say my exhibition went unnoticed.

Some time later I met James Bridie in the Art Club and he asked me what had gone wrong with my show. He was dumbfounded and could not believe my story. "You should have dined and wined the critics, and they would have eaten out of your hand."

The best known critic at that time was Eric Newton and he did not even mention my show although he wrote about Roberts. This infuriated Milly, and without telling me she decided to send him a note. She received a reply which was feeble and anaemic, and only then did she tell me about it. Had he been bold enough to say that he did not like my sculpture and saw little in it, I would have accepted his evaluation and been satisfied. His reply, however, demanded a letter from me, and I pointed out to him the fine opportunity he had missed by not comparing the two artists. One a painter, who produced contrived sculpture on a canvas, while the sculptor modelled realistically, sensitively, and followed no 'isms'.

A year or two later Newton was invited to the Glasgow Art Club to initiate a discussion on art criticism in Britain. He was really a very likeable person, and when I was introduced to him he began by saying that he wished the ground had opened there and then to swallow him. I tried to put him at his ease, for I seldom if ever harbour grievances against those who thoughtlessly offend me. It does not help one, for if you do, you only harm yourself.

I was asked to open the discussion. In my remarks I wanted to put the record straight and point out that in Britain, as against Europe, our critics are not corrupt, and to prove my point mentioned that I was excluded from my own show during the Press View. Dr. Honeyman was in the audience, for by then he had given up art dealing. "I knew that you would wait for a chance to get even with me for what I did to you in London during your show." His remark made it clear to me that he must have realised later that he had done me an injustice. I kept my peace, and in spite of it I did not break with him, although the failure of my exhibition did not allow me to ask for another in case I got a refusal.

When war broke out in 1939, I had no heart for exhibitions, and it was at least ten years, if not longer before I was ready for another. By then, Duncan was dead, and Lily, although a director of the firm, took no active part in the running of the gallery. MacNeill Reid had lost his influence — he could not even keep his own son in the business.

The young people who were running the gallery had no time for my work, as they had veered towards the very modern school, and I was only then emerging from realism, having been a late starter. Finally I decided to concentrate on my work and forget about London.

When I think of those years and what I had accomplished, I feel a certain satisfaction that they had prepared me to be able to accept the post in the School of Art. In some respects it was a success, and yet it closed one chapter of my life while opening up a new one. I used to work intuitively, without having to think or to explain to myself how I was working, but now I had to give an answer for every question asked.

I loved the School of Art. I loved the building, its novelty, its freshness, its surprises. In my life class there were 'T' irons projecting into the room near the top, and the ends were cut into three pieces and curled up into different shapes. None were alike, and this in itself was an object lesson that one should not be repetitive, but always find new ways of expressing the same idea. Even the design of the simple blue tiles in the concrete walls as one went up the side stairs surprised one with their touch of artistic simplicity and ingenuity of composition. The building became part of me and it must have affected my work. The students felt my attachment to the school and to them, and there was a growing understanding between us.

It is surprising how soon students can evaluate you and find out whether you measure up to the post you hold. When asked a question I never tried to talk round the subject, I gave a straight answer, and when I did not know, I said so. Students respect you for this, the subject being huge, and one is not expected to know every answer. I developed a keen and quick eye to see at a glance where a student went wrong, and the ability to correct the mistake with a few well chosen strokes. I had to demonstrate how to model, what to look out for, and how to achieve desired results.

I tried to be their friend, and was even bold enough to tell them that we, the staff, were in the school for their sake, not they for us. This the students took up like a clarion call and it was being aired all round till it came back to me as a question, "Who told them this?"

Yet all the time I was teaching in the School, I did not neglect my work in my own studio. I had created a clientele for myself before joining it, and was determined to keep it and enlarge it.

I well remember the broadcast on the Sunday morning, when Chamberlain announced to the British people that we were now at war with Germany, and that we had to prepare for a five year struggle. How did he know that the war would last five years? At the time I thought it strange, but he proved right.

With the beginning of the war, life became very complicated for me, very acute, very demanding and full of anxieties. When the Germans were advancing on Estonia in 1941, my sister's daughter, Sonja, was evacuated to the Urals, because she was pregnant, and thus she survived. But the trains could not cope with all the people who wanted to escape. When the Germans occupied Pärnu they hanged my sister Elsa and her husband Nanu, and many of my relations from their first floor windows, assisted by Estonians. You will understand why I never wanted to visit my homeland, just as I never want to set foot on German soil.

The Art School was closed for a few days, on the initiative of the then Director. W. O. Hutchison. "How can I keep it open when my own son is in the army?" was his remark to me. A strange philosophy. The Chairman of Governors had concurred with him. Then, however, came a directive from the Government that everything must carry on as usual, and the School opened again. All the younger teachers had to join the forces, and they were all assured that on return to civilian life they would get their posts back.

I was left single handed in my Department, and as I was also the nominal Head of the Pottery Department, and the person who taught in it had to join up, I began to get my students to make terra cottas to keep that department open and going. I was afraid that if it were to shut down, it might be difficult to start up again. My hands were full, but I was glad to be immersed in work, for it kept me from worrying and pondering on the fate of European Jewry, which seared my soul.

Yes, my hands were full. I made my students work, for we were in no mood to laugh, and the students felt privileged to be in the School of Art, instead of on the battlefield. I urged them on, and gave demonstrations of how to model, and generally how to use one's body when working.

And now, I will tell you how I model a head.

So many people constantly ask me how I manage to get life into a lump of clay, that I feel there is a real desire in the ordinary person to know how a sculptor goes about his job.

I will tell you not as colleagues, students, or amateurs, but just as individuals who would like to understand what goes on in my mind when I model a head and how I look at my subject. Every sculptor has his own method of working, and I can only speak of the one I practice and the result I try to achieve. I will try to explain my method simply, so that it can be easily followed. I can only give you my technique. The spirit of a work will enter it, whether I want it or not, for my dictum is that if I model the outside of a person correctly, the inside will reveal itself of its own accord.

I usually model with clay. Clay can be of different qualities and used for different purposes. There can be a very fine clay and a rougher one, and one uses that clay which will give the sculptor his desired result. There is a fairly light clay that fires white, and there is a reddish clay which when fired produces terra cotta. For many years I used white clay, and when I wanted to make a terra cotta, I had to mix into it a lot of red iron oxide. But for a long time now I have been using a clay from a brickworks between Glasgow and Edinburgh. It is dark greyish brown in colour, and fires a red brick. It has a rough texture, one that I like, one that gives my work the quality I want. Being dark in colour, I can model more correctly from the very start, and the shadows between white and dark are not as false as they might be when modelling with white clay.

I always make up my own clay, or have it made up for me by an assistant. I beat it with a knife-like iron, an eighth of an inch thick and about two inches wide. I take sufficient clay to be easily handled, put it on a board, roll it into a thick sausage, and cut it into thin slices, as with a knife. This I put together, slightly roll again, turn at right angles, and slice again. I repeat the process a number of times till I feel that my clay is homogeneous. I make several grades of clay, some harder, some softer. The reason for this will become obvious when I begin to model. I call beating the clay aerating the clay, filling it with air, giving it life.

Clay is heavy. Think of a brick, it is only fired clay with the water driven out, but feel how heavy it is. To model in clay one must have a support for it unless it is very stiff, and can support itself, but this is risky. This support is called an armature. I use a square iron about a quarter of an inch thick, or slightly more, its top bent into a loop, say four inches in diameter, and its lower end fixed into an opening made by three angle irons screwed to a board and securely wired together at the top. The height of the armature will depend on the size of the bust or the head to be modelled. I suspend, in the centre of the loop a butterfly — two bits of wood crossed together. If my head is going to be large I even hang butterflies to the botton of my armature. They act as shelves on which the clay rests.

When I am ready to begin my portrait I place the armature in profile with my sitter and make sure that I have bent the iron so that it will be in the centre of the head and the neck, which is seldom upright, but at an angle to the head. I begin by pressing fairly stiff clay into the loop and on to the butterfly, and continue to build clay round the armature and down to the board to prevent the clay from slipping.

Because of the method and the clay I use, I seldom work with my fingers. I may do so at first, when I put on the first lumps of clay, and I want to make sure that there are no holes or empty spaces in it. If you have to keep your work for any length of time, and the clay has to be occasionally watered to keep it pliable, the water may percolate into the holes, and gradually work its way to the outside, acting as a saw and making bits fall off. It has happened, for clay, being heavy, needs little assistance to disintegrate.

When I have built up a pear shaped lump as a basis for the head, I take a fairly large modelling tool — I use one that could be called a spatula, with a pointed end, and begin to lay more clay on with it, looking carefully at my model to make sure that I follow the structure of the head. When I begin to sketch in the features I start to use a slightly softer clay to make it easier for me to build the shapes, and finally finish with a soft clay that offers little resistance to my tool.

Softer clay is laid on top of stiffer clay, not the other way round. If one tried to put harder clay on to softer it would press into the clay already put on. I use soft clay for an additional reason; I find that there are sufficient problems to battle with, without having to fight with one's material. I want it to slide off my tool easily without my having to exert the pressure which stiff clay needs.

In the Paris art schools, the professors used to chant "Roulez, roulez", telling their students to roll out the clay into thin sticks, and then take bits and apply them to their work with their fingers. I take in my left hand a piece of clay the size of an egg and take bits of it with my tool and lay it on to the head wherever I feel it is needed. I use the term 'lay on' advisedly. I apply to this bit of clay the same pressure along its whole surface. I do not flick it on, decreasing the pressure from strong to nil. I control my clay from the beginning of my application to the end. I do not press it in or smooth it out on the work. I lay it on lightly, and this gives me the freshness of my surface. Just think of a singer sustaining a long note and holding it at the same strength to the end; you will then understand my application of the clay. I often use both

133

hands in modelling. I don't try for a rough surface; the method I have just described produces a lively, spontaneous and variable surface which helps to create of a portrait a work of art. The longer you work on a head the smoother the surface. Of course, every head needs its own treatment.

When I became a professional sculptor, it was fashionable to model with little pellets of clay which were pressed on to the work in tiny discs, or, as we used to call them 'threepenny bits'. It was to get away from the smooth surface, which was considered old fashioned. The 'threepenny' one looked artificial, contrived, and dull, even mechanical. I am glad that this phase is but a memory. I never used it.

In the company of a few professors a number of years ago, I happened to mention that I don't keep my clay in my left hand long. I change it often, as by handling it I feel that I squeeze all the life out of it. In other words, it becomes 'sad'. They were surprised to hear this from me, from one who is not a scientist, but who only works with it, and has a sympathy for his material. They told me that in the Glasgow University they were just then making experiments with clay and had discovered that it alters its chemical formula when it is kneaded a bit.

It is well to remember that modelling is the process of adding, of building up, as against carving, which is the art of cutting away. Michaelangelo was supposed to have said that the block of marble contains the figure, that all the sculptor needs to do is to cut away the superfluous material. With modelling it is the reverse. One begins with nothing, but gradually by adding one small lump to another almost anything can be built up so long as the clay has sufficient support for it.

The sculptor should build carefully round the armature, because the armature should remain in the centre of the head, and also because, by building thus, it is easier to visualise the finished work. A perfect modeller should never need to take off what he has already laid on, but should build unerringly till he or she has laid on the final skin. However, to model like this would take a very long time; so we are quite satisfied to work faster and to correct mistakes. There is nothing wrong with that. At one time I thought that Rodin was divinely inspired, and that when he put a lump or a pellet of clay on a head it remained there not to be touched again. Since then, I have read about his method from people who were present at his sittings, or from sitters themselves, and one person describes Rodin putting on a pellet of clay, studying it for a long time and then removing it.

To copy a head slavishly and exactly can be a laborious process, and it will never reveal the life we wish to express in our work. Living flesh is somewhat translucent. Light penetrates it slightly. Keep your eyes shut, and you will know if a light is switched on or off. Hold a torch in darkness against the palm of your hand, and you will see a glow through it.

On the other hand, clay and bronze are opaque substances. Therefore, in modelling a person one has to modify, clarify, and accentuate one's shapes and surfaces. The human face has colour, and it is the sculptor's job to try and translate this colour into form. A face all painted white as a clown's becomes unreadable, for we see only the strongly marked out eyes and the red painted mouth. In modelling a head, we expect to see it all, and more, though it is in one colour. It is a little different when carving in marble, which is also slightly translucent, especially when polished. But even when carving in marble the sculptor has to take care not to cut too deeply into the hollows, for the desired shadows may produce the opposite effect — reflected light.

If for nothing else, this by itself makes portraiture a very complex exercise and requires very careful study and invention. In art we have to use our imagination, to invent ways and means to get the same effect as skin and flesh. Years ago, I was giving a friend in the U.S.A. a lesson when I saw the head she was modelling. "Don't be afraid to tell a lie," I told her. I was thinking of Rodin's dictum of accentuating prominences and deepening hollows. I had not yet come across Picasso's dictum:

"Art is a lie which makes us realise the truth."

This philosophy must have run through many minds, but Picasso gave it voice in a short crisp sentence, brutal as his art, and nobody contradicted him. A painting with good perspective can give the feeling of a vista, yet it is painted on a flat surface. In other words, the painting is an illusion, not a lie, a truer meaning of what Picasso intended to convey.

I also take issue with him over the word 'truth'. What is Truth? Truth is ephemeral and transitory. Every generation, every individual has his own truth. I would replace it with 'reality'. Reality is the world we live in, the world we believe in and know, the knowledge we have amassed, the feelings we have experienced, the ideas we have stored up to help us live. So I would modify Picasso's dictum to:

"Art is an illusion which makes us understand the reality."

This may be a truer version than Picasso's, yet it lacks the force of his ten words, and I would not quarrel with him over it.

There is a story told about Turner, the great English painter, who had painted a sunset, and a lady who was looking at it exclaimed, "Mr. Turner, I have seen many wonderful sunsets, but I have never seen a sunset such as you have painted". "But madam, would you not like to?" was Turner's reply.

For some reason, perhaps because of their size and shape, the features of Michaelangelo's 'David' have become the standard features of the human face. In art schools they are used to teach modelling. When one knows the standard, it becomes easy to see how a feature differs from it, though to do this properly one would have to draw them and to explain how they work.

Anthropologists can reconstruct a head from a skull, because they can read the slightest variations in it, and make the necessary adjustments to create a living portrait of the individual. How much more easy then should it be to create a portrait when one has the sitter in front of one. In modelling, the bony structure becomes all important. One has to begin by studying the skull, at least the part of it that is visible to us. The forehead, the temples, the position of the cheekbones, the protrusion of the nose, the relative positions of the upper and lower lips, and then the chin.

One has to see at a glance whether the head is square, oblong, triangular, or oval; how the hair grows and what the shape of the back is like. In other words, the first thing the sculptor has to do is to formulate in his mind the general shape of the head he is going to model and how it sits on the neck. Sometimes I think it best if the sculptor does not know his sitter beforehand, for then he can get his first impressions clear and fresh. It is strange how we get used to a person's features, no matter how odd, if we see him or her often enough.

Therefore I look at the head. A horizontal line running through the centre of the eyes is supposed to divide the head into two equal parts. On the other hand, the face itself is supposed to be divided into three equal parts; the forehead to the bottom of the eyebrows; from there to the bottom of the nose; from the bottom of the nose to the bottom of the chin. It may sound strange, but nature has a way of compensating one part of the face at the expense of the other two. If the forehead is high, you can be sure that the nose will be short. If the forehead is of normal height and the nose long, the lower part of the face is sure to be small. If the face is square, all the features might be short, and the opposite if the face is long. So, when I look on my sitter's face, I examine first of all the features in relation to one another, not only from the front, but also from the side and from below. I try to model all parts at the same time, keeping the surface mobile, so that it will be easy to change parts, enlarge or reduce a feature as might be required.

I usually begin with the nose, because I begin by looking at my sitter in profile, and having observed the profile, it becomes a starting point. I draw an imaginary tangential line from the forehead to the tip of the nose and another touching the nose to the surface of the chin. This angle is most important, and I use it throughout my modelling as guide lines.

I seldom find that the nose continues the line of the forehead, which we find in a Greek profile, but it has a depression at the level of the eyes. I study the angle of the nose and its position on the face. When we speak of a large nose, it does not always mean that the person really has a big nose, it may only appear so, because it protrudes well forward on the face, by which I mean well forward of the upper lip. I try to sketch in the lips and the chin. At the same time I am also modelling the head

136

all round so that I get a better feeling of the mass, and I indicate the cheekbones and the ears. It is important to take account of the ears. A head can look narrow without them, and the sooner they are sketched in the better.

I always keep in mind that modelling is the art of addition, and as I begin to model, I go over the same parts time and time again as the head grows to its proper size. One of the reasons for this is that the neck grows thicker till it takes on the desired mass. I therefore look at my work from the profile to see that my neck has the outline of my sitter. I think of the chin, for the neck joins the head at a slight angle, and it is important to make sure that the chin projects the correct distance from the neck. It is this building of the neck that makes me build the face forward time and again.

This is no disadvantage; it familiarises me with the head and face of the sitter and his or her features, and enables me to model them finally with sureness and accuracy, and ease. As I lay on my clay, layer upon layer, I try to put it on just as I see it. I don't say to myself, "I will put it on approximately now and will correct it later". I try to have it right from the word 'go'. This may sound strange, because, I repeat, I remodel the features several times. I begin with the pear shaped mass, and with the nose right away. I consider it the central feature of my face, and when I enlarge the face I try to put more clay at the top of the head than at the bottom, for then the clay rests on the irons and butterflies, rather than being suspended, and depending on staying in position by its plasticity. At the same time, I try to make sure that the iron of my neck is well within the clay to allow for any alterations that I might want to make.

I mentioned the two imaginary lines I draw on the profile of the face. Now they become all important for the shape of the head. It can be fairly simple with the forehead and the nose, but the lower part can vary greatly from one person to another. One has to study the empty space that the line makes with the outline of the features. I might find that the upper lip touches the line, or there may be a considerable gap. This may depend on the shape of the chin, whether it is strong and protruding, or recedes, and it may also depend on the size of the nose and its position on the face.

When I am asked about modelling, my reply is that it is really just a case of one and one make two. It is a simple case of measurements. Most sculptors use callipers when modelling for measuring the features of a sitter. So did I for many years, but I discarded them long ago. I try to use my eyes. When sitters ask me, "Do you never measure, or use callipers?" my reply normally is, "Yes, I measure all the time, but my callipers are in my eyes".

The reason is simple; modelling is a composition of shapes and planes. They must all fit together irrespective of size, and as I now seldom model my sitters life size, but often a little larger, callipers are of no use to me. In any case, if one models for bronze, to model life size will result in the head turning out a little smaller, for molten bronze shrinks in cooling. Not only bronze, but most metals will contract in casting. A head will shrink about a quarter of an inch. It may sound little, but in bulk it is quite considerable. Some sculptors have made special scales for measuring, but it becomes a laborious process, a hindrance to spontaneous modelling.

In one's studio one works instinctively and without consciously observing oneself. It is only when one is watching someone else at work, as one does when instructing, that one becomes conscious of a right or a wrong way of working. I am now referring to one's stance, and the use of hands. When I model, I stand with my legs spread apart. I can lower myself by spreading out my legs more, and if I want to rise higher, all I need to do is to close my legs. This gives me a chance to see my sitter from below, or from above, up to a point. I have also noticed that some sculptors model with their left hand hanging loosely at their side. I could not work that way, for my movement would be restricted. When I stand and model, my movements are from the hip, my legs remaining firm, unless I want to go back from my work to see how it carries. Without realising it, I hold my hands almost together, first of all, because I need my left hand to hold my clay and be near my tool, but also because it creates a balance in my body, so that when I wish to turn, I turn with ease, naturally. At the same time my left hand helps me with some of the delicate parts, either both working together, or the left acting as a support for the right. Although I chiefly depend on a tool, calling it an extended finger, my fingers also do what a tool might not be able to accomplish.

I have so far not mentioned the individual features. They are, of course, the most important part of a head, but one must bear in mind that a person can be recognised from a distance not just by his or her features, but by the shape of the head alone. The shape of the head also then becomes all important and must be studied at the same time as the features.

Let us begin with the features. I will work downwards. At the moment I will forget the hair, which some call the crowning glory of a girl's head. Rodin made great use of hair even trying to express a person's character with it. Jacob Epstein did the same. But now I will begin with the forehead. Normally it slopes backwards, although it can rise straight up, strong and powerful, beginning to slope only from the point of the hair. It has several important features; the prominences over the eyes where normally the eyebrows grow; the depression above them, and the bulge of the cranium above. The horizontal bulges over the eyes continue sideways and upwards to join what we usually call the temples at the side of the forehead, and the latter can be well pronounced and indicate a ridge terminating the forehead.

I study carefully these temples which not only run towards the eybrows, but continue in a plane to join the cheekbones which contain the broadest part of the face. I study carefully the bulge which unites the forehead and disappears into the hair, the eye prominences which are broken by a depression at the nose, which can reach the centre of the forehead. I study the forehead in profile and get the correct angle as it appears to me. I try to stress the prominences, or deepen the depressions.

There is no part of a head that is more important than another. They all orchestrate to make a head live. Yet, most people consider that the eyes are the most important, probably because when we converse with a person, we look into his or her eyes and get the meaning of a person best by observing them. It has been said that the soul looks out of them. The eye in itself is a functional feature. The eyeball is not just round, but is slightly flattened from front to back, and the iris, the darker, coloured part with its radial lines bulges out in front. The top eyelid covers the iris more or less depending on the person, and therefore projects beyond the lower eyelid which only touches the iris. In addition, a careful study of the eyelids will reveal that the top one is slightly thicker than the lower one. The relative positions of both eyelids and their projections are most important. They follow the outline of the eyeball and they change with the position of the eyes. If the eyes look straight ahead, the highest point of the eyelids will be at the centre of the iris. If the eyes look to the side, it is the eyeball that turns, and the eyelids must take on the shape of the eyeball, and will project over the iris changing the shape of both eyes. The eye looking towards the nose will have an elongated outside, and a short, but wide inside, while the one looking away from the nose will have a short outside and a bigger inside.

I study the distance between the eyes and in profile their projection in relation to the nose. The eyelids meet at a point on their outside, but because the upper lid is slightly thicker, it continues a little beyond the lower one. At the side of the nose the eyelids join in a little curve and turn slightly on to the nose. This little pocket also has to be carefully studied, for it can run straight, or it can turn downwards, and a horizontal line from the outer point will indicate how the eye runs. The red patch on the curvature has to be noted and indicated. When the eyes look up, the top eyelid recedes beyond the lower one, and when they look down, the upper eyelid becomes most evident in the way it envelops the eyeball. When I model a female, I slightly break the end line of the eyelids, to indicate eyelashes, depending of course, on whether the person's eyelashes are prominent or not. The same can apply to a man.

Every part of our face moves with the change in our expression. The forehead can contract and frown. This causes the furrows in it, and each individual forms them in different ways. The eyes can open wide with wonder and contract with anger. The nose is not a stable feature, as most people imagine. It contracts with anger and broadens out with laughter, especially the nostrils, and even shortens. It is most important that all the features are modelled to be in harmony and to express the same mood. The nose widens a little where it joins the skull, narrows at the top as it descends towards the nostrils, and finishes in a bulbous mass. It can be broad or thin, widening as it joins the face. I study the profile of the nose and its relation to the forehead, the size of the depression at the eyes, and from the front, the thickness of the division between the nostrils at the bottom. The nostrils themselves are important, for they can be wide and sensitive. I usually say that they can "breathe". That is true. It is surprising how mobile a nose can be, but it must express part of the whole face. It dare not contradict the rest of the expression. The nostril curls into the hole of the nose, and so does the muscle of the bulb, both uniting inside. One has to study what happens to the nose between the eyes, whether it flows gently on to the forehead, or has a bulge running upwards due to the two grooves on each side of the nose. Sometimes it is not central.

When I come to the mouth I am almost lost in its complexity. The upper lip runs down from the nose and the cheeks in a slight curve, the centre from the division of the nose having a depression which curves forwards and terminates at the fleshy part of the mouth. The mouth itself curves from the centre to the sides. If the features of Michaelangelo's 'David' are to be taken as a guide, I have demonstrated to students that the line which divides the upper lip from the fleshy part of the mouth is almost exactly a semicircle. The fleshy part of the upper lip is divided into three parts; a small bulge in the centre below the middle depression, and two long prominences, one on each side. The lower lip is at most times recessed below the upper lip, and has its fleshy part divided into two portions; a depression corresponding to the small bulge in the middle of the top lip, and longish bulges on either side of the fleshy part. The corners of the mouth are very intriguing. The mouth is surrounded by a flat muscle. No matter what you take, be it a strip of clay, or dough, or plasticine, or anything that flexes, fold it while holding it flat and you will see that at the inside of the bend the matter will have creased up, while the outer flat edge will have thinned out. This is what happens with the corners of the mouth, they bulge out a little where the muscle turns round the mouth and creates those charming dimples in a woman's face when she smiles.

I was speaking of the fleshy part of the mouth, the red part. How do I overcome the colour bar? If one looks very carefully at the lip one will notice a thin raised part between the two, almost a line. This is very noticeable on the upper lip. It might be hidden by the fleshy bulges of the lower lip, but becomes very pronounced near the corners. Therefore, I indicate these by raised lines, or in some other way that may simulate the division. It is impossible to describe adequately one's method in words. This can only be demonstrated with clay, or on a work.

The chin may appear simple to model, but it is not so, for the whole face rests on it, and its shape must be carefully observed. It may be broad, strong, with a division near the bottom, or it can be narrow and sloping backwards. Its relation to the mouth, especially to the lower lip is most important. The band round the mouth can be seen at times running as a broad strip back from the lower lip to join the chin at a fairly sharp angle. This movement can take innumerable variations, and one has to study the profile to make sure of one's outline, remembering the imaginary line of the tangent from the nose to the projection of the chin.

From the chin the jaw runs back to the ear. The ear is normally contained in the space of the middle part of the face, meaning between the eyebrows and the bottom of the nose. I study its projection, the angle it makes with the cheek, and its general shape. Also its distance from the nose. One has to take care that both ears are at the same distance back. I love modelling ears. They are fascinating in their shapes, their flexibility, and intricacy. Even ears are mobile, and some people have the ability to shuggle them at will.

The jaw shapes the lower part of the face. It can make it square, oval or triangular from the cheekbones down to the chin. The jawbone can run almost horizontally back to the side of the face and rise vertically to the ear. Or it can run diagonally, almost touching the ear. Between these two extremes there can be many variations, and these have to be well observed. At all times the skull comes into evidence and the bony structure is vital in finalising a prominence created by it.

At last we come to the hair. I have been modelling the hair all the time I have been modelling all the other features, although I did not refer to it except in passing. I try to make the hair grow out of the head, it should not look as if stuck on, or like a wig. I try not to model each hair, so to speak, but try to give it mass, yet lightness where it is required and colour also, if possible. For dark hair I might give deeper partitions in the strands, although this has to be done with great care and due consideration. Hair is not just something that can be left to itself. I sometimes spend more time on hair than on a face, because it is so elusive, and never the same.

Then of course, comes the neck and its proper connection with the head. The shape of the neck changes with the position of the head, whether it looks straight ahead, or has turned to look sideways. The muscles from the skull, the mastoids attaching to the clavicle change in shape. Some people have an 'Adam's Apple' and the turn of the head changes its position.

141

If I have taken some time in describing the modelling of a head, I have in fact only slightly sketched in the rudiments of the process, how to proceed, and how to look at a model or sitter. There is a great deal more to it, such as the stressing of certain parts, accentuating characteristics, which every sculptor sees in his own way. It is this that distinguishes one sculptor from another. The giving of life to the inanimate clay, expression, vitality, and an interesting surface at the same time.

If a girl has beautiful luminous eyes, I model them slightly larger to compensate for the lack of colour. In a man the forehead may project like eaves over the eyes, so I give the eyebrows the protruberances they may have near the nose, or stress the furrows between the eyes and above the nose. The eyes must be made to look — the days of the solid eyeball have gone — and I give the iris a depression to simulate its darkness and the pupil its hole. I try to make the nostrils thin, so that one could imagine they could widen, or contract, as I mentioned earlier, able to 'breathe'. I give the mouth its characteristic lines and observe whether one corner is higher than the other, whether they droop or lift up, or are symmetrical.

When a person smiles, the lower eyelid straightens up, while the upper slightly closes, the corners rise and the mouth widens, and at the same time the lips narrow because they are being stretched. The cheeks begin to bulge and rise towards the eyes. The shape of the skull round the socket of the eye is still evident on the face. It curves round from the underside of the brow, forming a bulge towards the outer edge and curves round to the underside of the lower eyelid, thus forming the upper edge of the cheekbone. The cheekbone can be prominent, or otherwise.

One cannot just look at a head from the front and the sides. One has to look at it from many angles to get the forms right. One has to study a head from below to make sure that both sides project correctly forward, and from the front to observe how one side differs from the other. A head is never quite symmetrical, and its deviations are the touches that give it its visual truth.

I have only been discussing the mechanics of a head, leaving out the life that the process is intended to convey. Even to this day, and having been modelling portraits for so many, many years, when I see life beginning to emerge in a head I am modelling I am startled, excited and filled with some kind of fear. I tremble when under my fingers life begins to grow and flower.

For this words fail me, but it has been my axiom that if the sculptor has the vision and models the outside as he sees it, then the inside will shine through it and the life of the person will appear on the outside of the head. I make no excuse for repeating this axiom of mine several times, for within this Credo lies the secret of my modelling.

142

Of Men and Maestros

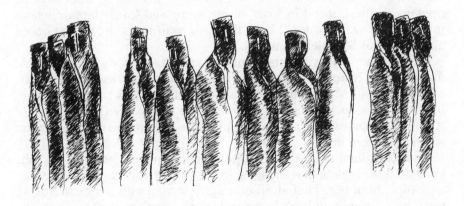

I have been told that Epstein took a week's sittings of at least two to three hours each for a portrait, and this he himself confirms in his autobiography. To model Joseph Conrad he took twenty one days. Living in London, the people he wished to model were usually at hand, and the time factor seldom, if ever, counted. Only occasionally had he to go to his subject's home, and this he disliked.

I used to have little choice in the matter of venue, for my sitters seldom lived in Glasgow, though now I ask them to come to my studio. When it came to modelling well known personalities, few of them were locally based, and I depended a great deal on professional artistes who would come to Glasgow usually for only one week of performances. During that time I would first have to get to know the actor, or actress, probably on Monday evening after the performance, arrange for sittings amounting to two at most, for there were matinee performances on the Wednesday and Saturday. This left only three days, one of which was usually taken up touring, as the visitor was probably in Glasgow for the first time, and was taken to see Scotland's wonderful scenery.

Therefore I had to model fast, at fever pitch, so to speak, and get into my work the essential characteristics of my sitter. In some respects this was an advantage, for I had to learn to model with precision and assurance, and many of my portraits were done in one, or at most two sittings. It gave my work freshness and spontaneity.

In 1933 I modelled Anna May Wong, the film actress. She managed to give me two sittings and was pleased with what I produced. She then told me that she had already been modelled several times, but each time the sculptor tried to give her European features, because her father was German. I had modelled her Chinese as I saw her, and as she was a Chinese Nationalist, she was delighted. I also felt that I had done myself justice.

I was becoming well known for my portraits, for shortly afterwards one Saturday afternoon there was a ring at my studio door and on opening it, there stood in front of me a fair and lovely female whose introductory words were "I hear that you want to model me, so here I am". This was Madeleine Carroll.

I did not remember having mentioned this to anybody, but perhaps I did, for I had heard that she was coming to Glasgow to see the location of a film about Mary, Queen of Scots, in which she was going to star, but which was never made. She might also have seen my bronze of Anna May Wong which had been displayed in the window of the Leicester Art Gallery, London.

I was delighted to model her. She was delicate and ethereal and she emanated the feeling that she lived in the clouds, for there was a certain unreality about her. That afternoon I got on well with her head, for we were by ourselves without interruption. She was to go touring on the Sunday, and when questioned as to where she had disappeared on the Saturday afternoon she had to admit where she had spent it. We had got on so well that the head only required the finishing touches, and she decided to forgo her tour and give me another sitting instead. Of course, by that time the Press was alerted and my doorbell did not stop ringing with reporters and photographers demanding admittance. This did not help my work, and after she left I decided to do a little more on my own. I managed to lose its freshness through my impetuousness, instead of leaving it to look at it later with a cool and critical eye.

This is a lesson I have never forgotten, and since then I have never touched a portrait without the sitter. Before then I used to uncover a head on which I was working, study the features and think, "Surely the nose cannot have that little twist", or "the mouth is not central", and many such thoughts would pass through my mind. Sometimes I would try to correct what seemed to me a mistake, only to discover when my sitter arrived that I was right in the first place. Now I refrain from uncovering a work in progress when my sitter is not present. I dislike belabouring a work, although I never destroy the head I discard. If I am not pleased with it I begin another and try to capture in it what escaped me in the first.

Quite a few of my sitters for portrait commissions did not live in Glasgow or London, some lived in the Midlands, and it was arranged that I model them in their homes. I therefore designed and made a collapsible wooden modelling stand, bought a sea chest, and was able to pack in it all that I needed for modelling and casting a head. It was a heavy load, but not conspicuous. Normally, I would arrive at my client's house on Friday afternoon and settle on a place for modelling. As my sitter would be free for the weekend I would begin modelling him on Saturday morning, continue after lunch, and finish on Sunday.

It was high pressure work, and my concentration had to be at concert pitch to produce a fine portrait. Later, when I had much experience in demonstration modelling I would be able to finish a bust, or a head, in three to five hours. On the Monday I would make the mould and return with it to my studio to cast it in Plaster of Paris to be sent to the foundry for a bronze. I trained myself to talk while modelling, to keep my sitter interested and alive, at the same time concentrating on my work. Laughingly I used to say that then I become schizophrenic, dividing my mind into two parts.

I am often asked which is my best portrait. How can one answer such a question? Each work contains something different, or brings back different memories. One might like a work for its sentimental associations and not at all for its sculptural values. A famous New York art dealer saw a little bronze of mine, 'Ghetto Jew', in the Reid Gallery and bought it. I was told that he bought it for purely sentimental reasons. Well, there are many reasons for wanting a work of art, and every reason is valid. What I find important is that the purchaser should continue to enjoy his acquisition for many years to come.

About this time, John Keppie brought me a plaster head of Henley, the poet, by Rodin. Rodin had been very friendly with Henley, and modelled him in appreciation of that friendship, but as Henley could not afford a bronze he either bought the plaster, or was presented with it by Rodin.

It now belonged to Henley's widow, and was deteriorating. The head had been kept in a damp place and its colouring was beginning to flake. Keppie asked me to make several casts of it, which I did. One he gave Mrs. Henley. Another he wanted for himself, and one is still in my possession. Later Keppie asked the Singer Foundry to cast a bronze from his plaster, which they did, including the turned plaster base, to which it was fixed, also with plaster.

In 1970 there was a special exhibition of Rodin's work in the Hayward Gallery on the South Bank in London. It included a whole room full of studies for his 'Balzac', leading up to the finished bronze. The exhibition also contained this Henley bronze, on loan from the Royal Scottish Academy, to whom Keppie had presented it when he was elected a full member. The exhibition catalogue simply stated 'No Foundry Mark'.

In the early thirties Milly and I had met a Mr. and Mrs. Donald Saxston. Mr. Saxston was an amateur painter and Mrs. Saxston dealt a little in antiques. They introduced me to their son-in-law, Harry Keir, who was by trade a decorator, but who, in his spare time made sketches of Glasgow tenement life.

I began to take an interest in his work, for to me it seemed genuine and full of artistic merit. His drawing developed and improved, and his line became free and facile. He tinted his drawings chiefly in browns, with a touch of green, and from the hints he would occasionally drop I gathered that paints being expensive, he used spirit stains from his decorating work.

He became a master at depicting the foibles of poverty, the life of the down-to-earth working man and his family, drawing them with brutal frankness, yet with the sympathy of one who not only understands them, but who is part of the scene. Harry Keir's sarcasm was biting, but it held no malice, just pity for the underdog. He lavished his sympathy on the poor, whose only relief was the pub.

For a number of years I was his mainstay, finding him clients and broadcasting his name. Ill health dogged his life, and he was not averse to alcohol. Robert Eadie drew Glasgow from all its angles, to preserve it for posterity at the time between the two Great Wars when Victorian Glasgow was beginning to be demolished. He even drew buildings in the course of being pulled down.

Well, Harry Keir did this for the ordinary Glasgow folk. He depicted the kitchen which was also the living room, and the 'jawbox' (the kitchen sink) which was used for washing up the dishes, and in which the children were bathed; the washing hung up to dry; the meals taken and the visitors entertained. He drew the beggar fiddling outside the pub, and the child sent to collect the father out of it. They are at a meal and the radio is on, and the title of the drawing is 'Baa. . .ch!' The expression on their faces is inimitable. The father and the mother sit at a table, somewhat inebriated, and look on with love and admiration at their small boy emptying the dregs from a bottle, some empty ones already standing below the table. The title of this dark tinted drawing is 'The Prodigy'. A man and his wife are standing at a barrow (Barrowland became indigenous to Glasgow) and are choosing some article which the corpulent woman is showing them. Its title is 'Rue de la Paix', the character drawing and the subject matter are superb.

It hurt me that in his heyday I was not able to persuade some influential people of the Press to gather some of Keir's drawings together and publish them in a portfolio. His output during the fifteen years of our close friendship was prodigious. He was a born illustrator, and given the opportunity, his name would have become a household word in Britain.

The two books he illustrated, *Oliver Twist,* and *A Tale of Two Cities* are proof that here we had a Grand Master, but because he lived in Glasgow he was in no man's land. He may have been too timid and perhaps he himself did not appreciate his own power as a draughtsman. Few can do two jobs at the same time successfully, and because his drawings were small they failed to make the impact they would have made today.

There was a time in the twenties, when an artist could have an exhibition of etchings and people might flock to see them. Nobody had then demonstrated that an artist can have an exhibition of drawings only. This privilege fell to Josef Herman many years later in London. Harry Keir was being taken advantage of by many, and this angered me, for he lacked *savoir faire.* After the Forties, we saw little of one another. There comes a time when you expect a person to stand on his own feet, at least you hope he will, for there are others who expect your help.

I wish to introduce another name into my memoirs, that of a Mr. William Boyd of Claremont, Broughty Ferry, near Dundee. Duncan Macdonald suggested that I accompany him to meet him, a client of his firm, then Aitken Dott's of Edinburgh. Mr. Boyd had been the owner of Keillers, the famous Dundee chocolate and jam manufacturers. He had sold his business and had just built a house for his retirement. This was also Duncan's first visit to Boyd's new home. He took us on a tour of the house and stopped in the dining room to show us a set of antique chairs he had bought.

As there were only eleven in the set, he had ordered a reproduction of one to make up the dozen. There was a fine firm of cabinetmakers in Dundee, Justice by name, and it was given the order for the twelfth. "You, Mr. Macdonald will not be able to tell me which is the genuine chair, and which is not, but Mr. Schotz will."

I was put on the spot. I had seen many antique pieces of furniture, but had never handled one. I did not dare to fail, and did not wish to take long about it, so I passed my hand over the back of one chair and then over the other and pointed out the genuine article. It was a revelation; one felt very friendly to the touch as if it had been used by many hands, very smooth from usage. It had lost its flatness and hardness, for it had many years of wear and tear. The other lacked the intimacy of the first, the newness shouting out from under my fingers. Only then did Mr. Boyd point out to us some of the other differences in the reproduction. The spars of the new chair were slightly coarser than in the old one. He had hoped that my keen eye would notice this, but I did not want to examine the two chairs minutely, and only went by the feel of the wood, and I was right.

Some years later I made a few friends in Dundee and had modelled there a Mr. Fimister, a master plumber. I also knew Mr. Souter, an architect. Lack of sales and commissions became intolerable to me, so one day I decided to pack a case with small bronzes, include an envelope of photographs, and take a trip to Dundee to try my luck there. It was going to take me a day to clean up my bronzes and pack them, so I decided to go the following morning.

That afternoon the telephone rang, and a man I knew from the Art Club asked me if I would be interested in a small commission. A memorial had been put up in the grounds of Glasgow University to one of the Hunter brothers, the famous professors after one of whom the Hunterian Museum is named. They had a residue of £400 and wanted to use it for a memorial in East Kilbride, half a mile from the Hunter's birthplace.

No, he could not see me right away, but we made an appointment for the following week. I did not cancel my earlier decision to visit Dundee. It made me even keener, hoping that the offer of a commission was a good omen.

On arrival I first telephoned Mr. Fimister. He told me that I had come at an awkward moment, for he was just going into hospital for an operation. I then telephoned Mr. Souter and was told that this was his day in Leuchars where he had another office. My last call was to Mr. Boyd. When I told him the reason for my visit, his reply was that he no longer bought, but was rather selling. Yet, seeing that I was in Dundee, he invited me to come over to show me what he had bought since he had last seen me. So I took the photographs out of my suitcase, deposited the latter in the left luggage, and started for 'Claremont'.

I was warmly received. Mr. Boyd had a fine collection of Impressionist paintings which he had acquired through the years from Alexander Reid, and others from the Scottish Gallery in Edinburgh. In Dundee there were a few individuals who had followed Reid's advice and had bought many Impressionist paintings. I was invited to stay for dinner, and had time to show Mr. Boyd the portraits I had been doing.

While William Boyd was still the owner of Keillers he had an affair with his secretary, which resulted in the birth of a baby girl. Everybody in Dundee knew of the affair, but so long as he was not married to the mother, society shut their eyes to it and he continued to be an honoured and welcome guest in their homes. Mr. Boyd was very fond of the child, and when she was four, he decided to marry her mother, whom he sent to a finishing school in Switzerland so that she would be able to entertain their visitors properly. But to his surprise, from then on he was ostracised by the Dundee gentry, and he became a lonely man.

To have an outlet for his energies he had built an Art Gallery in Broughty Ferry in memory of his parents. He also took a great interest in the Dundee School of Dentistry which was attached to St. Andrews University. He was also a patron of living artists, especially those with a local connection.

He even had a design made for a direct entrance to the Dundee Art Gallery to separate it from the Museum, offering to pay for the alteration. However his offer was turned down by the city. Mr. Boyd told me about his idea of a new entrance, and did not know why it was turned down, but I was told confidentially that those in authority considered that this would make him too important in the town.

That evening I met Joan, his young daughter. There was nothing special about her from the sculptural point of view. She had a fairly round full face, dark smooth hair with a fringe over her forehead, a face for a father to fondle and love. After dinner Mr. Boyd asked me if I would model Joan, and what would I charge for six bronzes. I gave him a very modest price, and for the extra bronzes I was only going to

150

charge him at cost. We settled on that. I returned home near midnight feeling happy and believing that my luck had turned. My suitcase had decided that it had had more than enough weight to carry, and the handle gave way. I put it in the left luggage, before rushing home to tell Milly the good news.

This was indeed a turning point. I accepted the Hunter Memorial commission, and Mr. Boyd became a true patron and friend to me. He was always on the lookout for commissions for me and Dundee became my second Scottish home. The firm there of Robertson and Bruce held one-man shows of mine in 1935 and 1937.

In 1935 the Duke and Duchess of Gloucester were about to be married, and Dundee was not sure what to give them for a wedding present. My exhibition solved the problem, for somebody had the bright idea to suggest a piece of sculpture and the choice fell on my daughter's head 'Cherna'. After the wedding, a photograph appeared in the Press of all the presents, and it was strange to see the little 'Cherna' among a forest of lamps and other large items. She looked so lonely and forlorn. Years later, when we got to know Miss Maxwell-Scott, a Lady in Waiting to the Duchess, we asked her about Cherna's head. "Oh, is it Benno's? We took it to be a French bronze. It is beautifully displayed in the entrance hall." I had forgotten to sign it.

When Mr. Boyd ordered the six copies of his daughter's head he told me that he wanted to give them to relatives, some of whom lived abroad. I discovered later that he had offered one to the Tate Gallery in London. Naturally it was refused. He could not have known that a gallery like the Tate would only accept an important and outstanding work of an artist. 'Joan' was a nice little head, carefully modelled, but had nothing to single it out for presentation to a gallery. What annoyed me was that he did not consult me in the matter, and the authorities there would have assumed that he had done so on my instigation. To this day the Tate has no work of mine, although I have created many worthy of its portals.

Mr. Boyd presented one of the 'Joan' bronzes to the newly erected Perth Art Gallery. I was staying at 'Claremont' on the day of the opening ceremony, and received an invitation through the good offices of Mr. Boyd. The Duke of York, later to be King George VI and his Duchess were to perform the opening. When I arrived I could not believe my eyes. The City had built an Art Gallery yet I was the only artist there, and this by mere chance. I knew almost all the members of the Royal Scottish Academy, but even its President was not there. If there was a single artist in the company, then I missed him.

Many years later Perth was still true to its form. The Scottish Arts Council was touring an exhibition of mine. In Perth I was not invited to the Private View. When it comes to official functions in Scotland, artists are usually ignored, and not in Perth alone.

Boyd had been instrumental in sponsoring several presentation busts, and I felt that something of the same nature should be done for him, in recognition of his efforts for, and generosity to the Dental School in Dundee. I approached Professor MacGillivray of MacGillivray, who was also his Clan Chieftain, and whom I had modelled, and suggested that a presentation bust of Mr. Boyd might be of considerable financial benefit to the Univeristy of St. Andrews, as Mr. Boyd might, as a consequence, endow a Chair of Dentistry there. What I kept to myself was that I hoped to plant the idea in Boyd's mind. The bait was taken but lukewarmly, though a sum was collected for me to model him. I was not greatly interested in the fee. I wanted him to receive that honour.

Mr. Boyd took up the idea of the Chair with enthusiasm, but it took him some time for its realisation, for he did not want to touch his capital, but hoped to raise the money by the sale of some of his paintings. In his collection he had the two now famous paintings of apple blossom by Van Gogh, but in 1938 people were beginning to be anxious about the political situation, and he could not get £3,000 each for them! Today in the saleroom they would fetch at least half a million each.

In the meantime I suggested to St. Andrews Unversity that they should confer a Doctorate on him. I was gratified that he did receive the LL.D. (*honoris causa*), but by then war had already broken out and I was prevented from being at the Graduation ceremony. Mr. Boyd died within the year, and I mourned a great friend, who believed in me and my future.

In 1935 I received a commission to model the Earl of Airlie, again through the good offices of Mr. Boyd and Robertson and Bruce. Two bronzes were to be cast, one for the Broughty Ferry Art Gallery, and the other to be presented to the Earl. As had become the custom, Mr. Boyd's Rolls Royce brought me to Cortachie Castle about eleven in the forenoon.

I had to meet my sitter, find a place where to model him, set up my collapsible modelling stand, and then relax a little before starting on the portrait. All this must have taken at least half an hour, if not more. When the Earl came into the hall where I had decided to work, his first question was "Will you be finished by lunchtime?" He was probably told that I took little time to complete a portrait and this was most likely stressed to persuade him to give me sittings. I replied that I was not a magician.

Photographers sometimes take hours to produce a fine photograph, yet I was expected to create a masterpiece in the twinkling of an eye. In the 'forties I began to give many demonstrations of modelling, and would produce in the course of a lecture a fairly competent likeness, but without the careful observation and depth that goes into the creation of a serious portrait.

In this case it was, of course, out of the question. For one thing, I had to work in difficult lighting and disturbed surroundings. The Earl was going to be busy in the afternoon, for his bailiff was ill, and he had to take his place. In the evening after dinner they took me for a walk. The Earl and Lady Airlie were very friendly and the conversation was general.

I asked how it came about that Jacob Epstein had never received a Royal commission. The Earl looked at me with a strange expression as if I had said something profane, or mentioned an absurdity. I had always felt that Epstein would have made a great portrait of King George V. It appeared that I only revealed my innocence and ignorance, for my remarks went unanswered. Years later I realised that there was a certain protocol in these matters, that such commissions are given not by Royalty, but by Royal societies, or suchlike bodies, and that the artist has to be approved by the personage in question.

When Gordon Wright was in the course of producing his illustrated biography of Hugh MacDiarmid, MacDiarmid told him that I knew more people than anyone else he had met. Working on these memoirs I find that, surprisingly enough, there seems to be some truth in that remark. Of course I've had quite a long innings in which to pile up my score.

James Bridie, the playwright, I met fairly often as he was a member of the Glasgow Art Club. Osborne Mavor (his real name) first came to prominence as a student at Glasgow University. In those days there was no time limit to one's study there, and his progress was very leisurely. He became the mainstay of *G.U.M.* the university magazine, contributing not only articles but also sketches and caricatures. The Students' Union was his domain, and several of the Union's most treasured traditions — such as Mad Friday — were born in his fertile mind.

During his time at the university he had as fellow students James Maxton and Walter Elliot. It was with the latter that he became very friendly, perhaps because both of them took up Medicine. I used to see all his plays in Glasgow, and sometimes also in London. We had many chats in the Art Club where he would gather round him some of the bright fellows after lunch and carry on a conversation to get material for his plays. I would join the round table when time permitted, but on one occasion I was in a hurry, and as I was passing on the way out he called to me, "Benno, come here, sit down and join the company". For some reason I was rather blunt in my reply, "You are doing your work here, while I have to do mine in my studio". I must have hit the nail on the head, for he playfully shook his fist at me.

I modelled him in 1938, but realised that my bust was too carefully modelled in a contemplative mood, so I later did another one, much stronger and better, which the Scottish Arts Council acquired. When

153

his *Mr. Gillie* was produced in the Glasgow King's Theatre, in which Mr. Gillie, although all his good intentions miscarry, goes to Heaven, I pointed out to Bridie that I understood that the road to Hell was paved with good intentions, and in my view Mr. Gillie should have gone to Hell. "Well Heaven is none the worse for a good paving!" was his response.

In his young days Mike (Dr. Michaelson) had an ambition to write poetry and plays. Having written a play on heredity, he sent it to Bridie for his criticism. What his reply was he did not tell me, probably because it was not very flattering. However, eighteen months later Bridie produced his *Sleeping Clergyman,* possibly his best play. Mike was full of admiration for it, and said that never in his wildest dreams could he have conceived such a plot and such a sequence. He did not consider that Bridie borrowed his idea. An idea once proclaimed becomes the property of mankind. The idea is only the starting point, the working out of the idea is the problem.

Sculpture is full of repetitive ideas, more than in any other form of art, yet nobody will claim or can claim proprietorship for a Venus, or for a Christ. As Mike himself said at the time, "But Bridie made something of it".

I modelled a small Sleeping Clergyman for Bridie to present to H. K. Ayliffe, his producer. We differed in one thing. Bridie considered that a play should entertain, and if it did, it had fulfilled its purpose, while I postulate that a play, (not all of course) should also educate, clarify, and release our emotions.

My father-in-law employed a girl by the name of Sonia Zam. She fell in love with a fellow of Irish descent, John Slane. When they married, her family cut her out of their lives and she lost all her Jewish friends. Milly had known her well, for she had worked beside her in her father's workroom, and she made an effort to find her, and she did.

They lived in Shettleston, a district in the East End of Glasgow, represented by James Maxton in Parliament. John Slane was a man of many sides and many talents. He began as a miner, but became an optician. Early in life he began to show great polemic talents, and the Labour Party were willing to train him for a Parliamentary career, but he decided not to accept the offer, as he did not want to lose his independence. At least, that is how he put it to me. Politically he was a Social Democrat, but as there was no such party then he joined the Independent Labour Party, which James Maxton represented. It was through him that I met most of the Members of Parliament representing the I.L.P., 'red Clydeside' constituting most of its members. Among them were George Buchanan, James Carmichael, Emrys Hughes, David Kirkwood, John McGovern and Peter Marshall. I used to meet them at their soirées.

When the trust wanted to commemorate Keir Hardie they came to me for it. The commission was for a bust to stand in front of the Council House in Old Cumnock. Later, casts were ordered for his constituency in Wales, then one for the House of Commons, and one for Glasgow. I had modelled James Maxton already — he was a gift from the gods for a sculptor — and he told me a strange story.

He had been modelled by Lady Caroline Scott, the wife of the explorer, and she had invited a number of celebrities for lunch to see the head, in clay. When George Bernard Shaw saw the head he said, "Maxton's head has a flat top" and with the side of his hand swept off a piece from the top. Jimmy Maxton told me that the head never recovered from that swipe.

Having modelled Keir Hardie I began to think about him more and more as time went on, for in him I recognised a personality towering in ideas and achievement. Then I conceived a statue for which I began to make a small maquette. It was almost complete when I received a phone call from Mr. Marshall who was the secretary of the Labour Party in Glasgow. He wanted to ask me for advice about a Keir Hardie monument, a cairn, or something else I might suggest. They did not know the exact spot where the house stood in which Keir Hardie was born, but an American firm which had built a factory nearby was offering them a plot of ground for the Memorial. They had £3000 for it. This was in 1957. Mr. Marshall's story came to me as a complete surprise, but such a coincidence has happened to me more than once, and I showed him my design. What he thought of it, or what passed through his mind, I could not tell. Perhaps he even thought that I knew about the fund all the time and was trying to get in on the ground floor at the very start. I know one thing; he had not expected to be confronted with a concrete idea. We began to talk round the subject, and I decided to call in Emrys Hughes, the M.P. who was married to Keir Hardie's daughter. It was decided that I send the plaster cast to a Labour Conference down south, and when it was returned to me and I saw Emrys Hughes he told me that I had not succeeded because I gave Keir Hardie big hands, clumsy shoes, an old suit, all the things that made him look a worker. Hardie, it seems, only spent a fortnight in the mines. He was a gentleman, with small hands, neat shoes, and there was always a crease in his trousers.

No, I had failed. How naive can a person be who knows little or nothing about art, and sculpture in particular. All his criticisms could have been corrected in the larger work. In the first sketch of the Earl Haig equestrian statue the horse looked like a cart horse. He did not look at the composition and poise of my figure or the strength of the personality I tried to express. I had met such people before and said "Amen". A couple of years ago I conceived a new composition for a statue, but whether it will fare any better, time alone will tell.

In reply to a note from me on the occasion of the dinner Members of Parliament gave him in 1968, the Rt. Hon. Arthur Woodburn P.C.,

D. Litt., M.P. wrote:

"Many thanks for your kind letter. Your bust of Keir Hardie is in one of the most often seen parts of the House. We all see it daily. The only improvement would be if we had a spotlight on it and I'll see what can be done. Incidentally, I never cease to admire your MacDiarmid head in the B.B.C.

We would all be amused at the E.H. attitude which my colleagues think is a little foolish. I am sure he was both a worker and a gentleman.

You may be interested in the following piece of history. Tom Williams M.P., when he was fighting Hammersmith, while canvassing was invited into her house by an elderly lady. She had been Keir Hardie's secretary when he was elected to Parliament. She said they had sent a wire to Cumnock to send on his top hat and frock coat. (Scots workers in these days were married in many cases in this garb. I used to play with my father's.) Unfortunately, or fortunately perhaps, they had not arrived by the time he had to go, so he was compelled to go in his cloth cap. So does truth conflict with legend."

The reason for this revelation may have been that some one on the radio had mentioned that he would have preferred to have seen Keir Hardie represented with his cloth cap on. Of course, but my bust was not intended for the House. In my statuette he was wearing his famous cap, and so he is in my new version.

In 1938 I was in Reid's Gallery in London, by appointment. Jimmy Maxton was going to take Dr. Honeyman and me to the House of Commons. As we were chatting, the conversation turned to trades and professions, and Tommy Honeyman suddenly exclaimed, "Look at us here, Benno was a draughtsman in John Brown's and is now a sculptor; I, a doctor, turned art dealer; you Jimmy, a school teacher became a politician. We have all been square pegs in round holes!" Then McNeill Reid, who was hovering about called out, "And look at me, I wanted to become an engineer, but my father made me come into the business". In the meantime a young man came into the gallery and began to go round the exhibition. Dr. Honeyman turned to him and asked him what his profession was, and he answered, "I am a painter". "Will you remain one?" was the next question. "If I can make ends meet without having to teach."

The trouble with so many talented business people is that they have a secure income and are afraid to give it up to follow their true bent. Milly used to say, "Throw your bread upon the water, and it may come back with ham and eggs on it". Of course, one needs real courage for such an act, and a belief in one's ability.

As we were walking towards the entrance to the House of Commons,

Jimmy Maxton pointed out to us two Members who were approaching. "The smaller one is Malcom Macdonald" he said. He was in lively conversation with his colleague, and when almost abreast he looked straight into my face. Our eyes met for a moment and his character revealed itself without reserve. His figure was neat and agile, and his face was shining with energy and success. His eyes were dark and brilliant, his smile triumphant. His whole expression exuded confidence and assurance, pride and defiance. He had been given the job of killing the Jewish National Home promised in the Balfour Declaration, by limiting the final admission of Jews to Palestine to seventy-five thousand. Three years later, when he was appointed High Commissioner to Canada I wondered whether this was a reward for his share in the treachery committed by the British Government. He remained in various high positions overseas till he retired. The Jewish National Home Bill was his swan song. He was out of real politics for good.

A good few years later there was an architectural conference in Glasgow, and one of the meetings was held in the Central Hotel. I was there for another function, but was impeded by architects streaming out of a hall. A friend hailed me, and introduced me to a tallish person emerging from the hall. He was a son of Ramsay Macdonald, and an architect. We shook hands and had a long chat together, in the course of which I told him that had he been Malcolm, I would have refused to shake hands with him. He excused his brother for his action over the Bill by telling me his hands were tied, and he was obliged to carry out Chamberlain's instructions.

When he was awarded the O.M. in retirement, Malcolm himself confessed that the Jews were small in numbers in Palestine at that time, and just did not count.

Early in 1939 the post of Director of the Glasgow Art Galleries became vacant, and two candidates were considered for it. One of them was Philip Hendy of the Manchester Art Gallery, the other was Tommy Honeyman, who felt that he had had enough of art dealing, and who also knew that war was at hand. The Lord Provost of Glasgow was then Patrick Dollan, with whom I was on a nodding acquaintance. He was a friend of Hugh Crawford, and between the two of them and W. O. Hutchison they had tried to get work for young artists such as decorating walls in public buildings. I had an uneasy feeling that Pat Dollan would have liked me to model him, but I had enough heads cluttering up my studio to engage in more, especially as Hugh Crawford might have felt that I was poaching on his preserves.

Philip Hendy was an academic historian full of art knowledge, who would have carried on the Kelvingrove Art Gallery as before, perhaps a little better. Tommy Honeyman told Paddy Dollan that he would bring the Gallery to the people, and Dollan, being a labourite and a socialist, decided on a new broom. Dr. Honeyman was appointed to the great disappointment and criticism of the learned fraternity, including Bill Hutchison.

It so happened that a year later the post of Director of the National Gallery in London became vacant, and Philip Hendy was appointed to it. How lucky for him that he did not get the Glasgow appointment, for then he might not have been able to apply so quickly for the more important post. I doubt if Glasgow would have suited him with its small minded people at the helm. For Tommy Honeyman it was an escape from London and from art dealing. What mattered to Glasgow was that he began to do what he promised.

He brought one exhibition after another of the Allied Artists to the Art Gallery, and this began to bring the people to Kelvingrove. He was a live wire and the Gallery became popular. When he ran out of Allied Exhibitions, he decided to stage what was called 'Holidays at Home'. In 1943, with the help of the British Institute of Adult Education, and C.E.M.A., he staged an exhibition 'The Artist at Work'. The painting section was arranged by H. Ruhemann, a refugee restorer from Germany, and I was given to deal with the sculpture section. It was the smaller part of the show, but involved a great deal of work. I had to produce a head in all its stages of modelling and casting, each stage having to be cast in plaster separately, but I was glad to be occupied, for Milly was in hospital to undergo an operation, and it helped to divert my mind.

During the exhibition demonstrations were being given in painting and sculpture. I gave a demonstration of modelling a head, and had to complete it in the course of a lecture lasting one hour or so. I had an audience of over five hundred, and it was so successful that after Glasgow, I had to give one in the National Gallery of Scotland in Edinburgh, and the following day in the High School in Edinburgh for the students.

It was surprising how popular these demonstrations were. I was in great demand, and carried out demonstrations for many years all over Scotland, till I decided that I had had enough. People began to think that it was easy when they saw me produce life out of a lump of clay without exerting myself, or so they thought. "There must be nothing to it" was their comment. They did not know what concentration I needed to work, to divide my mind in two, one seeing only my model, chosen at random from my audience, and producing a portrait in just over an hour, the other half making conversation to tie up with my work, yet light and amusing. I would be on edge for a couple of days before a demonstration, and for a few days afterwards, till I calmed down. It might go well, or it might misfire, and I did not dare to fail.

In 1946, Dr. Honeyman, to further his promise to Patrick Dollan, formed the Glasgow Art Galleries and Museums Association. It had a

158

formidable list of committee members, but when I looked through them I missed in it the name of the Director of the Art School, Bill Hutchison. When I pointed this out to Tommy, he remarked, "There are to be twenty members of Council, but you will see that only eighteen have been appointed. There is room for two more". Was this how T.J. paid Hutchison back for not backing him when he was applying for the Directorship of the Gallery? In his place, I would have brought him in, and made a friend of him instead of an enemy. When Hutchison left the School, the new Director was elected to the Council.

This incident annoyed me, for I am loyal to my friends. This was the reason I did not join the Association. In any case, it was formed to help the artists, and I was one of them. William Crosbie joined the Association "to keep the peace with Tommy" as he told me. I was never asked why I had not joined.

In 1952 the Glasgow Corporation bought the 'St. John of the Cross' by Salvador Dali and had paid £8,200 for it, when he was holding a one-man show in the Lefevre Gallery in London. In my opinion, the painting of Christ is in the style then seen in the Royal Academy. The lower part is very effective, although borrowed from other artists, but he gives without reserve his sources. There was a great outcry about the price, but that was quite irrelevant to me. On the contrary, I was glad to know that an artist could benefit from his painting while alive, instead of dealers or others in auction room sales.

I had a feeling that Dr. Honeyman wanted to make the painting into a religious spectacle. He, himself, was a religious man, and having been moved by it, he anticipated a similar reaction from others. He was right. He gave it a room with a theatrical setting and lighting, and there was an offertory box attached to one of the rods screening off the painting. You felt that you were in a church. Financially, this Dali became a money spinner, and it must have brought in more than it cost, and I suppose still brings in returns from postcards and reproductions.

As an art gallery director, Tommy Honeyman had one weakness — or strength. He always wanted to 'kill two birds with one stone' if at all possible. When he wanted to buy a William Crosbie, he bought his painting of Hugh MacDiarmid. Here then he had not only the painting by Crosbie, but also the portrait of the famous poet. When he wanted another of my sculptures for the gallery he bought my 'Duncan Macrae as MacGog' a famous character in a Bridie play. Macrae was well known, a first class actor in Scotland. To the Corporation of Glasgow on the other hand, this weakness may have been considered a virtue, getting full value out of a small budget, or perhaps he felt he had to do this to get his purchases accepted.

One day Milly returned from a meeting called to form the Saltire Society, and told me about a strange and magnetic woman she had met who impressed her very much. This lady was Margaret Morris, an adherent of the Greek dance movement, and well known in London. Everybody seemed aware of the coming war and tried to find roots elsewhere. Margaret Morris had recently come to Glasgow and opened a school of dancing.

She and J. D. Fergusson, the painter, had a more or less permanent relationship, and when he also came to Glasgow just before the war Milly and I made them welcome. He never forgot our gesture and occasionally would remark on it. He was responsible for creating the New Art Club, but on this hangs a tale.

He wanted to join the Glasgow Art Club, and was prepared to pay the annual subscription, but he considered it wrong for an artist to have to pay an entrance fee. His refusal was one of principle, and so, because he would not join the established club, he formed one for himself. He was able to do so by using Margaret Morris's premises which she had for her dancing school, and he needed to pay no rent. It looked as if he was doing a great deal for the young artists. Among its members however, there were hardly any who had real talent, or who had an art school training.

True, it became a focal point for aspiring artists and a talking shop. I myself never believed in talking art, I believed in doing it. Milly and I were invited to their soirées, but to me it had an artificial flavour, though for Margaret Morris and J. D. it served a useful purpose.

The Glasgow University conferred upon J. D. the LL.D. (*honoris causa*) for his efforts on behalf of the young artists. In my humble opinion, he did little for them, as posterity proved. He himself was a fine artist. Having originally studied art in Edinburgh he then spent almost his whole painting life in Paris. He had occasional exhibitions in the Reid and Lefevre Gallery, but on the whole sold little. Therefore, when he came to Glasgow, he had accumulated a great number of canvases which he was able to exhibit in the Kelvingrove Art Gallery, thanks to Tommy Honeyman. His work was impressive, but was of the past. In Glasgow he hardly painted at all.

It appeared to me that J. D. needed the artistic atmosphere of Paris to stimulate him in his work. Glasgow must have symbolised for him the very antithesis, and had a stultifying and deadening effect upon him. He was looked on as an outsider by many, but in the end he was elected an honorary member of the Glasgow Art Club, and so his early wish was fulfilled.

J. D. could talk about nothing endlessly, and when he did have a subject to talk about there was no stopping him; in the end perhaps, one was little the wiser. On one occasion he met his match. I had invited him to come to the exhibition of Jewish Art in 1942 to give a lecture, but instead of giving a lecture he went round the show and began to talk about the various paintings and artists, for here was a theme close to his heart, and for this he needed no preparation.

When he finished, I asked Mr. Moray Glasser to give the vote of thanks. I did not know what I had let myself in for, for Moray Glasser was of the same kidney, and how he did it is beyond me, but he must have taken as long, if not longer, for the vote of thanks, than J. D. took for his lecture. Fergusson was livid, but the company swallowed it hook, line, and sinker.

Margaret Morris was a true and faithful partner, and kept his work to the fore. I admired him as a painter, but I admired Margaret even more for her steadfastness and perseverance in keeping his name green. Both of them are now gone.

One day I opened the door to a ring, and there stood a fairly burly man who said, "I am Yankel Adler, the artist". He was a Polish refugee who had been living for some time with a minister just outside Glasgow, and had been given my name.

Milly and I made him welcome. He told us he could not stay with the minister much longer and was looking for help. We told him to return on the following Saturday afternoon when we would invite a few friends in. It so happened that that afternoon I was to open an exhibition of Harry Keir's work in a private house, and my great friend, Fred Nettler was to accompany me, for he had been buying Keir's drawings through my influence. When we arrived home, there was Yankel Adler with Moray Glasser, another close friend, and Milly in conversation.

The upshot of the meeting was that my friends each gave Adler enough money to allow him to work for six weeks, to produce enough paintings for a show. It was going to be difficult for me to ask a gallery to hold it, as I myself had not seen any of his work, although Adler was surprised that I did not know his name. I almost asked him, did he know mine? In any case, I decided to hold the exhibition in my own studio.

I cleared it completely and had it redecorated to look fresh to show off his paintings. I wrote thirty to forty personal letters to my business friends inviting them to the exhibition opening, provided tea for everybody, and we sold quite a few paintings. Yankel brought his paintings on the Thursday evening, our 'open' evening, and as they were being taken downstairs, in came William Crosbie. He must have got to know Crosbie in the interval. When Yankel saw Crosbie he turned to me and whispered, "Don't show him my paintings". It would never have occurred to me to show them to anybody before the exhibition, but I was taken aback, for it told me, not having looked as yet at the paintings, that while it was alright for me to sell them, he was ashamed to show them to Crosbie. Benno Schotz was good enough to be taken advantage of. I had wanted to keep the show going for a week, but Yankel insisted on one day only, the Sunday. During the week many people would have seen his work and got the wrong impression from them.

Later, when I met Josef Herman, and got to know him, he told me that this was what Adler would do in Poland. He would get hold of a wealthy businessman, get him to hold an exhibition of his work for one day, and then disappear. When I was hanging the show I could see that most of the paintings were pot boilers, but in spite of it, some of them proved he was a painter.

On the evening after the show he came in and we had a *tete-a-tete*, for Milly had gone out to visit friends. He wanted me to accept a painting for my trouble, but there was not one that I wanted. In any case, it would have been against my accepted principle to take presents from colleagues, but only to buy what I could afford. We began to talk in general terms, and really not knowing him, or his intentions, I suggested that if he intended to remain in Scotland, why not send a serious work to the Royal Scottish Academy? His reply was that he would first like to see what was being shown in the Academy, and that I did not really know his painting. Against this I replied, "Yankel, you have a dozen paintings next door, and at least in one of them you should be represented".

I did not know that I had touched him to the quick. He got up and left the house, I don't think he even said goodbye. He arrived the following morning to remove his paintings while I was at the School of Art, and never came back again. I only once saw him again, years later, in London in a Soho restaurant, and did not even recognise him until he spoke to me.

A couple of months later there was another ring at the door, and before me stood a smallish man in a soldier's overcoat. He handed me a note. It was from someone I did not know, but before me stood Josef Herman. He could speak no English, but our common language was Yiddish, and we invited him to join us for our Friday evening meal. We arranged to have some friends in who spoke Yiddish fluently. I told him, to his great suprise, that Yankel Adler was here, and directed him to his studio — which I had even found for him.

Herman turned up on the Friday evening and we had a lively time. There was only one fly in the ointment. We were about to leave Glasgow for the coast, where we would stay during the summer. But before leaving I asked my sister Hesse to give Josef a small room she had with a skylight where he could paint in the meantime. I was even able to arrange that both he and Adler should receive a subsidy from the Jewish Welfare Board.

Although my family were staying at Troon, I had to come up several times a week for fire-watching duties in the School of Art. Then I heard that all the Polish refugees had been rounded up and taken into the Polish Army as deserters. It so happened that they took a youth who could prove that he had been to school in Glasgow, and for some reason, because of this revelation, it was decided to free them all. In the army Herman met up with Itzick Manger, the Yiddish poet.

Josef was altogether a different person from Adler. He himself admitted that at the time he was influenced by Chagall, and his work was nostalgic of the circle in which he had lived. He had a great capacity for friendship, and this helped him to get to know many people in Glasgow. As I was on friendly terms with most of the private Art Galleries, it was easy for me to introduce Josef to them and to get the Connell sisters to give him a show. He did not really need much help in this, for his winning way did all that was necessary.

Tommy Honeyman once said to me, "Just look at Herman. If you do him a kindness or a good turn, he never forgets it, and mentions you if the occasion arises". I believe he was referring to Herman's Retrospective Exhibition in the Whitechapel Gallery, where he went out of his way to mention us. He certainly repaid Milly and me handsomely for our friendship by painting her early on during his stay in Glasgow, when he still used colour to express character. He painted Milly in a bluish green monotone. He should not have been surprised that she was not enamoured with it, because he did not in the least flatter her, but emphasised her strong character.

It so happened that a few days later Milly was discussing something with a friend and raised her voice. Josef was sitting with me a little distance away, and when he overheard what took place, he called out, as if to himself, "I knew that I was right!"

On one occasion he remarked to me that I was producing little. I could not tell him how the war affected me. I found it difficult to divide myself into two individuals; one that was living a social life with the refugees filling the house, and the other a sculptor and teacher. All the time I was searching for a symbol with which to express my feelings. This I finally found in my 'Lament' of 1943. I designed it a year or two earlier, but had to find wood for its carving, which had become very scarce, but I finally found a trunk of lignum vitae. No one who saw this piece would connect it with a lament of German Jewry, for I still followed the classical tradition of modelling and carving the nude, and trying to express in it my inner feelings.

The carving which I did the following year was the result of my decision to abandon Classical art, and to express myself in a direct manner. Also, the greater the persecution of European Jewry, the greater became my resolve to identify myself with them. I had wanted to express in it my own personal steadfastness and my belief in our religion and in my attachment to my people.

I searched the Psalms for a passage which would express this and I found it in Psalm 119, which has twenty three stanzas, each of which is called by the name of a letter of the Hebrew alphabet. I chose the stanza 'Resh', for it begins:

"Oh see mine afflication, and rescue me: for I do not forget Thy law." and continues later:

"Many are my persecutors and mine adversaries: yet have I not turned aside from Thy testimonies."

Orginally I exhibited it in the Royal Scottish Academy, and when another artist said to me, "She must have a strong character", I could not understand the remark, and decided to look it up in the catalogue. I discovered that the temporary assistant secretary had put my work down as 'R. Esh'! I wondered whether, had it been catalogued correctly it would have made any difference. I should have added 'from Psalm 119'. When Dr. Honeyman saw it he called out, "Ah, Unto the hills I lift mine eyes" and this was the title which I adopted, for it clarified my meaning.

The female figure stands in silent prayer and supplication, head lifted up to heaven, the ears turned out on to the raised shoulders, the quicker to hear the approach of deliverance, the hair like useless broken wings, and the hands pressed tight against her body to still the anguish of her soul.

When I began to look for wood for this work, of which I had already made a small maquette, I turned to Mr. H. Morris of the Glasgow furniture firm and he brought out a piece of timber from which the firm had cut away all the useable wood, because the rest of it had some shakes in it. Imagine my surprise when I saw that it even had the shape I needed for the work. It stands just over four feet and one inch high. When I had it carved, I invited Mr. Morris to see what I had done with his wood. He brought his son Neil with him to show him that there was another Jew in Glasgow who loved wood, and when he looked at my piece, and saw the shakes still open, he asked me if I would fill them in. When I replied that I was leaving them as they were, he said, "Quite right, they are the scars of life". I realised then that he loved more than just wood.

Sometime after Josef married and moved to London, I spent a weekend with him. On the Sunday morning he took me to meet some of his cronies. "Come, I will introduce you to some crackpots" was his comment. He introduced me to the two-in-one, Levitt-Him, whose advertising cartoons were then the talk of the town. I remember little about them. They could not have impressed me. He took me to meet Itzick Manger, the Yiddish poet. He was fairly tall, and emaciated, for he was tubercular. An English woman had befriended him, cared for him, and most likely loved him. He could only write his poetry at night, and when he wanted to write during the day, he would draw the curtains and light a candle to simulate night time.

The artist Josef most wanted me to meet was David Bomberg. He was not yet the famous painter he became after he died. He asked me about my work, and hearing what I had just done, he asked, "Has it

164

gone through the crucible of fire?" This was a new expression for me, but years later, when I saw his posthumous show, and his paintings mostly of mountains, it became clear to me what he meant.

I said to myself that there was one exhibition that Tommy Honeyman would not be able to arrange in the Kelvingrove Art Gallery, or even get permission for, were he willing. An exhibition that would never enter his mind — an exhibition of Jewish Art. The Jews were in the war just like any other people, if not more so, but who would consider them an entity, or deserving support and recognition? So I would have to do it myself. Josef Herman became my assistant in this enterprise.

The exhibition opened on 20th December 1942, just after the week of mourning for European Jewry, in the Jewish Institute in South Portland Street in the Gorbals, not the most fashionable part of Glasgow. People came from all over to visit it, because in this exhibition were shown artists who had never before been seen in Scotland, such as Modigliani, Chagall, Zadkine, Bomberg, Mané Katz, Soutine and many others. It was a great success. Tommy Honeyman bought the Zadkine 'Music Group' for the Kelvingrove Art Gallery. I had told him that if he did not buy it, I would. It was too cheap for words. I myself wrote the foreward to the catalogue:

"The exhibition has been organised to inaugurate an Art Collection in the Glasgow Jewish Institute. With it the Jewish Institute sets a new sign post in the service of the community. It does more — it focuses attention on the Jewish renaissance, and the gradual emergence of a Jewish Art. As the Jew of old had evolved a conception of life that differed in spirit from the Greek concept, so now the modern Jewish artist proclaims that he owes no allegiance to Greek Art, and can draw inspiration directly from life, freed from static tradition.

Today, when on the continent of Europe Jewish life and culture is being systematically and brutally uprooted and destroyed, there is an urgent necessity for Jews elsewhere to demonstrate their faith in themselves and their future. It is better for them to build afresh, to build stronger and better, in the certain knowledge that given faith, no power on earth can destroy the work of the spirit."

The first sentences require some clarification. That summer, Yankel Adler held a one-man show in the Annan Gallery at Charing Cross. Originally he had difficulty in securing the gallery, for financial reasons, by my intervention through Josef smoothed this out for him. The exhibition was taking place in the summer, when I was staying at the coast.

One fine day Josef materialised in Troon. "Benno, you must come to

165

Glasgow to save Yankel's show." He knew that Adler and I were no more on speaking terms, yet he also knew me, and therefore took the trouble to come. Although Adler was annoyed with me, I did not quarrel with his art. His paintings did not appeal to the general public, and to the Jews least of all.

I came back with Josef to Glasgow and began to telephone some of my friends to try to get them to buy some of the paintings. This proved more difficult than I had anticipated. They all said they could not hang them on their walls. Some promised but did not keep their word. So a new idea came into my mind. If they could not hang them on their own walls, why not get them to buy paintings and present them to the Glasgow community as the nucleus of a communal collection, to be housed meantime in the Jewish Institute, at that time the only possible place? I put them on the spot, and some could not refuse me.

It did not amount to much, but it was a good idea which unfortunately did not bear much fruit in later years. One had to give much time to such a venture, and my own affairs were becoming more and more demanding. Glasgow Jewry had not yet awakened to art, and one had to use sledge hammer techniques to make any impression upon them.

To make way for the redevelopment of the Gorbals the Institute was eventually pulled down. In any case it was no longer viable, for the community it served had long since moved out to the suburbs. Those then at the helm, did not know that the paintings and sculpture in the building did not belong to it, but was the property of the community at large. Everything was sent to Sotheby's, and sold before I got to know about it.

So far no one else has started a new communal collection, although many Glasgow Jews are now art conscious and have small collections themselves. Unfortunately London Jewry were no better. London had the Ben Uri Art Gallery, a non-profit making organisation for Jewish artists who could not show elsewhere, and later for Israeli artists. The gallery had a chequered career, and was obliged to move its location from place to place. It also owned a nice little art collection.

Someone had the bright idea of adding a storey to a Synagogue that was being completed in Soho, to become the new home for the Art Gallery. They built it before they had all the money to pay for it, as happens with most public buildings, and finally were short of £10,000 to pay off the balance. They could easily have gone round the Jewish businessmen with a hat, and collected the money in a forenoon, for by then the financial administration of the Gallery had been taken over by rich laymen; but no, they decided to sell a Modigliani drawing, the Kohinoor of their collection. In the saleroom it did not reach its reserve, but a private buyer was found for it. Artists have known for a long time that with businessmen sentiment plays no role. The artists would never have sold it.

166

I met Christopher Grieve — Hugh MacDiarmid, the world famous poet — at the beginning of the Second World War, when he came to live in Glasgow to find work. He was working on a boat, and during the Christmas postal rush would take on a job at the Post Office, anything that might help to keep body and soul together. In this respect he was one of those unique personalities who think that work does not demean, that man ennobles the work he does, no matter how menial it may be.

Milly and I got on very well with Grieve and his wife Valda, and they became frequent visitors to our home in West Campbell Street. I modelled him in 1941, but what happened to it is a mystery, for it disappeared after a London exhibition, and because of the war, and my disturbed mind, I did not pursue its loss.

As I got to know Grieve better I realised that he was too contrasting personalities in one. I dislike politics, in spite of the fact that I know many politicians; I never discussed politics with him. I knew he was a Communist, but it meant little to me, although he spoke of it openly, telling me that Russian Communism would not suit Scotland. It needed its own type. In spite of everything, his Presbyterian upbringing and his father's influence had taken root, and his bohemian behaviour was only skin deep.

He and Valda would visit us at odd times, not often during our open Thursday evenings. I doubt whether Grieve liked crowds. One Thursday evening, as he was passing the Art Club, out came Bridie with a friend. "Where are you going?" they asked him, and when he told them that he was going to the Schotzes, they said "He is also a friend of ours, we will join you."

Usually we would have twenty to thirty visitors, mostly artists. That evening we had a full house with Milly and I moving about between the livingroom and studio to talk to our visitors. There was a bottle of whisky on the table, tea was served, and the talk was frank and lively. During the evening Grieve came over to me in the studio and whispered, "I don't like this friend of Bridie's, every time you go out of the room he helps himself to the whisky bottle". It was there for everybody, and although Grieve liked a drink, he would never help himself, but would wait till his glass was filled. He had strict principles and objected if others did not behave likewise.

He was very touchy about his name and was annoyed if he was addressed by his first name unless he had given that person permission. It was late when our visitors left, and we were surprised to get a visit from Grieve the following forenoon. He had come to apologise to Milly, for seemingly he had addressed her by her first name the previous evening, although he said she had not given him permission to do so. He had remembered it later at home, and was annoyed with himself. This was Grieve in his private life and in his relationships with his friends. He was meticulous and correct, and expected the same behaviour from others.

When a number of his admirers, including Bridie and Walter Elliot got the idea that he should receive a Royal Bounty, knowing how little he earned, they came to ask me whether I thought Grieve would accept it. I must have sounded him out, though my memory is hazy on this point, but I do remember that he told me that he would not swear fealty to the Crown. Finally I told them that they should go ahead and that all would be well. He did get the Royal Bounty, and while it then amounted to only £75, it made a great difference to his income. The socialists, or labourites would have refused to promote it, because of his political views, but to his Conservative friends his politics did not matter.

What mattered was his poetry. To augment his income MacDiarmid began to copy his poems by hand and sell them. It was a laborious process, but he came by the idea from the many enquiries he received for his holograph manuscripts.

There was only one occasion when Grieve and I almost had a difference. It happened one Saturday night when Milly and I were visiting Walter Pritchard, a stained glass artist, mural painter and sculptor. He was also head of the Mural Department of the School of Art. His wife, Sally, was the sister of Robert MacLellan, the playwright, and was making a name for herself as a stained glass artist. Walter Pritchard had become a Catholic, and on one of their walls hung a crucifix. It was a beautiful cross, in ivory, and I used to admire it whenever I visited them.

Chris and Valda lodged in their basement flat and were with them that evening because of us. We also met a Frenchman there and it happened to be a day when something important was happening in France, something to do with a labour problem. Everybody was waiting to hear the news on the radio. I believe that the first item of the news was that U.N.O. had voted for a State of Israel. I was too excited to hear the rest of the news.

At the end everybody began to talk to the Frenchman about the French news. That Israel was declared a State passed unnoticed. So I got up and said to the company, "Will nobody congratulate us for the creation of our State, something we have been waiting for, for two thousand years?" There was silence. I think they were stunned by my outburst. So I continued, turning to our host, "The trouble with you people is that you have Christ on the wall", pointing to the crucifix, "but not in your hearts. Milly, this is no place for us, let us go".

Grieve tried to say something as an excuse, but I was too upset to listen to what he was saying, and we left.

One year Milly and I spent a holiday in Dingwall, and as Nigg was not far away I decided to visit Eric Linklater. He had quite an estate, and a long drive stretched from the imposing gate to the house, flanked by huge trees. It was late August, and leaves were already falling fast and filling the gutters. This gave me my opening remark. Autumn and falling leaves have always saddened me, to which Linklater replied that to him, falling leaves just meant good compost.

The table of the room he worked in was laden with journals, and he was working on some sort of article for a periodical. This brought our conversation round to professional writing, and then to MacDiarmid. He knew how friendly the two of us were, and could not refrain from remarking what a nice fellow MacDiarmid was to speak to, "But give him a pen in his hand and he goes berserk".

Because MacDiarmid's days were not fully occupied with writing poetry, and he had no teaching post, he had time to ponder over the cruelties of life, perhaps even his own, created by man, the inefficiency of Councillors, and their inability to help the poor. He was their champion, and he spared no invective to attack the Establishment, challenging its decisions in monthlies and weeklies he published. He spoke out boldly, but like John the Baptist, his voice was almost a cry in the wilderness. In this respect, however, he was luckier than others, because he lived to see at least some of his aims come into being.

When MacDiarmid was offered an LL.D. from Edinburgh University, Michael, his son, told me that his father did not sleep for two nights pondering whether he should accept the honour. We were all very glad that he did. It was probably a year later that I received my LL.D. from Strathclyde University, my Alma Mater, and it so happened that Milly and I went to a play in Edinburgh, and sitting near us was none other than Grieve. He was very pleased to see us, "So you have also joined the exclusive club", he remarked.

Many functions and evenings were arranged for his sixtieth birthday. At a luncheon he was presented with a drawing of himself by David Foggie. I was asked to be one of the speakers, and being the last one to speak, the Chairman whispered to me to be short, for they only had time for a short address. This took me off my theme completely, and I was a flop. After the meeting I was telling Bridie what I really wanted to say, and he said, "Why did you not say it, to hell with the Chairman, what you were going to say was vital". This was a lesson to me, to take my time in the future if I needed it.

During the years that MacDiarmid lived in Glasgow he had a crowd of hangers on. They would take him into a pub, and ply him with drink. They wanted to be his pals and to glean ideas and information from him. Were he alive, I am sure that Chris would not have minded my saying so, but even a very little drink went to his head. People began to say that he was seldom sober, but that was not true. He was never drunk, and could carry on a lucid conversation, even when he was not too steady on his feet. We tried hard to point out to him that these characters were not his friends, but his enemies. He was only able to shake them off when he went to live in a small isolated cottage near Biggar. Years later — again not socialists — added to the cottage a

169

kitchen and bathroom, and Valda said to us, "I now have everything I want from life. Now I am happy". I doubt whether jealousy was ever in their nature.

His son Michael lived within walking distance from me, and sometimes he would deposit his father at my place, especially when MacDiarmid had some engagement that evening, knowing that when he came to collect him after work, he would find him as fresh as when he brought him. One such afternoon Chris told me what he considered rather a humiliating experience. Valda, living a lifetime with a poet, knew about good and bad poetry, and decided to try her hand at writing some herself. She had published one privately, and it sounded quite good to me.

She decided to try her luck, and submitted another one to a magazine. To keep her company Chris sent one in also. Both were published, but to his astonishment Valda received a cheque for four guineas, while his was only for three! He was the most famous poet in Britain, if not in the world, but that was immaterial, — the magazine paid by the line, and Valda's poem was longer. His self esteem was shattered.

A portrait of MacDiarmid painted by Westwater was to be presented to him on his 70th birthday. Milly and I were invited and when we arrived, much to my surprise I was asked to make the presentation. I had no time for preparation, and began by comparing him with Burns, and how much better he had been served by the artists. The fashionable portrait painters of Edinburgh considered Burns a country versifier and had probably not even read his poetry. There was no money to be got out of him, so why bother to paint him. "How much luckier are you, Chris; you have been painted, modelled and drawn, and now you are being presented with a portrait specially commissioned to mark your seventieth birthday." Naturally I continued to enlarge on the occasion and finished by wishing Chris good health and continued inspiration.

Everybody congratulated me on my speech. They said I was best when I spoke impromptu. They did not think, of course, that to make a good speech one must have the right subject and the right theme.

The Royal Scottish Academy elected him our eighth Professor of Literature in 1974, but I was indisposed and could not go to the luncheon where he was to reply to his toast. He missed me, and I him. During the 150th anniversary celebrations of the R.S.A., Edinburgh City Council held a dinner in its honour. I could not attend for the same reason, but I heard one sentence of MacDiarmid's speech. "When Scotland was creating its Academy of Art one hundred and fifty years ago, London was creating its Zoo." Being an Anglophobe, he missed no opportunity to knock England hard when the occasion arose.

For quite a time he wanted to introduce me to Francis George Scott, the composer of Scottish songs, but held back at first in case we would not get on. F. G. Scott was originally a teacher in Grieve's school in

Langholm, in the Borders. Grieve used to show him his poems and other writings, and Scott began to take an interest in the youth's work. However, Scott became known as a composer. Scott and Grieve were reunited in the early 1920s and there developed between them a real friendship, with Scott becoming once again Grieve's mentor on many things.

One evening, Milly and I attended a poetry reading where Scott was in the chair, and after the meeting it was a simple matter for me to be introduced to him. He must have heard about me from Chris, and we had a good laugh at some of the incidents which happened before and during the reading session. This was the beginning of a friendship between our two families.

F. G.'s ambition was to re-create Scottish music, and there is little doubt that he laid its modern foundation. His strength lay in songs, and he set to music many of MacDiarmid's poems, some of Burns's and many others. He told me that having arrived back from college, and having had a cup of tea, he would relax in his easy chair. Gradually he would doze off. Then he would suddenly waken on hearing some notes in his head. These he would note down, and they would become the theme for a new song. F. G. had no voice to speak of, yet when he sat down at his tinny upright piano and began to sing to his own accompaniment, it was a most exciting experience, his flushed face and his inspired mood mesmerising his audience. It was especially so when he sang the ballad *John, my son John*, arguably one of his finest compositions.

When he composed a piece for a small orchestra, and it was going to be broadcast on the radio, he and his wife, and Chris and Valda came to West Campbell Street, to listen in, as we were their only friends who had a radio.

F. G. told me how one weekend Chris and Valda came to see them. Chris brought with him his draft of *A Drunk Man Looks at the Thistle*. Valda told me recently that Chris had the manuscript stuffed in all his pockets. F. G. read it through and straight away took charge. He told Chris, "A work has to have a beginning, a middle, and an end". I feel sure that Grieve was not prepared for such an analysis right away, but F. G. was so taken with the poem that he felt he had to edit it. So they shut themselves up in a bedroom, laid the poems out on the bed, and began. Scott felt that the beginning should have a vital poem and showed Grieve the one which he thought should come first. The end he also thought should be powerful, with the middle like an andante. So they set to work, and by the evening when the 'labour' was done, F. G. realised that Grieve had produced a masterpiece.

When Mr. George Bruce, the poet, was the Director of Art Features with BBC Scotland, he would call on me fairly frequently to give short talks on the radio, interviews, and to discuss the sculpture in the Royal

171

Scottish Academy on television. When it came to art, the B.B.C. felt that the public could not take more than five to ten minutes of it at a time.

On 12th December 1953, George Bruce, in his art programme *Counterpoint* decided to have five persons take part to give it a wide range of subject matter. The broadcast was to begin with me modelling a head; after five minutes or so Sir W. O. Hutchison was going to talk on Nasmyth, the Scottish portrait painter; then Sir Alexander Gray was to speak on his classical translations, and C. R. M. Brooks was going to recite some of them. In between the various sections I would be shown working on my portrait, to see its progress, and as MacDiarmid was to speak on the Scottish physiognomy I took him as my subject. Have you ever heard of such a dog's breakfast?

Well, things don't always turn out as planned, and just before going on the air, one of the two cameras stopped functioning. In desperation George Bruce turned to me and said, "Benno, will you carry on by yourself while the other camera is being repaired?" My answer was in the affirmative, as over the years I had given dozens of demonstrations, although Bruce had never seen one.

I began as if I were before a live, but invisible audience, not even knowing where the camera was. I chatted away, and I still remember saying, "I had better turn my bald patch away from you", forgetting that the camera could not be stationed behind me. I had twenty three minutes to myself on the screen, and from the correspondence received later it was rated the brightest television performance seen for a long time. They asked for more.

The Controller, sitting at home, became distressed when he heard about the breakdown of the camera, and came post haste to the studios to congratulate me on having got them out of a difficulty. What amused me was how the producer could not improvise. When the second camera became operative, they continued as if nothing had gone wrong, with Sir William talking about Nasmyth, with the result that the programme had no cohesion. They should have asked MacDiarmid to speak, as this would have rounded up my demonstration.

Because there was such excitement, and Sir Alexander Gray did not get a look in on the programme, he and his narrator, C. R. M. Brooks were greatly annoyed. Unbelievably, they refused to shake hands with me when leaving, saying, "You *willed* that camera to break down". I was stunned. "When you heard about the camera you said it was just what you needed." Did they really invest me with the evil eye?

The sculpture I modelled that evening was quite a good likeness for the time I had, except that when it was fired — I made it into a terra cotta — it looked small. My heads grow as I carry them to a conclusion.

This one I presented to the B.B.C.

As the Grieves were staying the night with us I asked Chris to come into my studio the following morning after breakfast, and said to him "*Now* I will model you". This is the head the B.B.C. bought in appreciation of my demonstration, the head which is displayed in the foyer of their Glasgow studios, and this is the head I consider the high water mark of my portraiture.

When Grieve died in 1978 I was given the honour of being one of his pallbearers. He was buried at Langholm, and as Valda said, "They did not make him a Freeman of the town, so now they will have him forever".

In the days when I used to give little dinners in the Art Club to my friends, whom, being a bachelor, I could not entertain at home, Sir John Richmond was always of the company. He had been painted more than once, but I always felt that no justice had been done to him, for he had a much deeper character than the artists portrayed.

I sometimes asked him to pose for me, but he was unwilling until he saw that I was really serious. His head was made for sculpture. It was strong, full, round to oval, and had the mass to make it not only a good head, but also a good piece of sculpture. During my second sitting something revealed itself that I had not noticed before, and I told him, "You know, Sir John, it is strange, but the more I work on your head, the more like a Buddha it becomes". So he came out with a story.

His niece was his housekeeper, and when they were sitting on a couch after dinner, he at one end, and she at the other, she would begin to tell him what needed to be done to the house, he would lend a dull ear to her remarks — he had a dull ear — till she would burst out and say, "There you sit like a Buddha and say nothing!"

It was then that he told me why he was loathe to be modelled. His school mates used to call him "Puddin' face" in coarse Scots, and he never got rid of that face. He felt that he would not make a good sculpture, and only realised his mistake when he saw my work. It was he who had bought the second head of the Lord Weir from me, to whom he was a half brother.

One day I happened to see a notice that Lord Boyd Orr was to give a lecture in the McLellan Galleries, which was only a few minutes walk from our home. Naturally, I had heard his name before, but I must confess that I knew little, if anything about him. The subject of the lecture must have interested me, otherwise I would not have gone to hear him.

When Boyd Orr came on to the platform, I was mesmerised by his head. I had never seen him before, nor did I remember ever seeing a photograph of him. He was made for sculpture. I doubt whether I heard one word he uttered. My mind was wholly occupied by studying his

173

features.

I seldom ask people whom I have never met to pose for me, except in my early days when I modelled artistes. However, I was so excited about Boyd Orr's head, that when the lecture was over I introduced myself, and asked him if he would allow me to model him. He must have heard about me, for he readily, even eagerly agreed.

My first sitting was fixed for the following morning, and in that morning I completed his head. Some heads are easier to model, while others are more difficult, but I had studied his features during his lecture, and I could have modelled him from memory. Some heads are subtle and delicate, but Boyd Orr's was chiselled and simple. I asked for another sitting, as I wanted to make a biggish bust, but after I had modelled it I discovered that the bust overpowered the head. The head was complete in itself and did not need any additional trappings to support it, so I only cast the head.

During my two sittings I got to know a lot about him. He was frank and communicative. He told me that Huxley Jones, who was the Head of the Sculpture Department of the Aberdeen College of Art had modelled him, and that the bust was in the Agricultural College there. I was glad I did not know this beforehand, for it would have inhibited me from asking him to sit for me. It might have looked as if I was trying to improve on the previous effort. Our methods were quite different, and so were our results. I almost imagined from our conversation that Lord Boyd Orr was not quite happy with what Huxley Jones had done, and was glad to give me the opportunity to see what I might produce. I have since seen a photograph of the other bust, but I refuse to judge a work from a photograph.

Talking with him about the United Nations, he told me in all seriousness that he was actually the first International Person, because when he was appointed the Head of the World Food Organisation, he had to swear fealty before every member of the United Nations. As my sittings were full of activity, and my chat on the light side I remember little else of our conversations, except one of my usual absurdities.

I had mentioned that Israel was entering on a five-year plan to become self sufficient in food production, and his remark was "The sooner they begin, the better". He had paid a visit to Israel, and knew much more about its agricultural capacity than I, and he smiled at my naïvety.

As long as I can remember, the Royal Scottish Academy used to invite painters and sculptors, and even architects to bolster up their annual exhibitions. To 'bolster up' may be the wrong expression. Artists from the South would only show in Scotland if invited, and all their costs paid. Scotland seemed isolated from the rest of the world, and the Academy was keen for the artists and the people to see what was being done beyond its borders.

This state of affairs only changed with the Edinburgh Festival, when special exhibitions were mounted by the joint efforts of the Festival Society, the Academy, and the Scottish Arts Council. For a long time I myself was a supporter of these invitations, in the hope that reciprocity might take place.

However, there was only a one-way traffic in the arts, and gradually I came to the conclusion that it was time we stood on our own feet, and did not depend on stimulation from outside.

In 1949 I was asked by the Academy to go to Italy and invite a collection of sculpture. This was really the first time I had left Britain since I came to settle here, and Milly joined me on the trip. Our first stop was Milan, and I was surprised to see Douglas Young, the poet, Greek scholar, and Scottish Nationalist standing at the station, a full head above all the other people there. He was two metres high, and could not be easily missed.

The International P.E.N. Club were holding their annual conference in Venice that year, and it suited him to attend it, for he was writing a book about a neglected Greek poet, Theognis. He describes episodes of his journey in *Chasing an Ancient Greek.*

To me, Florence was a vast museum. No matter where one looked, treasures met your eye. One can have a surfeit of art and antiquity, and a museum can become stuffy for lack of fresh air and change. Milan did not appeal to me, and its Gallery was closed as war damage was being repaired. Yet it was in Milan that I saw an early Marini in a dealer's gallery, a horse. It was smooth and delicately finished and showed a Chinese influence. Not at all the style in which he came into prominence.

We arrived in Rome in the afternoon, and when we took our first look around — there had been a drought — everything was dusty, the fountains dry and neglected and sad looking. Later in the evening clouds began to gather threateningly, and all of a sudden the heavens broke loose. Flashing and fork lighting and prolonged peals of thunder tore through the stillness.

Milly stuck her head under the blankets, being afraid, but for me it was a reminder of my young days at home, when we experienced such storms now and again. But never before had I seen such heavenly splendour lasting for hours. I could not tear myself away from the window till the thunder and lighting ceased, though the rain continued to fall unabated. We woke the next morning to bright sunshine, and when we went forth, the city had undergone a metamorphosis. Everything sparkled, the fountains were playing, spouting and overflowing. Our own spirits were uplifted, and I began my visits to the sculptors I had in mind.

Rome had a wonderful new museum. Almost every Italian sculptor of any eminence was represented in it. One only needed to walk round it to get a fair idea of whom to invite. It was in Rome that I met Manzù,

Mirko Basaldello and Greco. At that time Greco lived in the German Prix de Rome building, and was anxious to retain it, hoping it would not be given back to the Germans.

At the time he was so poor that to offer us a cup of coffee must have involved a sacrifice. He was taken up by the London gallery, Roland Browse and Delbanco, after the pieces I had chosen were shown in London, and sometime later seeing one of his figures in their gallery I remarked that, had it been done by an Englishman, no one would have looked at it. Dr. Roland replied, "But see how Italian it is". A strange way of thinking. I thought that there was only one standard by which to judge a work.

Manzù did not know a single word of English, or French, and he had to call in an interpreter. He showed me a series of twelve bronze panels, reliefs dealing with the war, but I pointed out to him that they had to be shown in toto, and I could invite at most only four pieces from each sculptor. So he sent us a life size reclining figure.

Rome became hot, and when I went to see Mirko, I found him working in the nude. He compromised, and put on a pair of swim trunks when he realised I had Milly with me. I found him very amiable and full of vigour, and he was working on a pair of gates. He had just composed a work he called 'Tobias and the Angel', the same title as a play which James Bridie had recently written. I invited it to Edinburgh, but because of my remarks and reference to Bridie, he changed its title to 'Heroic Motive'.

It was in Venice that I unearthed Viani, and met Marini. The latter was not keen to send to a group show, and said that there might be other occasions for showing in Britain. I don't think he was ever taken up by a gallery. In Venice, in the Guggenheim Museum I saw his equestrian group with the penis that can be screwed in and out. Miss Peggy Guggenheim wanted it that way. All the Italian sculptors who exhibited in the R.S.A. in Edinburgh in 1950 showed in Britain for the first time, except for Manzù, who already had a small work in the Tate.

In Venice I met up with Edwin Muir, and feeling I was being hemmed in by the past all around, I mentioned that it would do no harm to have some modern architecture here and there. Out of the blue he asked me, "Would you destroy San Marco?" 'Destroying' never came into the picture, but I being bold replied, "Yes, if I thought I could build better". He asked me a singular and straight question, which had no bearing on our conversation, and I had to answer honestly, and at that time, this was my opinion. He turned away from me, and hardly spoke to me again, except when I was the host at dinner.

Douglas Young was present at my meeting with Edwin Muir. His remarks about Dante Zamboni and my conversations with that sculptor in his book are correct, but not my outburst in Venice. His narrative was romantic and not verbatim. Self expression can be poor, dull, and without imagination.

Venice had an exhibition of Bellini that year. Everywhere there were huge posters 'Mostra Bellini', they stared at you, no matter where you turned. I took the opportunity to contact the organisers of the 'Biennale' to ask why Scottish artists were never invited to their exhibitions, which took place every two years, then the only Biennale in the world. The reply I received was to the point. Scotland was not an independent country. Protocol demanded that the invitation be sent to the Foreign Office in London, and the Foreign Office passed it on to the British Council. There it got into the hands of a Mrs. Somerville, who, I understand, decided what the exhibits were to be. Scotland never came into the picture. As far as Mrs. Somerville was concerned, it did not exist.

That year I modelled Douglas Young in the pose of Theognis, as on the cover of his book, and exhibited it as a terra cotta in the Royal Glasgow Institute of the Fine Arts. When it was being placed in the sculpture section I received a telephone call from the gallery. A young assistant, seventeen years of age, looking at my sculpture, suddenly discovered that I had modelled both feet the same. They were either both right, or both left feet, I forget which. What should they do about it? "Nothing" was my answer, "I will deal with it on the varnishing day." It did not take long to rectify, but it just proves how easily one can make a mistake, which we all missed, to be discovered by an observant youth.

It was on the score of two similar hands, that one of Stanley Spencer's paintings was rejected from the Royal Academy when he was already an Associate of that exclusive 'club' — Eric Kennington's phrase to me. It created quite a stir, as works of elected members are not *sub judice*. For weeks it was *the* topic of conversation among artists all over Britain. Veracity in anatomy can be a very dull affair. Art does not just deal with anatomical veracity, and should not be judged on that score. Even Michaelangelo carved muscles which did not exist.

I related that when I was elected an Associate of the Academy, I was given the opportunity to bring a Henry Moore sculpture to our annual exhibition. Then my invitation was by letter, and from the few pieces he had available, I chose one from a photograph, a piece of Aztec influence. Years later I wanted to have a special exhibition of Henry Moore's sculpture in the Academy, and this time I paid him a visit, and I chose nine sculptures for our show of 1956. These were also shown in Scotland for the first time.

Henry Moore took me round his studios, where his assistants were enlarging his maquettes, and he also took me into his private studio, where he was designing his sculptures. It was cluttered with sketches, and in his cases were bits and pieces from which he derived his ideas. He was rather keen that I invite his 'Mother and Child', the one where the Child's head is a large beak ready to snap at the mother's breast.

We all know that a child lives off the mother from its very conception, and to me the allusion was literary rather than sculptural. In this respect Henry Moore follows the Egyptian and Aztec traditions. Many of the Egyptian gods were modelled naturalistically, even though stylised, till they came to the head. Then they gave the figures a lion's head, a vulture's, or some other, depending on the deity it was supposed to depict.

The Aztecs did the same, and Moore was greatly influenced by their sculpture in his early years. He did this with his 'Warrior' war memorial, and also with his 'King and Queen'. They harmonise well, yet I am left with a doubtful feeling. Is it right for us to use such emblems today? The Aztecs and the Egyptians believed them to be gods, but do we?

Moore showed me five pillar-like sculptures he had designed, because he told me he had received a commission for such a composition from a client in Italy. Henry Moore has received few commissions for sited sculpture, and when he is asked for a piece he expects his clients to choose something he has already designed. It is interesting and instructive to note that Moore was not satisfied with one design, but designed five.

He had done the same thing when years earlier he received a commision for a 'Madonna and Child'. Then he even designed family groups, which later he was able to enlarge. These pillars are really the only vertical sculptures I have seen by Henry Moore, except for a winged figure. At first only one of these was executed in its full size. At the time of my visit it was being enlarged in one of his studios in two parts, as the ceiling was too low to enable it to be enlarged in one piece. Since then I have seen one or two of the others enlarged.

Since I am on the subject, I may as well admit that I was surprised when the first one was named 'Glenkin Cross', the name deriving probably from its siting in Scotland. But why 'Cross'? I see the top part as a seated female figure, draped in Moore's characteristic fashion, the arms folded at right angles to the body, as it squats on its square pedestal. Is it a case of the King and his robe?

As I had been interested for a long time in Moore's two 'Warriors', the standing skeletal ones, especially in their shields, I asked him about them. He was frank and open. He told me that he wanted to design them for a long time, but only managed to do so after he had paid a visit to Africa.

What interested me most were the shields which the warriors held. Had they any significance? Why were they triangular? I showered him with these questions, but he could not enlighten me on these points. They just happened. This I could easily understand. An artist designs, and allows the subconscious to take over. The sculptor becomes the

178

tool, the inspiration is given free reign. Only afterwards does the sculptor go over his creation with a critical eye, and then, only then does he make sure that the work has logic, and reads from every angle, and that the shapes conform and belong.

I asked Moore whether he knew that in some concentration camps the Germans used to tattoo the Jews with triangles before their numbers, one for men and another for women? No, he did not know. I did not expect him to know, because even in Israel, where I expected that everything would be known about the Holocaust, well informed Jews did not know about this. I was almost made to look a fool when I assured them that I had read about it in a reputable journal, but at the time did not take note of the journal, nor of the writer. However I did receive proof that the article about the triangles was true in 1978, when I met Professor Eli Wiesel who is considered an authority on the Holocaust. As a boy he had been an inmate of a camp, and has published a number of books on the subject. He told me that I was right and he himself had seen these triangles on former concentration camp inmates. The men had the point of the triangle on top, because this was how the hair grows in a man's pubis, coming up almost to a point below the navel. In the case of a woman, the triangle was inverted, to match her pubic hair. For the Germans the reason was simple. A man could not disguise himself as a woman, were he set on escape, because the triangle would tell the authorities the person's gender. The same applied to a woman.

But this was not *my* problem. Mine was, how did we come to adopt the Shield of David, better known as the Star of David, for our symbol? Historians assert that we did not invent it, that we borrowed it. The Encyclopaedia Judaica tells us that the hexagon was known from as early as the bronze age — possibly as a magical sign, in many civilisations and in many regions. The first undisputed example is on a seal from the seventh century B.C.

In my analysis the answer is simple. The Star of David consists of the male and female triangles superimposed one on top of the other. At its lowest level, the Star of David becomes a fertility sign, one of procreation, as Isaac said to Jacob, "Be fruitful and multiply" (Genesis XXVIII 3). At its highest level, on the other hand it becomes a symbol of eternal life, of perpetuation, survival, and constant renewal.

Is it not remarkable that we Jews should have chosen the Shield of David as our own? It is so appropriate for the Jewish race, since they have been able to survive every persecution and slaughter throughout the generations, and flower again.

The year 1950 stands out in my mind as one of great activity, responsibility, and committee meetings. Periodically, London used to stage a Judaica book exhibition, and Glasgow would follow suit, involving the Mitchell Library in the venture. London held an exhibition early in 1950, and I was approached to arrange one in Glasgow.

The 1951 Festival of Britain was already being planned. Glasgow had more than once led the field in Jewish matters, and it was nearly ten years since we had staged our first Jewish Art Exhibition. Why then limit our venture to books alone? Why not embrace the whole gamut of Jewish culture in a Festival of Jewish Art as part of the Festival of Britain?

This was a bold idea, but could it be brought to fruition? I discussed the project with a few friends, and found great enthusiasm in the idea, so we collected a number of intellectuals to discuss the subject fully. The Festival was to consist of an art exhibition, a book exhibition, an exhibition of ritual objects from various sources, a concert, a dramatic performance, lectures, and a section dealing with the Holocaust. It turned out to be a vast project, but I managed to gather round me a nucleus of enthusiasts who carried the burden willingly and worked endlessly and ungrudgingly to get the best results.

The Jewish community talked of little else for months. Our publicity reached everywhere, and our art exhibition even included works from the United States. For the first time a Jewish exhibition had a fully illustrated catalogue. Our Festival took place in February 1951, and we were all satisfied and relieved to have accomplished what we set out to do.

We had put in a year's work on the undertaking, with innumerable meetings, travelling, and collecting exhibits. We were able to carry out such a tremendous task because we were a closely knit community. Had we been a large community like London, it would have been difficult to find people who would work in harmony and unison.

I lost a year's work through being the co-ordinator of all the sections. There were only eight British artists in the whole exhibition, and when Joe Ancill asked me why he was not included — he should have looked at the names before asking me this question — my reply was that if I had not been so closely connected with the enterprise, I might not have been among the exhibitors. It was this trivial matter that finally severed our friendship.

After our Festival it became imperative for London Jewry to do something, so in due course they staged an art exhibition which was hardly even an echo of ours. All I remember of it are some poles wrapped round with red, white and blue ribbons by way of their patriotic intentions.

We invited Martin Buber to give one of the lectures; a concert by Ida Haendal and the young American pianist Abbey Simon; drama — *The Dybbuk*; music on records during lunchtime, and many other events. It again attracted the attention of the non-Jewish public to the cultural contribution of the Jews to the world, at a time when it was needed.

The Haendal/Simon recital created great excitement, and the hall

PRINCIPAL FESTIVAL EVENTS

Sunday, 4th February —McLellan Galleries, 3 p.m.—
Festival Opening.   Private View.

Tuesday, 6th February —McLellan Galleries, 7.45 p.m.—
Lecture by Josef Herman on " Jewish Art."

Wednesday, 7th February—Berkeley Hall, 7.30 p.m.—
Concert by Hirsch String Quartet.

Sunday, 11th February —Cranston's Cinema, 3.30 and 7.15 p.m.—
Film Show.   " The Last Chance " and " Tomorrow is a Wonderful Day."

Thursday, 15th February—McLellan Galleries, 7.45 p.m.—
Lecture by Professor Martin Buber.

Saturday, 17th February —Institute Little Theatre, 8 p.m.—
" The Dybbuk."   Gala Opening.

Tuesday, 20th February —Berkeley Hall, 7.30 p.m.—
Concert by Ida Haendel and Abbey Simon.

Thursday, 22nd February—McLellan Galleries, 7.45 p.m.—
Lecture by Joseph Leftwich on "Yiddish Literature."

Saturday, 24th February —Festival Ball.

Sunday, 25th February —Close of Festival.

Programme of events at the Festival of Jewish Arts, Glasgow 1951.

was packed. Abbey Simon was such a success in his part of the programme, having to give several encores, that we wondered whether the temperamental Ida Haendal might become offended. Not a bit of it! After the interval she swept, beaming onto the stage, struck a heroic pose, and in equally heroic tones launched into her first offering. The applause was thunderous. The climax came with the two artists' most moving performance of Ernest Bloch's *Nigun,* from his *Baal Shem* suite, one of the greatest musical expressions of the Jewish soul.

One week in September 1952, Glasgow seemed to be invaded by sailors, mostly American. They were everywhere. A N.A.T.O. exercise 'Mainbrace' was to take place in the North Atlantic the following week, and seventy warships of various nations were anchored in the Clyde. Elizabeth Mary Watt, an artist and decorator of china with whom Hesse shared a flat, was annoyed. She complained to Hesse how forward the sailors were, for many of them were parading in the streets, arm in arm with Scottish girls. To this Hesse replied jokingly, "For all you know they may be related. I have American relations myself, and if one of them happened to be a sailor and came ashore in Glasgow, I might be walking with him arm in arm myself".

That Friday evening, as was usual, Hesse joined us for dinner, and shortly after we had finished our meal there was a ring at our door. Cherna answered it and was confronted by an American sailor who asked, "Is this the Schotz residence?" When assured that it was, he continued, "I think Mr. Schotz is my uncle".

When I went into the hall, there stood before me a most handsome youth. He was Paul Schoenbaum, the youngest son of my cousin Essie, the daughter of my Uncle Elias. Essie knew that she had relations in Britain, and when Paul was conscripted into the Navy, she made him promise that should he ever touch a British port he would try to find out something about us.

He kept his promise, and when his ship first berthed in Britain, I forget where, he contacted the Rabbi there, who found my name and address in *Who's Who.* When his ship finally berthed at Greenock his company was the last to get shore leave on the Friday afternoon. He spent some time looking for a present for his mother, and then he and his buddy had a meal. When his friend went to a dance hall nearby, Paul himself asked in the restaurant where Kirklee Road was, — we had moved a couple of years before — or Benno Schotz. Someone knew, and actually walked him all the way from Charing Cross.

There was great excitement in our home, and we were delighted to discover our lost relations in the United States. We soon received a glowing letter from Essie expressing her happiness in finding us. She wrote that although she received the news from Paul on the Eve of one of our High Festivals, when she was very busy in the kitchen, she 'burned

182

up the wires' phoning all her relatives with the news.

One of her brothers, Seymour Schotz, was a doctor and held the post of Head of Anaesthesia in the Presbyterian Hospital in Philadelphia. He and his wife Helen took advantage of a conference in Europe to pay us a visit. We became dear and close friends. Tragically Essie died before we could visit the United States. I was very upset, and a great urge came over me to see my other cousins, Louis and Max, and their families. I was afraid that if I did not do so quickly one or the other of us might die before we met.

I am glad to say that on frequent trips to the States since then I have visited them several times, though it is with Seymour and Helen that I have a true relationship which goes far beyond mere family connections.

About the same time I received a visit from a Mr. Dillon, a dealer in old paintings. When handing me his visiting card he told me that it was an alias, and that his real name was Paul Heimovici. My name had been given to him by my Rabbi, whose wife came from the same town in Rumania as he. He had become stateless as a result of the war, and was hidden for two and a half years by a Dutch woman in her cellar, to escape the Germans.

We made him welcome, and I gave him as much help and advice as I could. He visited us several times, and finally I suggested that to find the paintings he wanted his best bet was to go to Edinburgh. There he became friendly with a well known antique dealer, Mrs. Esta Henry, a woman of extraordinary character — not surprising in one who ran away from home in Sunderland at the age of nine, and opened a shop in Edinburgh — who decided that here was a person with whom she could again share her life.

She was then seventy years of age and Paul was fifty, but she guessed that Paul would not reject her proposal, for to him she would be an anchor. She was right. One evening in her rooms above her shop she asked to see his false passport, threw it on the fire, and told him, "Now go and give yourself up to the Police". Esta Henry considered that with her influence (she had also at one time been a City Councillor) she would have no difficulty in getting him permission to stay in Britain, so that she could marry him in his real name.

In this she was mistaken. The police kept him in prison for several months, for apparently Interpol were looking for a Paul Heimovici in connection with some heinous crime. The name, we were told, is as common in Rumania as John Smith is in Scotland. He was even taken to the Rumanian Embassy in London to show himself to the authorities, to prove that he was not the Paul Heimovici they were looking for. Esta mounted a campaign for his release, the Press was alerted, and finally a clever lawyer found a loophole to have him released. Esta made a great occasion of it, hired a band, and a pony and trap to take her and her

'Prince' back home.

When they married, he took on the family name of Henry, and because of Paul's interest in paintings, Esta wanted to celebrate their marriage by a double painting. But Paul persuaded her to ask me to model them both instead, probably as a reward for my interest in him in Glasgow. This I did. The composition called for Paul to hold something in his hand, and Amiel suggested that I give him one of the eccentric rings Esta delighted in. I created my own ring in the form of an Adam and Eve design, and it provided the right touch to round off the work.

When Esta asked me the meaning of the ring, and I explained it to her, she exclaimed, "Oh, you naughty boy!" Later I enlarged the design on the ring, and it became a sculpture in its own right.

Paul told us that he had cousins in Israel with whom he was very close, and asked us if we could try and find them as we were soon to leave for Israel. It so happens that in Israel there are also many Heimovicis, but the first people we managed to contact were the right ones! They later came to Britain to visit him.

However, there is a tragic end to this story. Their building in the High Street in Edinburgh adjoined John Knox's House, and Esta intended to leave it, with her wonderful collection of antique silver, over which my double bust would have presided, to the nation, but some years later, before she had arranged it, they were both flying to South America, when the plane crashed, and there were no survivors.

Shortly after the war, my friend Fred Nettler came to visit me one evening with a Mrs. Ivy Paterson, whom he introduced as being Orde Wingate's mother-in-law. This started a friendship which lasted for many years and I gradually got to know her history.

As a girl, while travelling from Australia to continue her violin studies in London, she met her future husband on the ship. Although she was already giving concert recitals in Australia and the Far East, after her marriage, her violin was put away for good. Years later, returning from Australia where Ivy had taken her daughter Lorna to meet her grandmother, Lorna met a young subaltern, Orde Wingate, and they fell in love. Lorna was then sixteen, and they married just before her eighteenth birthday.

Ivy Paterson told me that when he was sent to Palestine he listened on the boat to officers instructing soldiers on how to deal with the Jews. This shocked the young man, who had been brought up in a strictly religious home, and who considered the Jews as the rightful heirs to the Holy Land.

After the Second World War, Sir Gilmour Menzies Anderson, who happened to be my lawyer, asked me why we Jews make such a fuss over Orde Wingate. He himself was a Brigadier to him in the Chindit campaign, and considered Wingate a great man, but knew that the then

Brigadier General was not loved by his officers. I then explained that but for Orde Wingate Israel might not have existed today. With the consent of the authorities he began to train the men from the Kibbutzim and elsewhere in self-defence, then forming the Jewish Defence Forces, the Hagana.

He also showed them how to use their meagre forces in attack, although this was in defiance of British regulations. "Yes" I told Sir Gilmour, "without Wingate's training the Jews would not have been able to withstand the Arab attack and the invasion of Israel in 1948. He instilled into them courage and belief in themselves, and profoundly affected their military thinking and planning".

Mrs. Paterson became friendly with Major Malcolm Vivian Hay of Seaton, Aberdeen, whom she later married after her husband died. Major Hay had been seriously wounded in the Great War. When the German Red Cross were going round the field after the battle and stopped to examine him, he knew he must do something to show them that he was alive. With great power of concentration he managed to open one eye, and survived.

To occupy his time he began to write historical books. He was a Roman Catholic, but his books were excluded from the shelves of their libraries, for as a historian, Malcolm Hay believed in the truth. In one book on anti-semitism, *The Foot of Pride* he described Paul as the first anti-semite.

For a year or so Ivy had been pressing me to model him. "Come over for a week's holiday, and model Malcolm at the same time." It just shows how little people understand what goes on in an artist's mind when he is working on a portrait. I cannot have a holiday while I am working, for my mind is wholly taken up with my subject, and any deviation can affect it. Yet, in the end, I went and stayed with Malcolm for a week.

He then told me the story of his estate. As Major Hay, he was not a wealthy man, and wanting to avoid his son having to pay heavy estate duties, he transferred the estate into the son's name some years before I met him. The son was half French, and perhaps did not feel the same attachment to the estate as his father, for as soon as it became his, he sold it to the Aberdeen Corporation, on the understanding that his father would be allowed to remain in Seaton House as long as he lived.

The house was allowed to deteriorate, the father having no good reason for keeping it up. It looked sad and forlorn, and Malcolm himself, I am sure, did not feel at home in it any more. He seemed a sad and broken man.

Ivy had a lovely home in Aberdeen, but Malcolm was not fated to enjoy his new married life for long. He had to undergo surgery and something went wrong. He suffered terrible pain before he died, and in our home Ivy shed bitter tears, crying "The doctors crucified him, they crucified him!"

Sholem Asch was a Jewish author and dramatist of outstanding merit. In the last few years of his life he came to live with his daughter in London. In Glasgow, the Friends of the Hebrew University of Jerusalem held an annual dinner. I was their President for a number of years, and I suggested that we bring him as our speaker to one of our dinners.

To make the invitation more tempting I suggested that I would like to model him at the same time. There was quite a time lag between our invitation and our dinner. He might have mentioned it to some of his friends, and this must have come to the ears of Epstein. The upshot of it was that Jacob Epstein modelled him before me.

At the time I knew nothing about it, for Sholem Asch never whispered to me what had taken place. He must have felt embarrassed over the incident, indeed, his wife later complained to me about it. The speech worried him, and when I was trying to model him he could not settle down. I got twenty minutes from him, and finished the head while he was reclining on a *chaise longue* outside my studio door, brooding and snoozing, for he and his daughter were staying with us. The morning after the dinner he said to me, "Now, let us go into the studio", but my reply was that I had finished.

That summer a Cezanne exhibition was being held in the Royal Scottish Academy as a Festival attraction, and Sholem Asch was keen to see the show. As we were going to spend some hours in Edinburgh, I phoned up Compton MacKenzie the famous author the night before, and arranged to bring him over for a chat.

At four o'clock the taxi delivered us at Compton MacKenzie's house. Before getting out of the taxi Sholem Asch asked me what MacKenzie wrote about. I managed to give him a fair idea in a few words. When we entered, we were taken into MacKenzie's library where he seemingly worked. After the proper introductions, they began to discuss their respective methods of writing, and became engaged in a lengthy conversation.

Then Sholem Asch had to excuse himself, and while he was away Sir Compton asked me, "What does he write?" I could understand that Sholem Asch might not know what Compton MacKenzie wrote, but Sholem Asch had enraged the Jews with his trilogy about Mary, the Nazarene, and St. John. They were novels by a Jew about the birth of Christianity, and MacKenzie having become a Catholic as a young man, I presumed that he might have heard about them. It just proves that writers have no time to read each others novels, for they are too busy with their own.

Sholem Asch was aware of course, of the animosity his novels created among the Jews, and during our walks together he told me that he had to write them to get them out of his system. Just as one day our Rabbi asked us what I was doing, and Milly answered, "Dr. Gottlieb, you will not be pleased with what you will see in our place just now. It is full of crosses". He did not seem to be in the least surprised, and smilingly replied, "Well, He was one of us".

In 1957 I leased a studio in London, 10, Chelsea Manor Studios, in Flood Street. London had always attracted me. I was a member of the Chelsea Art Club for many years and usually stayed there during my trips. I wanted a studio in Chelsea, but they were at a premium. So many of them had been taken over by wealthy amateurs, by actors, writers, and musicians. The professional artists were being squeezed out.

On one of my visits to London I was lucky. A studio became available, and I was fortunate to get it. I used it during the vacations. I enjoyed Chelsea, the Embankment, the gardens in front of its houses, the strange little buildings, The Court Theatre at Sloane Square, the restaurants, the shops.

We did not live a Bohemian life, no parties, no wine, no beer, just a few old friends who helped me with sales and commissions. I have never been a head hunter, as the portrait sculptors were called in London. I modelled as many figurative subjects as portraits.

I could only renew the lease for three years at a time, and in 1964 the building was bought by a man who wanted to convert it into an Art School. At least, that is what he told us, though the project never materialised, for he could not eject two artists whose only home it was. Mine was just a *pied-a-terre,* so I could not claim security of tenure. Also I had discovered that it was not the best place for modelling portraits. I tried to find another studio at short notice, but without success. However, at that time I was very busy in Glasgow, working with two assistants, so I decided that one studio was sufficient, and so it remained. Why chase the wind and work for the landlord? There is no benefit in it.

Isaac Eban and his wife were old friends. Mrs. Eban's son Aubrey became well known as Abba Eban after he emigrated to Palestine, and was one of the chief spokesmen at U.N.O. for the creation of Israel, and later the Israeli Foreign Minister.

Mrs. Eban was determined that I should model him during one of his stops in London between New York and Jerusalem. She brought him up to my Flood Street studio one Sunday forenoon, accompanied by Jon Kimche, who was then the editor of *The Middle East Review,* and who was to interview him while I was working. He also had with him his book of speeches he had delivered at U.N.O., which he was correcting at the same time. Mrs. Eban carried on a lively conversation with Milly.

I did not want to insult Mrs. Eban, otherwise I would have told her that I could not model a portrait in a market place. Yet in the hour and a half I produced not a bad sketch. So I decided to cast the head, and bring it back to Glasgow where I remodelled it, for in my sketch I had enough information to work from, and from my visual memory to produce a properly considered head. I made it into a terra cotta, and not being commercially inclined, I never showed it to the Ebans, or to Abba himself. I only exhibited it for the first time in my Retrospective Portrait Exhibition in Kelvingrove in 1978, as it was chosen by the organisers, and it held its own among my best works on show.

My great friend, Fred Nettler, visited us frequently at Flood Street, as he was often in London on business. One afternoon in 1958, he arrived with a big and powerfully built man, a Mr. Ezra Danin. He was a Jew of Iraqui origin, and amongst other things he had been the manager of Fred's Israeli orange grove. He spoke Arabic faultlessly, and English well. Golda Meir mentions him in her autobiography, *My Life,* as the person who accompanied her to King Abdullah of Transjordan when she tried to persuade him not to attack Israel after the British Forces evacuated Palestine. He told me that the sumptuous feast which had been prepared for her was left uneaten, as Golda was too distressed and left without touching the food.

Fred had a reason for bringing him to meet me, for after a few preliminary remarks he said to me, "Hasn't Ezra a magnificent head?" True, he did have a powerful head, a veritable chunk of stone. The idea was that I should model him, and without wasting much time, I made a quick sketch of him in clay. He could only give me an hour and a half, but what I accomplished in that time made me want to make a proper study of him. "I will be in Glasgow in a few months, so then I can give you all the time you will need."

As things turned out, the few months extended to nearly a year and a half, for on returning to Israel he became ill, and was only cured when he was made to lose weight — from twenty-two stone to eighteen! When he came to Glasgow I had the opportunity to prove myself. His is the most solid head I have ever modelled. He had a certain peculiarity in his eyes — a family trait. I did not ask him whether I caught it or not, but he told me of an occasion when he had to go back to Iraq on a secret mission. He returned to his home town to be identified, and those who had known his family examined him carefully and searchingly for the eye peculiarity common to his family. Later he became a Minister without Portfolio, and was responsible for all Arab broadcasts from Israel.

He told me a rather humorous story about Eban's head. Seemingly in company my name came up, and Eban, who was there mentioned that I had modelled him, but made him look brainless. He had hardly looked at the head. When Ezra heard this he said, "Why blame Benno? Let

188

him have it out with his mother!"

Zipora, Danin's wife, was a personality in her own right, as an authority on cooking fish. She had published a book with one hundred recipes on how to prepare it. We used to visit them almost every time we were in Israel. On one occasion they insisted we stay to lunch, and after the meal I mentioned to Zipora that we had expected to be served fish. "You had it!" she replied. Ezra himself kept fishponds, for in Israel, fish are cultivated that way. But eventually the government told him to stop, as the water was needed for irrigation in the kibbutzim. He then turned to growing roses. They would be cut at dawn and sold in the shops in Sweden, and other European countries in the late afternoon. At that time they were too expensive for the British market, but now they are to be seen everywhere.

I met Marc Chagall the artist in 1959, when he came to Glasgow to receive the LL.D. which Glasgow University had conferred upon him. Mr. Andrew MacLaren Young, then a lecturer in Fine Art, and later Professor of the Department, had put him forward for the Doctorate. MacLaren Young told me that the first time he put Chagall forward, nobody knew anything about him, and it was a full time job canvassing for his election the following year.

After the Graduation, when we were all leaving the Bute Hall, Professor Walton asked me to stay behind so that he could introduce me to Chagall. When we shook hands, I addressed him in Yiddish, knowing that it was his mother tongue. I was surprised that he did not say a word, but just looked at me blankly, as if I had spoken a Martian language. I just could not understand his attitude. I said to myself, "Why is he pretending he knows no Yiddish? Is he ashamed to be heard speaking it? Everybody in Britain who is at all interested in art knows that he comes from Vitebsk, and that he is a Jew". It left a bad taste in my mouth.

Some days earlier, I had been in touch with our Lord Provost, Myer Galpern, the first Jew in Glasgow to reach that position. I told him about Chagall's visit, and suggested that it would be proper for the City to entertain him. The Lord Provost agreed to arrange a Civic Luncheon for him, the day after the Graduation.

At the Graduation Ball, to which Milly and I were then on the permanent guest list, Myer Galpern came over to me and said, "Benno, tomorrow I am giving Marc Chagall a luncheon, yet so far I have not met him, and I don't even know what language he speaks besides French. Introduce him to me". I did not see Chagall, but I found his wife, who was French. She assured me that besides French, he spoke Yiddish and Russian. She got hold of her husband, and the introductions over, the three of us began to chatter away in Yiddish to our heart's delight. He tried to bluff out our previous introduction, explaining that

189

in France, if three people had been heard talking Yiddish, there would have been a pogrom.

Did he take us for such fools? Myer Galpern answered him "Here I am a Jew and Head of the City". A man who is not afraid to paint Jewish themes and who makes a good living out of it, yet speaking as he did, cannot be sincere. Had I known he was two-faced, I would never have gone to the trouble of suggesting a Civic Luncheon for him.

I took the opportunity to tell him about our Festival of Jewish Art, in which he had featured with some paintings. I promised to bring him a catalogue of the exhibition to the luncheon at the City Chambers the following day. When he read all the international names of the participants, and saw all the reproductions he asked peevishly, "Why did you not write to me about it?" Then I had the satisfaction of telling him that we *had* written to him, but had not received a reply. We had even invited him to come to open the exhibition, but again we received no reply. That silenced him.

Since then I have always had my doubts about Chagall's integrity, and his Jewishness. I began to feel that he brought the Ghetto with him to Paris, and has been trying to paint it out of his system all those years.

I met Chaim Potok in Philadelphia shortly after he published his first novel, *The Chosen*. Since then I have continued to meet him and his charming wife whenever I happen to be in Jerusalem where he lives for part of each year. He was connected with the Jewish Publication Society of Philadelphia and wanted to become a full time author.

The first time I visited Potok in Jerusalem, he took me into a room full of his paintings. It was his studio. I did not know that he was also a painter. I should have guessed this from his book, *My Name is Asher Lev,* as it is full of painting idioms, and deep understanding of the mental complex of an artist. While his novels move me deeply, because they are impregnated with feeling and tradition, his paintings seem to me stark and hard. They have precision, careful composition and a cerebral vision, which may be his release from long concentration on a novel.

But this is not my reason for mentioning Potok. While we were having a cup of tea, he brought up in conversation Marc Chagall, perhaps because at that time Chagall was engaged in designing the tapestry for the *Knesset*. I explained to him that the early Chagalls were really illustrations on canvas of Yiddish sayings.

I gave him several examples, such as *Green und Gell* — Green and Yellow. So Chagall paints a man with one side of his face green and the other yellow; *Sie hot feigelech in kop* — She has birds in her head, so he paints a girl with flowers, and a nest, and birds on top of her head instead of hair; *Zei fliean uebern gasse* — They fly over the street, so he paints a couple flying high above the town; *Er hot fardreit ihr kop* — He has turned her head, so he paints a couple flying out of a window, the girl's head twisted backwards.

I gave Potok many more. He became quite excited over it, for he had never thought or read about it, and then he asked me where I had read it. My reply was, "Does one have to read everything? I read his paintings, and that was enough for me". I have never seen it in print, but Milly and I saw it more or less at the same time in his work.

I was on a nodding acquaintance with Walter Elliot, C.H., Member of Parliament for Kelvingrove for many years, for he would occasionally visit the Glasgow Art Club, being a friend of James Bridie, and he was one of the people who sponsored the application for a Royal Bounty for Hugh MacDiarmid. He was the Lord High Commissioner of the General Assembly of the Church of Scotland in 1956, and knowing that he was bound to be in Scotland for at least a week, I invited him to pose for me. He accepted willingly.

I had been working on a new sketch for a figure, and on entering my studio for the first time his eye caught sight of it and he exclaimed, "Oh, a dryad", and 'Dryad' became its name. Sometimes it is very difficult to find titles for one's work, and once I even invited Francis Scarfe, the poet, who was a lecturer in the Glasgow University French Department, to help me name a series of drawings.

This was for an exhibition of Drawings and Related Sculpture I was holding in the Glasgow Fine Art Institute Rooms in Blythswood Square. Scarfe had been writing a novel about a sculptor, and since he wanted to meet one, Professor Boase, the Head of his Department, introduced us. He must have been surprised to discover that I knew his poetry and even had his books on my shelves, just as I was surprised to discover that he lived in Glasgow.

While I was working on placing and hanging this exhibition, Walter Elliot happened to drop in for an hour, and became interested in the naming process. He even made a couple of suggestions. Then he exclaimed, "This is almost as fascinating as naming racehorses!" Quite a fitting remark, since he was almost as enthusiastic for art as he was for the Noble Sport, and we had a good laugh about it.

Elliot said that, talking about his political career, he could have been elevated to the Peerage, but when the suggestion was put to him by Winston Churchill, he replied that if he went to the Upper House, the Conservatives would lose Kelvingrove, the constituency he represented. His prediction turned out to be true, for when he died suddenly, the seat was won by Labour.

He was rather sore about one thing. He felt that Glasgow should have made him a Freeman. He deserved it from Glasgow for the long service he had rendered it in Parliament. He considered that his politics should not have come into question where service to the country was concerned. Glasgow Corporation was Labour controlled, and it would have gone against their principles to honour a dedicated Conservative in such a way. Yes, they did make Sir Isaac Woolfson a Freeman years later, but we all know that money talks. Also, he had no official connection with the Conservative Party, and had benefited Glasgow culturally.

Elliot told me how he saved Westminster Hall from being destroyed, if not the whole of the Palace of Westminster from being burned to the ground during one of the air raids on London. He happened to be near the House, when an incendiary bomb hit the Hall. He loved the Houses of Parliament, and fire-watched there almost nightly. Firemen were on the spot immediately, but as the building was a Royal Palace they had no authority to touch it. This enraged Elliot, and he said to them, "I am a Privy Councillor, and I am allowed to do what is required. Give me your axe". So he broke the great doors and let the firemen put out the fire.

When in December 1956 my bust of Keir Hardie was being presented to the House of Commons, Walter Elliot, while making his speech, revealed that when they were both at Glasgow University, he and Jimmie Maxton were in opposite camps. Maxton was a Conservative, while he, Elliot, was a Socialist. Strange how the ideas of people can change with experience and circumstance. This happens only to thinking people. Hitler prided himself on the fact that his ideas never changed since he was seventeen years old.

Some months after I modelled him, I received a letter from Elliot asking me to let him have a note of the statues I had executed. There was talk of a statue for Lloyd George, and he wanted to put my name forward. I had to disillusion him. There had been no bronze statue put up in Scotland for about twenty-five years. He could hardly believe it, but this was the case. The last statue put up in Scotland was that to King Edward VII in the grounds of the Palace of Holyrood House. Another was only put up in 1975 — my 'Rob Roy'.

Early in May, 1972, I received a visit from a Mr. Adam McGregor Dick of Kilmarnock. He was a distant descendant of Rob Roy, albeit on the wrong side of the blanket. At least, this is how he put it. He wanted to commission a statue of his famous antecedent. I asked him why he came to me, and he told me that Mr. Johnson of the Dick Institute at Kilmarnock had suggested my name. I knew Mr. Johnson, as he had bought for the Institute my bronze 'John Cairney as Robert Burns'. This proved to me Mr. Dick's credibility, and we discussed his project.

The idea excited my imagination, as naturally I had no statue to my name. He brought me what was purported to be a contemporary portrait, which he wished me to copy. It represented Rob Roy as a dandy, in a dancing rather than a fighting pose. I told Mr. Dick that if he wanted me to carry out the commission, I would make Rob Roy a man of action, the man he was, though not as one ready for attack. I would represent him with his sword at the ready, in defence of his right, full of confidence in his power and proud in his stance.

At the time he intended the statue for Kilmarnock, but friends suggested Edinburgh. As a site there did not materialise, he approached Stirling, who provided a fine site in their town centre. However, I was happy to continue in the meantime with my maquettes and full scale figure, in spite of much friction between Mr. Dick and myself. It is best to draw a veil over our transactions. The price of a commission has always been of secondary consideration to me, and as has often been the case, I underestimated my costs, which I had put in writing to Mr. Dick. Nor could I foresee the introduction of Value Added Tax, before the statue had been completed. Mr. Dick certainly lacked the largesse, and humour of his forebear, and kept me to my original price, and by rights I am a part donor of the finished work.

My design for the plinth was rejected in favour of one by the Stirling town architect; I was not even invited to see that the statue was properly erected, by which time Mr. Dick had died. To add insult to injury, his widow would not allow Stirling District Council to invite me to the unveiling. Nevertheless, it stands proud and alive, beside Campbell-Bannerman and Robert Burns, for posterity.

Fulfilment

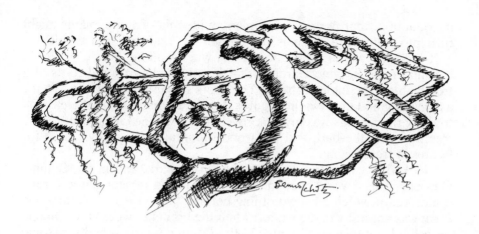

In 1975 the Scottish Arts Council mounted an exhibition arranged by Dr. David Irvin, which had as its title 'The Need to Draw'. It contained two of my drawings. From the very beginning of my studies to become an artist, I considered drawing very important — it almost became a passion — first, to conquer its resistance, then as an instantaneous medium of expressing moods and ideas for sculpture.

Prehistoric man was already an incisive draughtsman with a keen eye for observation far beyond his other accomplishments. Who taught him to draw? Eric van Daniken tells us that man was taught to draw by beings who visited this earth from outer space and who had a high cultural attainment! No matter how, drawing is the quickest and simplest way of expressing an idea. It is the artist's shorthand for memorising an experience, or a feeling.

I consider drawing the most abstract of all the arts. For drawing one uses a line, and a few lines can enclose space and give it not only volume, but also mass. Yet there is no such thing as a line in nature, it is man's singular invention. The nearest approach to a line in nature is the juxtaposition of two planes, but this line is only imaginary, because it has no thickness, while a line drawn by primitive man, or the contemporary artists has a thickness which even varies in strength.

Some people are natural draughtsmen. Others have to slave at it to conquer its secrets. One must love to draw, otherwise it can become a drudgery. I had to develop a faculty for it, but it can be acquired with patience and hard work. I wanted to master it, and to draw well, because it was something that baffled my imagination, something that haunted me.

What I loved most was to draw trees, and when on holiday would spend most of my time doing that. I would draw trees as trees, because I felt a kinship with them, my mind turning back to my student days, when reading the poems of Heinrich Heine, who writes in one

197

introduction, that perhaps after many millennia of years, plants might turn into animal life, animals into human life, and men into angels.

It was on a winter's day about 1950, when walking beside the River Kelvin, in the Botanic Gardens that I noticed the exposed roots of a tree high on the inclined bank. The roots suggested themselves to me as reclining and intertwining figures. I rushed home for my sketchbook to draw them. This was my first revelation that one can see more in a tree than just the bark and the wood it contains. Thus my search for figures in trees began.

I looked at every tree in the Kelvingrove Park, and in the Botanic Gardens. A new world opened up for me. I found subject matter for my sculpture, of which I knew nothing before. The best time for drawing them was naturally in the winter, when the branches were bare. On one occasion I notice a small hedge in the Botanic Gardens and saw some interesting shapes among the small trunks. I never went out without my sketchbook then, so I drew a few of them, and they made an interesting frieze. At home, when I examined my drawing, I decided that I could improve upon it. As there seemed no urgency about it, it was about a couple of weeks before I went back to the spot to re-draw it. With surprise and chagrin I discovered that in the interval the hedge had been cut down! Yet I liked that drawing, framed it and hung it in our sitting room.

Some years later, when Mr. A. Buchanan Campbell, an architect, asked me to design two groups for a school, and I began to look through my drawings for an idea, Amiel said to me, "Daddy, I like this drawing, why not use it?" This made me think, and the result was a group I named 'Saraband'. Two pieces from that group I later enlarged from my maquette into separate sculptures. Another drawing, which I had made not far from Milngavie inspired the other group.

My whole sculptural development took on a new slant. It always had a human angle, but now it clarified itself for me. Just as some people see figures, or faces, in the fire, so I began to see figures in tree trunks and their branches. When I began to analyse the reason for this development, as an artist seldom does anything without a reason, my only deduction was that I was merely projecting on to the trees my latent, perhaps even subconscious emotions. I began to see in them my yearnings, frustrations, sorrows, and joys. They became the poems I have been trying to write, but which lacked the suggestive quality I was able to infuse into my drawings.

My 'Ezekiel's Vision' and 'Earthbound II' were inspired from a book of olive trees with photographs of their fantastic shapes. My original group of 'Earthbound' I designed when I was invited to participate in an art exhibition in Moscow in 1959 as part of a Youth Festival. It represents two youths, one on the shoulders of the other, trying to catch Maeterlinck's elusive Blue Bird. Its design suggested itself to me years earlier, when on one of my walks I noticed a sapling growing at an angle, and a thin branch — it had only one — growing almost as a counterbalance to the main stock. From its top fluttered a single leaf. Although I noticed it only in passing, yet when I was thinking of a subject for the Youth Festival, this sapling became significant to me and symbolic in working out my design. I remembered the spot where I had seen it, but when I went to draw it, I could no more find it. It was probably uprooted not to grow into a 'queer' shaped tree. I wanted to draw it to illustrate how an idea can evolve into an important work from the simplest trifle, so long as you notice and remember it. This theme of the Blue Bird, the striving for the unobtainable, for perfection, has become recurrent in my sculpture. I have already done three 'Earthbounds' and more are waiting to be given life.

When in 1960 I was recovering from a coronary, Milly took me to Portpatrick, near Stranraer, to convalesce, because it was flat, and had a rocky shore. She realised that these I might want to draw, and this would relieve my monotony and keep me from being low spirited. As I was still very weak, we would hire a chauffeur-driven car to see some well known spots in the district, and to enjoy the scenery and parks.

On one drive I suddenly noticed a high trunk of a tree with no top to it, just a bare trunk. It must have been struck by lightening, for long jagged splinters were jutting upwards from its top like wings. "Ah," I said to myself, "an angel" because at the time I was working on the Stations of the Cross for St. Charles, in Glasgow, and on a sculpture for St. Paul's at Glenrothes. One becomes attuned to the work one is involved in, and symbols become associated with them. Then I said to myself, "Why an angel, why not a Victory? I will make a Victory to celebrate my recovery."

This was not the first time that I produced sculpture which was the result of an illness. In 1925, when I recovered from my burst duodenum I modelled a Job, of which only one small bronze exists. The result of the idea for a Victory was the modelling of seven, because I realised that victory has many facets.

When I discovered in Israel the endless material to be found in the olive trees which grow there in abundance, my visits became frequent. I began to love olive trees, they possessed me. It is almost impossible to kill an olive tree. I have seen them charred out of recognition, yet when one examines such a tree, studying it for a sign of life, one will find at the top, a tiny branch beginning to grow, with a leaf on its end. When I used to come across such a tree, I would think how similar it is to the Jewish people, who can survive and flourish again after every massacre.

By now I have filled sketchbook after sketchbook with drawings of olive trees, and my drawings have become fairly complicated, for they are made up of a number of tree trunks joined together to create a feeling of fantasy. In 1967 I spent my whole visit in the Garden of

199

Gethsemane drawing the eight trees that were still there then. Now there are only seven left. Milly used to say that I would take root in the Garden. I made about twenty drawings, but when I showed them to the Scottish Arts Council with the idea of producing a portfolio of a selected number, it found no favour, as portfolios were not being printed in Britain at the time.

Trees in Israel are precious, and afforestation plays an important role in the building of the country. Permission has to be obtained to cut down a tree, and a good reason is needed for doing so. Near where I stayed in Jerusalem was a small open space on low ground with some olive trees on it. One day I saw building beginning to take place. Lorries were bringing earth to level the ground to the height of the surrounding area, and in the process were burying the olive trees in the hollow. It hurt me to see this act of vandalism. The builders could argue that they cut down no trees, but I felt as if they were burying living bodies and I called this spot the cemetery of olive trees.

While I am drawing I really don't know what the result might be. Only later, when I study it after completion, its subject matter begins to shine through. At the time of drawing, all I am concerned about is a unity of composition and a harmony of feeling. When I combine a few trees into one page I have to make sure that they all express the same mood, and that their shapes compliment each other.

We all see differently, and even I, when I go back to the tree I have drawn to reassure myself that I had seen right, would hardly recognise it again, for it all depends on the light and the time of day, and on my own mental and spiritual condition of the moment.

Pebbles on the Mediterranean coast have also become subject matter for my sculpture. Dora and her husband have a coast house at Beit Yanai, not far from Natanya, and there I find my treasure trove. I have drawn many of them, and some inspired me with ideas.

My brother-in-law, Dr. Isaac Camrass, Dora's husband, had spent the six years of the war as a Captain in the Medical Corps, attached to the 51st. Highland Light Infantry in Egypt, North Africa and Italy. He did not want to be immured in a hospital behind the lines, and volunteered to go with the army to the Front. He travelled in a jeep 250 miles daily to visit his gun batteries. His covered jeep was riddled with bullets, but he came through the whole war without a scratch, and was awarded the M.B.E. for saving his colonel from drowning during the invasion of Sicily.

On his return to civilian life he found himself in the same situation in London, as Dr. Michaelson had done in Glasgow. He and Dora were very active Zionists, and when the State of Israel was created he was invited to organise the Israeli Nursing Service. They emigrated in 1949.

With our friends the Michaelsons, they were very keen that we should visit them. The Michaelsons found a way to tempt us to come. They managed to arrange an invitation for me to hold a one-man show in the Municipal Gallery in Haifa. They also arranged that the Bezalel Art Gallery in Jerusalem invite me as well. The new Museum was not yet built, but as Jerusalem was the capital, it was agreed between them that my show would first take place in Jerusalem and then it would go to Haifa.

I received the invitation in May, 1954, and it gave me an impetus I would not have believed. That same morning, the weather being warm, I sat down in front of our house, on the lawn, and looking at the branches of a tree in our neighbour's garden conceived a composition of a mother and child, or of an elder sister playing with her younger brother. I called it 'Playtime'. This was the beginning of a series of compositions which otherwise would never have developed. An artist sometimes needs an incentive for a burst of his energy and creativity, and these two one-man shows did this for me. The experience of finding inspiration in trees stimulated my imagination and guided me into new avenues of composition and design.

For some reason my cases of sculpture missed being loaded onto the intended cargo boat, although they were waiting at the dock. They were put on the next boat, which would still arrive in time for the show. My exhibition was to open in Jerusalem on Saturday 1st. January 1955. December, January and February are the rainy months in Israel, and one can never be sure how the weather might turn out. The boat duly arrived in Haifa, but the rain came down in torrents, and when it rained in Israel in those days, the docks closed, for no goods could be taken out of the holds. The docks were closed for three days, and my ear was glued to the telephone all the time, waiting for news. At last, on the Friday morning three cases were unloaded, but the fourth failed to appear. It was the very last case to come out of the hold. As everybody was tense with waiting, knowing how important it was, a jubilant cheer went up when it did.

By then it was Friday afternoon, when everything closes early. A special lorry was hired and waiting to take the cases to Jerusalem, and special labour was arranged for their unloading. It was a tense moment for me, to see the cases in the Gallery at four in the afternoon, when the Curator and his assistant started arranging the show.

Exhibitions in Israel usually open on a Saturday forenoon, after the Synagogue services. Tickets for admission are bought during the week, while many patrons have a season ticket. I had no idea what might take place. Great was my surprise when the opening ceremony was performed by the Hon. Edwin Samuel, (later Lord Samuel), whom I knew. He spoke in Hebrew, of course, but beside me stood my friend Misha Louvish, formerly of Glasgow, who translated the opening address for me, word for word.

201

I was too excited to absorb what was said. I had gone through a week of torture, and the release of the tension elated me. I moved about as in a trance, shaking hands with friends of long ago, doing things mechanically, speaking without thinking what I was saying, but everybody seemed pleased with the show and congratulations were on every hand.

The Curator did a fine job in arranging the show. The catalogue was a simple folded sheet with a reproduction at the front and back. We looked for Press notices, but they were not forthcoming. Somebody had the bright idea of buttonholing one of the foremost art critics in Jerusalem. When he came into the exhibition he was surprised to see my more advanced work. The reproductions on the catalogue were of a head and a torso, not my choice. I was not consulted.

The critic said, "If I had known of the modern pieces I would have come right away." From the illustrations he expected an old fashioned show and would not have come to see it if he had not been, so to speak, dragged in.

The exhibition was a success, and I was asked to allow it to remain open for an extra weekend, for it broke all previous records of attendance. Some months earlier Marc Chagall had an exhibition there, but my attendance exceeded his. He was not then too well known in Israel, nor was I, but there had been few if any sculpture exhibitions before mine.

No time was lost between my show in Bezalel and the one in Haifa. What was more, one morning I was told that I was expected to make a speech about my work on the radio at noon. I had quickly to compose a short address, and as I began to speak in English a Hebrew voice took over gradually and mine was faded out. I have no written record of my remarks, but I remember that I likened the freeing of my sculpture from solidity and tension to the freeing of the Jews by the creation of Israel. That might have been true, who knows, or it might just have been my personal development.

The Mayor of Haifa, Abba Khushi, was well known all over Israel for his diligence in keeping Haifa an example for all the other Israeli cities. At five in the morning he would begin to go round the streets to see that they were kept clean. After that he would start his office work. I rather took to him and asked him if he would pose for me.

For such people 'posing' meant that you model them while they carry on with their work. I often used to be asked whether a person posing for me had to sit without moving, or changing the position of their head. My reply was that a person does not change no matter what his position is. It is the sculptor's job to catch the likeness whenever possible, retain it in his mind, and transfer it into the clay, then, or later.

The Mayor wanted me to come to his office at six o'clock in the morning, before he really got busy, but we compromised and I used to arrive at eight! I decided to make a terra cotta of it, as this appeared to be the simplest way of making the work permanent. I found a potter who had a kiln and brought the head to her when it was not yet quite dry. I suggested that she put it into the kiln with the door open to dry it off properly. I forgot to tell her to turn the head occasionally to make sure that all the sides would dry evenly, but expected that, being a potter, she would know this much. If left as it was the side that was facing the open door would not dry as well as the rest.

We were setting out with the Camrasses from Jerusalem for their seaside villa at Beit Yanai when the phone rang. It was the potter to tell me that when she looked into the kiln she saw a piece of the cheek facing the kiln door had fallen off. What should she do about it? I had expected this to happen when I heard her question. "Carry on firing" was my reply. There could be no other.

Later, when I returned to Haifa and went to see her and collected the head, I asked her if she had isinglass. This she had. In half an hour I had the piece glued on and the seams touched up so well that I could not see myself where the breaks were. The potter was pleasantly surprised, and it was an object lesson for her. One has to know one's technique, otherwise one's work can be ruined.

Abba Khushi must have also taken a liking to me for he asked me if I would be willing to come to Haifa and open an Art School there. It meant not only uprooting myself and my family, but more or less giving up my life—sculpture, for to create a School of Art is a big undertaking, and I had seen how little time the Directors of the Glasgow School had to devote to their art. I declined his offer, generous though it was, considering I would have been provided with a house, and all kinds of facilities.

One incident in my Haifa exhibition moved me greatly. I visited my show very seldom, but I was told about a woman who visited it daily, to look at a work which I then called 'The Mourners', but which I later renamed 'Requiem'. She was keen to buy it, but because of British Government restrictions I had no right to sell—the exhibition being for prestige only.

Finally a meeting was arranged between us in the Gallery and I asked her why she was so keen on this particular work. She then told me that she and her husband had come from Germany, and each day when he returned from work in the evening, and she would see him safe and sound, this was how they would stand together in their hall, for several minutes in prayer and thanksgiving. I was deeply moved by her story and had to let her have the work. Years later, after the Six Day War, we met again at a concert in Jerusalem and they told me that they lost their only son in that war. What can one say in the face of such a tragedy? "We have 'The Mourners' " she reminded me. Now they had it for succour and support.

Dora was a lecturer in the English Department of the Hebrew University of Jerusalem, and so was a Mrs. Shulamit Nardi, with whom she became firm friends. It was natural for me to get to know her and her husband, Dr, Noah Nardi. I believe that Mrs. Nardi was instrumental in Milly and I receiving an invitation to visit the President of Israel, Ben Zvi, one morning.

As this was our first visit to the country, we wanted to see as much of it as we possibly could, especially as a car and a chaffeur were put at our disposal. We had arranged to go touring that day, and it was our intention to decline the invitation. Dora and Issac were furious. "What do you mean by going to decline the invitation? In Israel this is a command." This silenced us, and we duly presented ourselves at the President's residence at twelve noon, as requested. We were the only visitors, and the President himself showed us around, and also showed great interest in us. His sister-in-law was also a sculptress, Batya Lishansky, and there were some of her works in the *Beit Hanassi*, the Hebrew name for his Residence.

At the time it consisted of three huts joined together, but to us they looked beautiful. The President told us that the previous day he had to show round some Americans, and they said it was not quite like the White House, but his reply was that on the previous Saturday he went to the Synagogue, and was given to recite the most important portion of the week's Torah, and that this the President of America could never get. This visit was a most edifying experience, and one we have always cherished.

When my sculptures came back from Israel, I decided that it was time that I had another exhibition in Edinburgh. By that time Bill Macaulay was already a partner in Aitken Dott's. He had been an assistant in the Kelvingrove Art Gallery. When we got to know him and his wife, they lived in a flat in Great Western Terrace, one of the finest terraces in Glasgow. We became so friendly that when a house became vacant in the Terrace, we almost took it together. The drawback was that we needed an extra room, and that we could not have.

Macaulay was not satisfied with his position at Kelvingrove, and was on the lookout for something better, when he was offered the partnership in the firm of Aitken Dott & Co. Leaving Glasgow, he said to me that there would always be a Benno Schotz in his gallery. Our relationship was such that I could not ask him for a show. The invitation had to come from him. It never came, yet we continued on friendly terms, although we could not meet as often, for they had bought a property not far from Edinburgh, and neither Milly nor I could drive.

So I decided to exhibit in a rival gallery, Doig, Wilson and Wheatley. Bill Macaulay came to the opening and bought a work. Whether it was a salve to his conscience, I cannot tell. The show, if not a sell out, did not do too badly, but my clients were from Glasgow or further afield. I doubt whether I sold a single work to an Edinburgian. They remained true to their nature.

My work must have been seen by American sculptors visiting Edinburgh and the Academy, for one day in 1956 I received a letter from the President of the National Sculpture Society of New York, telling me that I seemed to have numerous friends in the Society, and would I allow my name to go forward as a corresponding member? I believe that, that year, they had only three names on their list, two from Britain, and one from Belgium. Later I discovered that the other British name was non other than that of Sir William Reid Dick, the then Sculptor-in-Ordinary to the Queen in Scotland.

On one occasion I was in the States when they had a meeting which I decided to attend. I travelled from Philadelphia for it. Imagine my surprise, when on entering their Art Club, I could have mistaken it for the Glasgow, or the Edinburgh one, or even the Chelsea Art Club in London. They all seem to acquire the same stamp. The rooms might be different, but the spirit they emanate and the atmosphere they evoke is one that unites us.

Charles Wheeler, who later became the President of the Royal Academy, felt that some of us sculptors in Britain lacked a venue to show portraits. So along with some others who lived in and around London he founded the Society of Portrait Sculptors. They formed themselves into a committee, and put down the names of sculptors they would like to have in the Society. They elected them members, and then wrote to them inviting them to join. This was a stroke of vision.

When I received a letter telling me that I had been unanimously elected a member of the newly formed Society, I accepted willingly, if for no other reason than to show solidarity with my fellow sculptors. I was never a member of the Society of British Sculptors. I have never applied for membership to any society where I could be blackballed. To send photographs of my work to prove that I was worthy of membership of this moribund Society was disdainful to me. In later years, more than one President wanted me to join, and my reply used to be, "Elect me a member and I will join." But this they did not do. They were too hidebound by their rules. Eventually I was elected an Honorary Fellow in November 1980. I did not need the Society, it was they who needed me. I don't look for honours, and when they come, they come as a surprise.

When I meet people and converse with them, I find them either interesting or dull, but I seldom try to analyse them as characters and pigeonhole them. It never occurs to me to read their lives from their faces. Life would be intolerable were I always to do this. If they have striking heads I might think, "How good it would be to model them"—especially when I meet a lovely woman.

It is only in a train, in the underground, or on a bus, that I begin to study the physiognomy of the people sitting opposite, or in company where I am just an onlooker. Then their faces begin to speak volumes, and were I an author, I would weave stories around them. Their features, their expressions, when in repose, speak to me of their past, and I unconsciously let my imagination roam about them.

Do I do this when I model people? Very, very seldom. Sometimes the person posing for me becomes a confidant. There must be a harmony between the sitter and myself, but sometimes I have to originate this in order to create the atmosphere in which I can produce my best work. It has happened that a sitter has drawn a curtain between himself and me, and I sense it and know that if I cannot tear it down, my portrait will be only a mask, and that his personality will escape me, that what I will depict will remain a shell which will certainly not satisfy me.

I am not just modelling a person, I unconsciously read into their souls and they reveal themselves to me. That person becomes part of myself and remains part of me all my life. But as I am normally happy when I model, I transmit my feelings to my sitters, and they become involved in what I do and respond openheartedly.

In 1919 I modelled a Miss Boston. When I was nearing the end of her sittings she thanked me, and revealed that while I was modelling her something strange happened to her. She began to feel as if a great load was being lifted off her shoulders. She told me she had been depressed, and had some personal unhappiness and difficult problems, but posing for me had made her very happy. I was very surprised, and I began to think, "Is there something more to modelling a person than just reproducing an image?"

One day I had met Robert Sivell in the company of other artists, and as I happened to mention that I was engaged on a commissioned portrait he asked, "Are you a lucky sculptor?" I looked at him in surprise, not knowing what he meant, and not wanting to ask him in the presence of others. "Surely he cannot be so superstitious." To my knowledge he had only been given one commission in his early years, to paint twins, and I have never seen a portrait of his which might have been a commission. Yet he painted his wife and daughter many times, so he must have considered it lucky. Did he consider Art a supernatural gift, just like myself, and feel that an artist could become like an African medicine man?

I had a similar experience when modelling Dr. Alec Lerner. He was a director of Marks and Spencer and I used to meet him at the dinners of the Glasgow Friends of the Hebrew University. On one occasion he asked me to model him and as he lived in London it was easy for him to sit for me in my Flood Street studio.

It happened during the darkest days of his life. His wife had left him, and was just then going to marry someone else. Perhaps he wanted something to distract him from his personal troubles, perhaps he wanted to do me a good turn, who can tell? Because I knew all the circumstances of his life. I decided to give him, not the sad expression and feelings he had, but to express in my work a man who can not only brave the storm, but look into the future with a clear eye, and almost with a smile.

I seldom, if ever, have difficulty in portraying what I see in a person, but here I had made up my mind beforehand what my aim should be. I never struggled over a portrait as I did over my Alec Lerner. I began to feel a weight on my shoulders, as if I was transferring upon myself his unhappiness and trauma. He himself saw my condition, and remarked to Milly, who was watching me, "See, how he is perspiring"—something that had never happened to me before. I wondered whether he himself was feeling more content and at peace.

When the head was completed, my troubles were not at an end. I should have asked him what colour of patina he would like the bronze to be. I gave it a golden patina, a discovery I had made, and which no one else could achieve without electrolysis. He came to see it and was surprised. He wanted a green patina, which was difficult to produce in my London studio,—I mean a stable green, not one which lasts only a few years — as I did not keep so many chemicals there. I had to take it back to Glasgow with me.

As I was slow in returning it I received a rather stern note from him. In transit, the nose got rubbed, and when exhibited did not look its best. It had to be returned to be re-toned. Afterwards I said to myself, "It serves you right to model what you do not see!"

I remember as a young man I met a girl who interested me, and I asked her to pose for me. As soon as I began to model her a silliness began to appear in her head. If I model the outside as I see it, the inside will reveal itself, and her true nature appeared. It was sufficient for me to make some sort of excuse not to finish it. Although I say that I don't set myself up as a judge of the people I model, yet if the portrait reveals the character of the person, I just have to accept the result.

I saw Paul Robeson for the first time in a Glasgow theatre long before he became famous not only as a singer but also as a political figure. I must have heard him in *Show Boat*. I still see him sitting on a log and whittling a piece of wood singing *Old Man River*. At the time I was thinking that here was a new Chaliapin. I did not think of him as black or white. All I heard was a voice that had music in it. A bass can sound coarse and dull, but here even the low notes vibrated with an entrancing musical tone.

I did not think of him again, although his name used to crop up in the Press occasionally, until one day when I saw a photograph of a bronze Jacob Epstein had modelled of him. I was thrilled by this portrait, marvelled at Epstein's mystique, and how he could have produced such

207

a head. Then I was anxious to meet Robeson, to see him at close range, and to analyse how Epstein obtained his result.

This opportunity came to me in 1948 when Robeson came on a visit to Glasgow to give some recitals. One day, Willison Taylor, a painter, who had studied sculpture with me for a year, invited us to a reception in the McLellan Galleries which he was arranging for Robeson. By then Robeson was well known as a Communist, but this didn't matter to me.

I was overjoyed at the opportunity to meet him and see the man whose head I so admired. Here was a man who was able to overcome the terrible disadvantage of colour, one who broke through the barrier of race and became famous because of his voice. Even these sentiments meant little to me, as I wanted only to study his features and to learn from them the mystery of Epstein's art.

When I saw the man, I realised that he had put on some weight since Epstein had modelled him, but I could still read his features and compare them in my mind with the bronze as against the reality. I remember little about the evening, except for a remark that Robeson made during a speech of thanks, and that stayed in my mind. "Africa is on the move, though here you don't yet know about it," We all know how true his words turned out to be.

He sang a few songs, and while he was singing, he held his hand to his ear, as if he was listening to his own voice. Later, when I had an opportunity to have a few words with him, I asked him the reason for it. He explained that when he sang to a small audience in a large room, he tried not to strain his voice, and by cupping his hand to his ear he could gauge its strength.

Some years later, I asked my architect friend, Jack Coia, why I was on the black list of the Catholic Church, for I had heard rumours to that effect, and his reply was short and crisp, "You were seen at the reception to Paul Robeson." I told him my reason for being there.

When I look at the Robeson bronze now, it no longer holds its mystery for me. I judge it simply as a good Epstein.

However, one day I had a visit from none other than Jack Coia. He was building one of his Catholic Churches not far from my home and studio, and he had a problem. It was a big church, with a heavy horizontal beam projecting about eighteen inches from the side walls, dividing them into upper and lower sections. The lower part accommodated the side altars and confessionals. What troubled him was what to do with the top part, which was of plain red brick, and extended up all of twenty feet from the beam. Not long before another architect had put up a triangular church with a Madonna in mosaic on its front elevation, so he felt he couldn't use mosaic. What could I suggest?

When I visited St. Charles, I saw that the walls were also divided by vertical beams running up to the roof. These created four large panels along both sides of the church. I felt they would form an ideal framework for Stations of the Cross. On each side, one important Station could occupy a whole panel, while the other panels could each hold two. Terra cotta would blend in with the brick, and would unify the walls.

Jack agreed with my idea, and when we were driving to his office, he asked me casually what it might cost. I gave him an approximate figure, before having given it any thought. The financial side of my work was never of prime importance to me, although one does not wish to be exploited. For me it was a challenge, and I felt that I was uniquely able to execute this great undertaking in terra cotta. When I made my design, a series of small drawings, I realised that the figure I had mentioned would be quite inadequate, but with a few minor adjustments Jack kept me to it.

He employed two chief assistants at the time. Isi Metzstein, and Andrew MacMillan. They were very avant garde and their churches made them famous throughout Britain. At the time of writing, Andrew MacMillan is Professor of Architecture at Glasgow University. When I arrived with my sketches of the Stations I heard Jack say to them, "I told you he'd be able to do it!"

The figures were about three-quarter life size, in very high relief; some were actually in the round, and there were sixty-four of them! The crosses were seven feet overall. I was still at the Art School and this made it possible for me to fire them myself. In my department we had a large flat kiln, about six feet long and three feet wide, though only about eighteen inches high. Without this kiln I could never have undertaken the project, which took altogether two years to complete. I even had to invent a method of modelling the figures so that they could be hollowed out from the back and then laid flat to dry.

After I had modelled about a dozen figures I realised that if I continued without models a certain uniformity would dull the effect. So I began to ask members of my family and quite a number of my friends to pose for me. Even the priest himself is there, instructing a child. Jack Coia I modelled as a Christ, though he said that he thought I would have wanted to represent him as the devil! Milly was annoyed with me for giving her a weeping expression, though I told her it was in the spirit of the group of Women of Jerusalem. The child in the group is Madeleine Coia. I myself, am an onlooker.

The fixing of the figures to the wall was something of a problem, but my training in mechanical engineering stood me in good stead, and I found a simple solution. All I needed were hooks, which were made individually and screwed into the wall at predetermined points. The figures, with fixing points provided in the terra cotta were then simply hung on to the hooks.

This was not the only work I created for St. Charles. There is a seventeen foot high Altar Cross with a five foot high aureola of thorns and beams of light. It incorporates a Crucifixion and two supporting figures of Mary and St. John. I also made a Lamb of Glory for the front of the Altar Table. When another priest, Father Grace, for whom I was also working at the time, came in and saw the design of the relief, I told him I was taking it from the Old Testament, the ram caught in the thicket. He was deeply moved and replied "I'm sure Father O'Sullivan does not know what he is getting."

Finally, I designed and made the Sanctuary Lamp, hanging by a chain from a life-size flying angel holding cymbals. For the angel I wanted to achieve something neither male nor female, but which transcended sexuality. Then I happened to notice our cleaning lady. Beneath her careworn exterior her face was severe, almost ascetic, yet with a slender serenity. I asked her if she would be willing to sit for me, and her reaction was quite touching, with its mixture of incredulity that I should wish to model her as an angel, then pride and trepidation. She duly arrived for her sitting, with her hair specially done for the occasion. Altogether, St. Charles was a formidable undertaking.

It was while working on the 'Stations' that I received a visit from Andrew MacMillan one Sunday morning. He had a sad story to tell. He was building a church, St. Paul's in Glenrothes and needed an Altar Cross. They had given it to a firm of architectural brassworkers, who had engaged a designer from Edinburgh. After a couple of months, or thereabouts, the designer came to MacMillan with the doleful tale that he had no idea what to do. They now had only six weeks till the consecration of the church. Was there anything I could do?

If nothing else, this was proof that they only came to me when they were in a jam. By rights, I should have sent him packing, but when there was a challenge I was always ready to pick it up. He had the design of the church with him, and the type of Cross he wanted was cinemascope, three dimensional, in the style of the Catalan Crosses of Spain. It was quite an order for the time in hand.

I wanted to show them I was not stumped for ideas, and started right away. By next afternoon I had a maquette ready in wire, and asked Andy, as we called him, to look in on his way home. He lived nearby. He was surprised to see how quickly I had produced a design to his specification. I just wanted to make some slight adjustments, which I did the following day.

We took the train to Kirkcaldy on the Wednesday morning, and there Father Grace met us. We adjourned to a tea room for a cup of coffee, I showed him my maquette, and he accepted it without reserve. Then we went to see the church in construction, and I was able to decide how big the Cross should be. It had to be the main focal point, there being nothing else to distract one's view.

I asked a student of mine, Alan Fletcher, who had just received his

Diploma, to help me with the Cross, and both of us started work on making it. I had to create the figures and the emblems of the Passion, while Fletcher was putting together the Cross itself. We worked day and night. It was an original design in many respects, and because of the shortness of time, the figures had to be modelled in plastic metal.

It was actually never assembled till the evening before it was transported to Glenrothes, Father Grace never having seen it in the interim. Even a few days earlier, Jack Coia was not sure if the design was right. He had never seen such a Cross, and wondered how it would be received. The designer for the brass company was keen to see it, and so I invited him to come on the Friday evening when I knew it would be assembled. He was astounded, and admitted that he could never have conceived such an idea.

When Father Grace saw it up in his church he realised that he had received something very special. Archbishop Gray of Edinburgh and St. Andrews, now Cardinal Gray, must have arrived that evening for the consecration the following morning, and early on Sunday morning he asked Father Grace if he could go into the church and see it before the others.

Father Grace had been acutely criticised for having asked Gillespie Kidd and Coia to build his church, and when they saw it in progress he was advised more than once to have it pulled down and have the design given to someone else. The outside was completely bare, not a single window breaking the severity of the brick walls. When the Archbishop went into the church he stopped at the Cross and asked who had done it. Father Grace, not being sure how the Archbishop would react to the fact that a Jew had designed it, replied, "A bloke from Glasgow did it."

The only light which came in from outside was from a window at the entrance, and a shaft of light from a concealed window high in the roof above the Altar, which lit the Cross beautifully. Not being at the consecration, I had no idea how it was received, and was naturally anxious. The following morning, however, Jack Coia telephoned me to say that "We have broken through with a modern building and a modern Cross."

A week later Milly and I paid a visit to the church because I wanted to photograph the Cross. There was also a Presbyterian church in Glenrothes, and its minister would frequently come into St. Paul's, for as he used to say to Father Grace, he preferred to pray in this church than in his own. I happened to be busy photographing when he came in. Father Grace told him I was the sculptor. "Is he an R.C.?" asked the minister. "No, he isn't." "Is he one of us?" continued the minister. "So I had to spill the beans" confessed Father Grace to me afterwards. "How can a Jew make such a devotional Cross?" was the minister's next question. "Because he is a devotional Jew" was the prompt reply. One does not often meet such a broadminded priest.

211

A month or so later, Emilio Coia, the caricaturist and art critic, met the Archbishop in Edinburgh, and was asked if he had seen Benno Schotz's Cross in Glenrothes. Emilio had not. "You must go and see it. It is fit for the Vatican". Can one have greater praise? This High Altar Cross was designed in 1958. Two years later, in 1960, Father Grace asked me to design the Lady Altar Piece.

Alan Fletcher was of Romany stock, and was a veritable throw back, black haired, a striking head, and with long Roman features. When he came to the Art School after his military service, he wanted to become a painter. But his unconventional nature, combined with rather difficult home circumstances led him to neglect the more formal aspects of his studies in the first two years of the General Course. He was in danger of not being accepted by the Drawing and Painting Department. Being already mature in his outlook, he wanted to study under someone whose work he respected, and in whom he had faith. He wanted his Diploma, but to him it did not matter in which department he obtained it. Well, he approached me, and, sensing his originality and potential, I accepted him into the Sculpture Department. In the end he amply repaid my trust in him.

He used to come late to class, and only when we got to know one another better did he tell me the reason. He would work at home on his painting late into the night, and in the morning, before coming to the School, he would visit the local baths, to have a swim and freshen up. When he became my assistant he would arrive about lunchtime, but then we would work till perhaps eleven at night. When he got home, his pals would be waiting for him, and would keep him up till the early hours of the morning.

He never left my place without cleaning my tools and laying them out ready for use next morning. Perhaps his life was chaotic, but where art was concerned he was orderly. In fact he began to mechanise me, making me buy electric drills, saws, and other equipment to ease my work. Before, I used to do everything by hand. I became very fond of him, and so did Milly, and he used to eat with us. Once, when I said to him, "Alan, you are like a son to me," he riposted, "And I'm like a father to you."

My belief in his qualities was vindicated when he finally took his Diploma with great credit, being awarded a travelling scholarship. He decided to go to Italy. One night, at a hostel in Milan, it was too hot to sleep and a few of them were sitting at the front door talking late into the night. Perhaps he intended to play a trick on them; jump over a parapet in the courtyard and then reappear from another gate. It seems that he did jump over the parapet, but in the dark he did not realise that there was a drop of twenty feet on the other side. His friends wondered where he had got to, but eventually went to bed. He was discovered only the following afternoon, dead.

We were heartbroken at the news. When we went to condole his parents we saw for the first time where he lived. His room was cluttered up with all kinds of things, and how he was able to paint in it was beyond my understanding. Yet he had left a great many paintings and sketches. He was even exhibiting in the R.S.A. in the year that the Duke of Edinburgh began his periodical purchases from the Academy. He had purchased a painting by Carole Gibbons, Alan's girl friend. Fletcher had painted a platter on which he was going to paint some fruit, but then something suggested a sheep's head to him, and this was the painting which was hung in the Academy. Afterwards he said with levity and perhaps a touch of regret, "I wish the Duke liked sheep's head."

After his tragic death I felt that some kind of posthumous show should be given him, for in painting in Scotland he was a Gaudier-Brzeshka. So I got in touch with Mrs. Charles Kemp, who then dealt with the Art Section of the Arts Council—Scottish Committee. An exhibition materialised, and took place in the McLellan Galleries in June 1959, and included paintings, drawings and sculpture.

In my introduction to the catalogue I said:

". . . In retrospect Fletcher's paintings can now be seen as autobiographical and subjective. His self portraits and portraits of his friends, his lamps and ladder carriers, and above all, his 'Man on the Wheel', so precariously balanced, so tense and full of fear. Alan Fletcher had an inherent fear of accidents, and he made no secret of it, as if he had a premonition that one day fate would play a trick on him.

There is no trace in him of provincialism. His work was in the broad stream of the modern movement, and we, as we look on his paintings now, are left wondering what might not his future have been in terms of paint and invention. . ."

From all the Art Schools in Britain students can enter for what is called the Prix de Rome Scholarship. It is a yearly competition, and the winner gets a large award, enough to keep him, or her to study in Rome for three years. It is held in all branches of art, and is the apogee of a student's attainment. On several occasions I have sent students to compete. It is hardly the correct expression, for a student sends a work to a specified place, and a committee judges the entries.

Maurice Lambert, whose brother was Constant Lambert, the conductor, was considered a young avant-garde sculptor, and I used to admire his small carvings in green marble, or in alabaster. When he returned from the 1939-45 war, he decided to become a classical sculptor, and to prove his conversion, he dumped all his old plasters on a van and took them to a rubbish dump.

From then on, his name was hardly ever heard, although he exhibited in the Royal Academy, was elected as Associate, and in due course an Academician. Then he was appointed Professor of Sculpture at the Royal Academy Schools, and yearly sent a student to compete for the Prix de Rome.

In 1959 I sent up a student with what I considered was a winner, and it so happened I was in London at the same time. So I took the trouble to go up to see that my pupil's work was properly displayed. What then was my surprise, that the attendant did not allow my pupil to place his work in an empty space, because that area was reserved for another student. The room was small, and my student's work had to be placed against the wall, although it was intended to be seen all round. I realised that somebody must have influence, and decided to get to the bottom of it.

Soon afterwards our own Diplomas were to be judged, and that year Gilbert Ledward, R.A. came to do the adjudication. When he saw the mounted group my student had sent to London, he was surprised, and remarked that they must have made a mistake in the judging of the Prix de Rome.

He then told me how Maurice Lambert annually exerted pressure on the committee to have his pupil elected winner, and always threatened that he would resign if his student was not chosen. This had gone on for six years, and they were getting fed up with his domination. The following year he again presented a student whose work nobody liked, and again he threatened to resign. This time, however, they stood their ground, and chose another. True to his word, Lambert went home and sent in his resignation from the committee.

In the spring of 1960 Milly and I spent a week in Paris. We visited galleries, we saw exhibitions, we paid a visit to Zadkine, when he invited us to his studio, the only occasion that I met him. Having seen his work in galleries and in reproductions, I knew him well long before the meeting. Walking around with him in his spacious studios, I tried to compare him with the picture I had created of him in my mind's eye. His exhibition in Cologne was just about to open, and so he had only smallish terra cottas around, and a few large pieces, including a plaster Orpheus—a variation on one of his favourite themes.

Outside in the yard an assistant was carving a granite figure on which chalk marks indicated what the maestro wanted him to do. A figure was being enlarged in clay from a smaller version, and I was not surprised to observe how Zadkine stopped before it, and with meticulous care, touched up a blemish he had noticed in passing.

This work was an object lesson in enlarging, for the modern sculptor no longer trusts mechanical enlargement, realising that every scale

214

demands its own treatment, mass and proportions, in order to retain the feeling of the original inspiration.

It is a misconception that sculptors have to be massive and muscular to enable them to handle heavy material and to carve hard stone. Many sculptors I have known have been slight in build. But the sculptor has to be wiry; it is the brain that controls the sensitive fingers, the vision which imprints itself upon the work. Zadkine was slight in build, and just above medium height. When one looked at him, one wondered how such a delicate frame had been able to create so many large figures and complex compositions.

It was in 1941 that I saw my first Zadkine bronze. I was in London looking for works for the Glasgow Jewish Art Exhibition of 1942. This bronze, which greatly attracted me, was a variation of his 'The Musicians'. I was thrilled to invite it. It was the first Zadkine to be exhibited in Scotland, and was purchased by the Kelvingrove Art Gallery.

Zadkine's early carvings follow a general pattern evolved by the young and advanced school of sculptors in the early decades of this century. In Britain their chief exponents were Henri Gaudier Brzeshka and Frank Dobson. They evoke a feeling of sadness, even nostalgia, by their sentiment, soft contours and gentle forms. His polychrome carvings, suggesting a collage relief in the round, were new, fresh and decorative, but they in themselves would not have attained for him the premier place in sculpture which he attained, however revolutionary they might have been in their day. They were but a stage in his pilgrimage of research and discovery. It is his later development which makes him such an important sculptor.

His pilgrimage brought him right back to the direct road of true tradition. The term 'tradition' is often used loosely to denote works carried out in the manner of a former period, or master. This outward manifestation of tradition, this copying of a style leads to stagnation and sterility. The real value of tradition is in a tangible expressive continuation and development of a way of thinking.

Zadkine demonstrates that he is carrying on the tradition initiated by Rodin, however startling such a statement may appear at first. Rodin was the sculptor of the expressionist movement. While the painters were able to break up light and colour into their prismatic equivalents on their canvases, Rodin obtained the same result by breaking up his modelled surface to achieve heightened brilliance, a quality likened to sunlight dancing upon rippled water, by using light as an *active* agent, an aid to expression. Until his advent, light had been only a passive agent, an aid to seeing. This approach set sculpture on a new path along which it could develop.

But Rodin seemed at first a lone voice. Antoine Bourdelle, who had at one time worked in Rodin's studio, turned back to archaic Greece, and his other famous contemporary, Aristide Maillol, cast envious eyes on Praxiteles. Germaine Richier alone has been acclaimed the rightful and legitimate successor to Rodin, but in what way has she developed the ideas initiated by him?

Zadkine alone, in my opinion, understood this new 'light' on sculpture, whether consciously or subconsciously, and so created works in which light plays an active and a vital role. What distinguishes him above all, is his application of the concave form.

When light is cast on a concave form at a certain angle, it can give the illusion of a convex one. The negative takes on a positive appearance. The ancient engravers of intaglios understood and used this effect, and it is still used to this day. These forms began to predominate in Zadkine's work. His use of concave surfaces side by side with convex gives his work its flickering light effects and his figures the appearance of movement. By this device, which he has made wholly his own, they spring to life.

In addition, where Rodin breaks up his modelled surface, Zadkine goes one stage further—he breaks up his figures, or forms, in order to put the parts together again, having hollowed some parts out, or flattened others, to recreate a new image, and a new reality.

No more is his sculpture solid and static. The tree inspires him. His groups are like trunks and branches thrown together, stacked as if for a bonfire, and firing the imagination. They are organic and breathe life. Light and air play through them, for they are trellised in composition, but their openings and holes are not accidental. They derive from new ideas in three-dimensional design, giving modern sculpture a lightness and mobility.

When giving lectures on modern sculpture, I used to finish with Zadkine, and show a slide of his 'Sculptor', a wood carving of 1933. In it were all the elements of his art, and it fully expressed his Credo.

Art was to Zadkine not the copying of nature, but the use of its elements in whole or in part, reassembled and recreated to express his emotions. Reality meant a great deal to him, and his 'Sculptor' carves a figure, but that figure is the creation of his own imagination and is conceived in concave shapes. The sculptor himself is carved in flats and in flat relief to give it a feeling of lightness in spite of its bulk—pure Cubism. In this work Zadkine tells us that to express his inward self he must create a new reality, be it only a world of shadows, but shadows that speak and have a being.

Zadkine is a great romantic like his master Rodin, and believes in humanity's ultimate goodness and redemption. He is a poet in stone and bronze, and in wood he can charm and play like Pan upon a reed. His work agitates, arrests, and stimulates thought. Thus he is no iconoclast. He is not a destroyer of tradition, although he refuses to accept an outworn creed. Rather he refreshes and invigorates the oldest art in the world.

216

Our Paris trip must have moved me, or exhausted me greatly. Whatever the reason, a week after our return to my London studio, and while on a visit to my foundry, I suffered a coronary. We decided to return to Glasgow, despite my condition. Then, for many weeks I was laid up in our bedroom, Milly rationing my visitors till I was over the worst.

While still in bed, and having nothing better to do, I began to make designs for the Lady Altar piece for St. Paul's, Glenrothes. It really amounted to doodling, but it gave my imagination something to do, and this helped my recovery.

When I finally came downstairs and began to take an interest in my studio, Andy MacMillan brought me a sheet of paper with a few ideas he had on the subject. They followed the accepted pattern of what was considered right. For some days I tried to work out one or two of them, but I could not produce anything that would have satisfied me. Then Milly said to me, "Benno, I have seen your doodles upstairs. Why don't you try and work out one of those?" I took her advice, and in a day I had my design.

My wire maquette is not quite like the finished work. which represents part of an open flower; the back petal is like a drawing in wire rising high and curving forward to a point. From it projects the Star of Bethlehem. The stem rises from the ground and terminates in a Cross, on top of which stands Mary with the Child; on one side are represented the emblems of Mary, and on the other, those of the Child. One of these is a Phoenix, as a symbol of the Resurrection.

I chose the Phoenix for my own symbol as well, as a sign of my recovery. I was then reading Robert Graves' *The White Goddess* and this gave me the idea of incorporating the crescent and the waning moons with the Star of Bethlehem as a sign of eternal life. Some consider the completed work even better than the High Altar Cross. I was glad to be able to bypass accepted conventions again, and produce something new. Not having been hemmed in by the past, I could take a fresh look with a completely detached mind and an objective eye, at a problem that might have defeated one of the Catholic faith.

It was then that Father Grace asked me to design the 'Stations of the Cross' for his church. It took me about five years to work out my design. Not that I worked on it. I was looking for a new idea. Every time I used to meet Father Grace he would say to me, "I see you keep quiet about the Stations". The working out takes little time, so long as one has an idea.

Suddenly one came to me. In the Catholic religion, Alpha and Omega feature prominently. These two letters solved my problem. In thirty-six hours I had my design. I depicted Christ receiving the Cross in the form of an Alpha, and the Descent from the Cross I made into an Omega. This gave me the key to the composition, and it became logical to make the whole design as a script. It was to be set on a simple white painted brick wall, and was to be twenty-five feet long.

However, Father Grace had one problem. The Stations were dearer than the other pieces I had designed for the church, and he had not enough money for them. We arranged that we would go to see Archbishop Gray and get his blessing for the enterprise, which would have completed the church with the work of one sculptor to give it unity. What we both forgot was that by the time I would have finished the 'Stations' he would have accumulated all the money needed.

But is was not to be. Father Grace had suffered a heart attack before I met him, and he sadly died from another before we could complete his plan. The new priest did not want to carry out the former priest's wishes. He told me that Stations of the Cross were going out of fashion. I knew, however, that there was talk of adding a fifteenth Station, the Resurrection, to the existing fourteen.

One day Josef Herman came to stay, and when he entered the studio my design immediately caught his eye. "Well, well, so many artists have tried to make new Stations of the Cross, including Matisse, and here you come along and produce what they have all failed to achieve." The plasticine maquette still hangs in my studio and will probably never be executed, although I worked out and exhibited the figure of Christ on the Cross, and the Omega.

The end of 1961 saw a change in my life. I was then already seventy, and retirement from teaching was called for. It was a wrench, because I loved it. Twenty three years of my life I spent in the School, and I felt like a stone built into its fabric. Yet it placed its own stone on my shoulders, and when I left that stone fell off, the School's responsibilities no longer weighing me down. I began to work in my studio with greater zest, accountable only to myself and my clients.

Nevertheless, when I had taken on the post in 1938 I had expected to hold it for five to ten years at the most, and as the time for my departure drew near I became concerned about the future. We depended now on my monthly salary, and the question was, how would I fare without it? Not being superannuated, (when I joined the School the scheme was voluntary and I was advised against it) I could only rely on my old age pension.

I asked the Director's advice about the possibility of getting an ex-gratia payment in recognition of all the years I had taught in the School. His reply was discouraging. "We tried it for a janitor without success." I was rather amused at the comparison, but went ahead on my own and applied for one anyway. The decision was favourable, if not overly generous. I was offered the choice of a golden handshake amounting to a little more than a year's salary, or a small annuity of about one fifth of the lump sum. Everybody advised me to take the cash, but being an optimist I opted for the annuity. As can be seen, my decision was right!

Because my relations with some members of the Staff were occasionally strained, I did not want to be given a parting gift. I didn't want to keep something which some people might have contributed to out of duty, but not from the heart. But since a sum of money had been collected I asked that they give it to me as a cheque, which I then handed to the School for a Drawing Prize in the Sculpture Department, with a promise to enlarge it as time went on. This I have done on several occasions, but the Sculpture Department has completely changed its face, and, since I doubt that any serious drawing is still being done there, my prize now applies to the whole School, and is one of its major prizes.

Shortly before leaving I had an opportunity to acquire a number of pieces of furniture by Charles Rennie Mackintosh. I presented the School with a unique sample chest with sixty flat drawers, which he had specially designed for a friend, a Mr. Douglas, who was in the decorating business, as a momento of my happy years there.

My anxiety about my future turned out to be groundless, for as soon as it got around that I had left the School, potential clients, even architects, realised that I would be free to take on large commissions. In addition, my visits to my London studio were no longer restricted, and I commuted between Glasgow and London, as the occasion arose. Milly then regretted that I had not resigned ten years earlier, seeing me so happy and carefree. I had not realised till then what a responsibility looking after my students had been, for I shared their anxieties, problems, and perplexities. I heard recently from a former student that when I entered a class they used to tremble. I was surprised, for my sympathies were with them. Yes, I would speak with conviction and would even raise my voice, but this was part of my nature and it did not mean anger or annoyance. Even in my own home I would be told at times not to shout, when I was only expressing myself with enthusiasm.

At the end of the year I received a letter from the Arts Council (Scottish Committee) which read, ". . . It is to mark this occasion (my retirement) that at a recent meeting of the Committee here, it was suggested that an exhibition of your work might be shown in our Gallery." The letter was signed by William Buchanan, the newly appointed Exhibition Officer, as yet a stranger to me, but soon to become known to us as our friend Bill. Perhaps I was too excited to take in the letter as written, for there had never been a sculpture exhibition at the Scottish Arts Council Headquarters in Rothesay Terrace in Edinburgh, and my mind was running on a retrospective one. Therefore I replied that I considered myself not yet ready for a retrospective exhibition, but if they would accept a contemporary show, I would be happy to provide them with one. As this was what they had in mind all along, they readily agreed. I knew that in London artists have retrospective shows at forty, or even younger, but this was not my way. Who wants to be a Madame Tetrazzini, giving farewell concerts for years on end?

It is significant what an impetus such an offer can give an artist. In six months or so I produced seventeen new works, among them a seven foot high figure and a six foot wide high-relief.

Catalogues, by the way, are notoriously difficult to compile, and mistakes and omissions so easily slip in. This exhibition was to travel to several towns, but their dates had not yet been settled at the time of printing. Therefore in this case I have a catalogue of an important show of new pieces, virtually the only record that remains at the end of an exhibition without any dates as to when it was actually held!

The foreword was written by Hugh MacDiarmid, and after opening in Edinburgh the show went to Aberdeen, Dundee, Perth, and finally Glasgow. The tour took ten months. Some galleries invited me to the opening, but some, true to their tradition, ignored me. Such are the ways of the City Fathers of some of our towns, such is their *savoir faire!*

Milly and I had not visited Israel for eight years, and so our friends held out a carrot to us, by arranging for me to model David Ben Gurion, the Prime Minister, should I come to Jerusalem. Paula Ben Gurion, the Prime Minister's wife, persuaded him to sit for me. In this case sitting was the right word, for he sat behind his desk, and I had to model him while he was busy writing. My best time to study him was when the news came on, for then his ear was glued to the radio, and I was able to see him properly. I was to get two sittings, but they were to be in the evenings, in artificial light. I was never left alone with him. When Madame Ben Gurion could not be there, a plain clothed security man came to sit in the small study.

I have a habit of sometimes modelling a little larger than life, and when Madame Ben Gurion saw that I had begun with the nose, she said in her forthright way, "You are giving him too large a nose." All I could reply was, "Madame, don't worry, it will be alright." However, the following morning she met my friend, Professor Michaelson, and told him. "He is quite a good sculptor." She had seen how well the portrait was progressing and realised that if I were given a little more time, I would really make something worthwhile.

So she suggested that her husband should give me another half hour, after my second sitting. When I came into his study he said to me, "I thought you had had your two sittings, why are you here again?" "First of all, because you really did not pose for me, you carried on with your work, and secondly because Madame Paula is so impressed, she would like me to finish it."

That silenced him, and he came out from behind his desk, and stood beside me for the half hour, which I badly needed to produce a work worthy of the man.

The day before I began to model him, Milly and I were given tickets to the visitors' gallery of the Knesset so that I could see him in action.

That afternoon he was the main speaker and while he was talking a terrible rumpus broke out, and he could not carry on. The session had to be adjourned.

There was a curtain at the back through which speakers emerged, and it was known that Paula Ben Gurion would often sit behind the curtain to hear what was going on. On this occasion she even came out from her hiding place to see who the protesters were. Knowing no modern Hebrew we could not follow the proceedings, but apparently Ben Gurion had referred to the days when the Hagana and the Irgun were at loggerheads, and to an incident that in some ways already was ancient history and had been resolved.

In Israeli politics, however, memories are long, and he was not the man to retract. Rather than give in he decided to step down. I did not know when I was modelling him that he was probably composing his resignation speech.

I brought the clay head back to Dora's house to take a mould of it. When their Yemenite daily saw the head she exclaimed "Oh, they're just like two drops of water!"—meaning Ben Gurion himself and the portrait. How very poetic this sounds besides our 'like two peas in a pod'. But then, water in the East is so very precious.

When, by the way, the head was eventually unveiled at the Israel Museum in Jerusalem, it was accepted by Teddy Kollek, who had just been elected Mayor of the city. It was, in fact his very first official act in his new role.

On the morning of 30th. January, 1963, shortly before leaving for Israel, I received what appeared to be an official letter in a blue envelope with a seal on it. "Could it be a commission?" Milly wondered. It was in fact, a letter from the Secretary of State for Scotland, the Rt. Hon. Michael Noble.

Dear Mr. Schotz,
As you will probably know, the post of Queen's Sculptor in Ordinary for Scotland fell vacant on the death of Sir William Reid Dick in October 1961. I feel that the time has now come when the position should be filled and I am sure that your appointment would be widely acceptable in artistic circles in Scotland.
I should be very glad to know whether you are willing that I should submit your name to Her Majesty. The post is purely honorary: it carries no duties, nor, I am afraid, any remuneration.

Yours very sincerely,
Michael Noble.

A few days after I received this letter, Sir William and Lady

MacTaggart were dining with us. Sir William was at that time President of the Royal Scottish Academy. After dinner I handed him the letter in my studio, and asked him if he knew anything about. "Yes," was his reply. Some weeks before, he had received a telephone call from St. Andrews House, Edinburgh. He was asked which of three names he was given he considered best, and chose mine. As he had been puzzled by the inquiry, he went the following morning to St. Andrews House to find out more about it, and had been told the reason.

I indicated my acceptance, and received a formal acknowledgment the next day. When the Warrant arrived it read:

ELIZABETH THE SECOND by the Grace of God of
the United Kingdom of Great Britain and
Northern Ireland and of Our other Realms
and Territories QUEEN, Head of the
Commonwealth, Defender of the Faith, to
all to whom these presents shall come.

GREETING!

WHEREAS the office of Our Sculptor in Ordinary for Scotland is now vacant by the death of Sir William Reid Dick, Knight Commander of the Royal Victorian Order, Royal Academician, and WE being well informed of the abilities and good endowments of Benno Schotz, Esquire, Academician of the Royal Scottish Academy, whereby he is well qualified to fill the said office.

NOW BE IT KNOWN that WE have nominated constituted and appointed like as WE do by these presents nominate constitute and appoint the said Benno Schotz, Esquire, to be Our Sculptor in Ordinary for Scotland.

GIVING AND GRANTING unto him the said Office to have, hold exercise and enjoy, but without salary, during his natural life.
Given at Our Court at Windsor this sixteenth day of April 1963 in the Twelfth Year of Our Reign.

'In Ordinary' means that it is in the gift of Her Majesty, and not of her Ministers.

For many years the Office of Sculptor in Ordinary was in abeyance, unitl it was revived by King George V and its mantle fell on Pittendrigh Macgillivray. When he died, Sir William Reid Dick, who lived and worked in London was appointed to the Office. The Scottish sculptors were very angry over this appointment, and rightly so, for it became a title without a meaning. There were then several sculptors in Scotland who could have held the post with dignity and decorum. This time St. Andrews House did not want to commit a similar mistake, although I believe a London Scot was also on the list. That I was singled out was a great surprise to me, and certainly an utter surprise to my colleagues. Only when the news became public did I myself realise the importance of the appointment.

Naturally it created a certain amount of jealousy in the Royal Scottish Academy and in the Glasgow Art Club, where my appointment was greeted with silence. The public and the Press, on the other hand, were delighted. For some reason the Press always considered me publicity value, and used to proclaim me as the torch bearer of Scottish sculpture, sometimes to my utter embarrassment. For the Jewish community it was proof that in Britain creed and race do not matter, only merit, for here was I, who had come to Scotland as a youth of twenty, and who, by sheer willpower, talent and stamina had reached this unique position.

The Scottish Jewish community wanted to acknowledge my appointment in some tangible form, and some friends put the proposition to me that they buy two casts of the Ben Gurion head, one to be presented to Israel, and the other to the Glasgow Art Gallery. I did not like the idea of benefiting financially from their project, yet I liked the idea of having the Ben Gurion in Israel. It was therefore agreed that the bronze should go to Israel, but I suggested that the remainder of the money collected should be given to the Royal Scottish Academy as an annual sculpture prize bearing my name.

At that time the Fairfield shipyard Company was building the *Nili* for an Israeli company, and Madame Levi Eshkol, the wife of the Israeli Prime Minister, was coming to Glasgow to launch it. The organisers of the fund decided that this would be an ideal opportunity to ask Madame Eshkol to accept the bronze on behalf of the Israeli Government and at the same time to present a cheque to the President of the Royal Scottish Academy to inaugurate the prize in my name.

The platform party foregathered in a reception room, and Madame Eshkol said to me that she would accept the head for presentation to the Israeli Museum only on one condition, that I model her husband on my next visit. This I promised to do.

Milly and I have always stayed with the Camrasses when in Jerusalem. Dora's friend, Mrs. Nardi, as well as teaching in the Hebrew University of Jerusalem, was also an assistant secretary to President Zalman Shazar. As a consequence, she introduced us to the President and his wife, and a friendship developed between us. We were often invited to their home for dinner, and were usually the sole guests.

This friendship with Shazar resulted in my modelling him. Like Ben Gurion, he continued to sit behind his desk, and carried on with his work, and I preferred not to inconvenience him, although the light in his study was not so good during the day. When I cast the head in Plaster of Paris I was not satisfied with the result, and decided to remodel him on my next visit. He was then gracious enough to ask me why I had

223

not told him what I required of him the first time. This second head I cast in bronze, and later presented it to the *Beit Hanassi,* the Presidents official residence where it joined two other heads of former Presidents.

He had asked me to send him a copy of a lecture I had given about my work, and complained one day that he had not yet received it. I had to explain that the lecture was built around slides of my sculpture, and without the slides the lecture would make little sense. What was more, I had to condense it to last only just under an hour, the time a lecture takes in Britain. When his wife heard this, she nudged me and said, "Tell him this again." In Israel a speech is no speech unless it lasts at least two hours, and Shazar was known for his lengthy speeches!

On one visit Milly made me bring a sketchbook I had just filled with drawings during a weekend I had spent on the Golan Heights. Milly's idea was, that should the conversation flag, I could liven it up by showing them what I had produced in the weekend. As usual, she was right, and the President even named one of the drawings, which of course, I framed and presented to him.

During the same visit I fulfilled Madame Eshkol's request to model her husband. Although I was modelling Levi Eshkol in the official residence of the Prime Minister, it was not upstairs in Ben Gurion's small study, but downstairs in their dining room near a broad opening into another room. I chose the position where the light was best, since as usual, I had to work at night. I would finish near ten o'clock, and I was never allowed to leave without the two of us having a cup of coffee and a piece of cheesecake.

When I took the head to the Bezalel Art School to be fired as a terra cotta, before bringing it back to Britain, the pottery teacher remarked, "You must have modelled this head with love." True, never before had I felt such harmony in a home. There were no outsiders present, and no guards, when we were left alone to get on with the work. One felt their love permeating the whole house. It was a strange experience which I have never encountered before or since.

I feel guilty in never having sent Madame Eshkol a photograph of the bronze. Firstly, it was some time before I managed to obtain a successful photograph of it. Secondly, I did not want her to think that I was trying to sell her the head, or cultivate her acquaintance. This was invariably my practice. If a friendship grew out of my work I welcomed it, but I had no taste for pursuing people in order to benefit from their friendship. We loved company, and as it happens always had more friends than was good for my work.

When we visited Israel in 1970, we tried to travel incognito as Amiel was getting married in Jerusalem, and I wanted to spend what spare time I had drawing my olive trees. However, the news soon went around that I was there, and when President Shazar heard, he was quite annoyed. "Why has he not come?" he asked Shulamit. "Tell him to come."

When Mrs Nardi tried to arrange a visit with the official secretary, the latter could not find any spare time in her appointment book. So a scheme was devised by Shulamit and the President; I should call at the office ostensibly to see Mrs. Nardi, and while I was chatting with her the President would come out of his room on some pretext, and find me there!

"Ah, Benno Schotz! You are here again," he exclaimed, "how nice to see you, come into my room and let us have a chat." We talked about my trip, and how I intended to spend it. "Is there no one you would like to model?" he went on. I hesitated, as I had not intended to do any modelling on this trip. "Yes" I replied, "Golda Meir." "Why don't you ask her?" was his next question. So I explained that had she still been the Foreign Secretary I might have asked her, but now that she was the Prime Minister, she must be far too busy. "Wait a minute, just sit down and have a little rest." Having said this, he went into the outer office and returned five minutes later. "I have had a political discussion. You will hear from Golda Meir in the course of a day or two" he remarked.

On the Friday afternoon, just as we were about to leave Jerusalem for a weekend at Dora and Isaac's seaside home, Shulamit rang up to tell us that I would get a sitting from Mrs. Meir the next day, between five and seven, after her Sabbath rest. On Friday afternoon everything closes early, but I managed to alert the brickworks from whom I usually got my clay, unloaded our weekend bags from the car, and hurried to collect the clay.

To save a few precious minutes I built up the pear shape of the head beforehand, something I had never done before, and put what I considered sufficient clay in a basin for modelling the head.

I was going to model Mrs. Meir in the same room as I had previously modelled Levi Eshkol. Already knowing the best spot, I set up my collapsible modelling stand, and when Mrs. Meir came donwstairs from her rest, she looked refreshed and ready to sit for me without preliminaries. I worked well, for we were free and easy with one another, and I knew the room well. "I see you don't make me smiling" was one of her remarks, to which I replied, "Madame Prime Minister, it would not be right to make you smiling at this stage of Israel's history." "You are quite right," she replied. I felt inspired, and I was at grips with the features, and a likeness had already emerged, when after about an hour her doctor came in. She seemingly asked how long I had been working, and showed surprise at the result so far. Although my Hebrew is almost non existent, physical expression can tell a lot.

I carried on for about another half hour, and when I bent down to take a ball of clay from my basin, I discovered to my surprise and chagrin that I had used up every lump. I had, for once, miscalculated the amount of clay I would need, and did not bring enough. I began to tear off pieces from here and there, and Mrs. Meir, suddenly realising what had happened, exclaimed, for she had noticed my distress, "What can you expect from a person with such a bun and such a nose?" I had to counter her remark, and said, "Madame Prime Minister, I have recently read an article about our uncrushed noses." I could see that my reply pleased her, and she offered me another sitting, "for I know how you must feel."

I had to wait ten days for this next sitting, and it was arranged to take place from nine to eleven p.m., so late in the evening! When I arrived I discovered that an Italian artist was also going to sketch her while I would be modelling. I was rather surprised, for this was going to cramp my style. She would have to sit still for the artist, while my conversation with her would lose its intimacy, something I had established with her during my first sitting. What was worse, the Italian brought his wife with him, and she sat beside him while he was working. I felt he did not show sufficient respect to Israel's Prime Minister. It had never occurred to me to bring Milly with *me,* which I am sure she would have cherished, and this thought annoyed me intensely, and disturbed my equanimity and concentration.

Mrs. Meir was half an hour late arriving home, and began to apologise to me for being late. "Please, you need not apologise for being late. I know how busy you are. I know that you did not go to the movies" I said to her. "Nor did I play cards," was her reply. She hated Israeli women who spent their time playing bridge.

Because of the Italian, Mrs. Meir was trying to keep a still pose, and I had to jump about, bend down and stretch upwards, strain myself unduly, in order to see my sitter from all angles, and I could not make as good a work as I would have done had I been on my own. However, when I brought it back to Glasgow, I remodelled it and it is now one of my most powerful pieces.

She was a homely and unassuming woman, and when Isaac came to collect me after the sitting, she herself opened the door to him, to his and my great surprise. Since then, more than one sculptor had tried to model her. Some from photographs, one, I believe, from life. What amuses me is that when our Jewish philanthropical societies, even those connected with Israeli art, decide to have a charity auction, they remember that in Glasgow lives a fairly well known sculptor. They then put pressure on me to donate a work, and don't give up till they have succeeded. However, when it comes to a commission for Israel, then Benno Schotz is completely forgotten, and the commission goes to a fashionable London sculptor. Such are the vagaries of those who think they know best and are doing public good. My one relief and thankfulness is that I have never depended on a Jewish clientele.

When I accepted the post of Sculptor in Ordinary I decided that it should not be just a title. I had already tried to act on behalf of our

Scottish artists, but now I felt that I had the authority which I badly needed.

For many years I had felt frustrated by architects' neglect of sculpture. I realised, nevertheless, that the fault was not theirs, but that of their clients, who wished to save costs. The President of the Royal Society of British Sculptors had written to me that they had made numerous recommendations, but those in power usually decided 'to sit on cold eggs'. Also, as I have previously mentioned, I had been told when I visited Italy on behalf of the R.S.A. that Scottish artists were excluded from international exhibitions such as the Venice Biennale through no fault of the organisers. Their hands were tied, as the invitation went to the Foreign Office in London.

Sir Myer Galpern, M.P. suggested that I write to Miss Jennie Lee, who was the Minister with special responsibility for the Arts, a new Office, of which she was the first holder. This I did, asking her to receive a deputation to discuss ". . . the matter of a percentage allocation for Decoration on Public Buildings and with regard to the strange position in which Scotland finds itself with regard to exhibitions abroad. . ."

The meeting took place at the end of May, 1965, and our deputation consisted of the President of the R.S.A. Sir William MacTaggart, to represent painting, William Kininmonth, the Secretary, to represent architecture, and myself. Miss Lee was accompanied by her private secretary and Mr. A. R. Maxwell-Hyslop, from the Scottish Office.

She straight away took the field and waved in her hand a memorandum she had received from Mrs. Somerville, who, for many years had been the power at the British Council, or so we were led to believe. It apparently detailed the successes her direction had enjoyed, and stated that a number of Scots had been invited. This referred, of course, to London Scots, whom we considered a species lost to Scotland. We were never given an opportunity to read this memorandum, and at a later date, when I asked for a copy, I was given to understand that it was for Miss Lee's personal use.

We then turned to the allocation of a percentage of funds to be set aside for the decoration of public buildings. As we had anticipated, the Minister was quite non-committal, although we gave her statistics of the various countries which had passed laws making it imperative that one per cent, and in some cases even more, be spent on sculptural decoration. I had collected information from thirteen countries which had passed such legislation, and Mr. Kininmonth, who was dealing with this subject, pointed out that of the many thousand pounds which he himself had allocated for sculpture on his public buildings, perhaps one or two hundred was all that was allowed him by his clients.

We were not politicians, and could not convince her that we had justice on our side. My personal hope lay in the fact that Miss Lee was a Scottish lassie when she first entered Parliament, and that her sympathies might still be for her native land. Yet we felt after the meeting that we had achieved nothing, and the subsequent correspondence proved us right.

In reply to a note to Miss Lee, thanking her for the meeting, I received a letter from her Private Secretary, dated 3rd. June, 1965, in which he said that Miss Lee's Department, and the Ministry of Public Buildings and Works would be giving further thoughts to the question of sculptural decoration on building projects. Miss Lee also promised to forward our grievances about the British Council to the Foreign Office, with whom responsibility for the Council's work lay.

This letter was followed by another, retracting everything she had said earlier, after seemingly discussing the matter with the Ministry of Public Works.

This letter was dated *15th. July, 1965;* in it Miss Lee's secretary made a point about my letter of 31st. May, apologising that it had not been possible, because of pressure of other work, to write to me about it earlier. She said that their recollection was not at all that Miss Lee expressed any intent to take action about sculptural decoration on building projects, although not denying that buildings should, in appropriate cases, have some decoration, perhaps sculptural. . .

Also, I was asked to agree, should I address the Royal Society of British Sculptors on the subject, that this represented a fair summary of the position!

After my one and only exercise in art politics I decided that there was no point in knocking one's head against a brick wall. I wanted to remain whole and sane, and the only way to do so was to work and to create.

It will appear from what I am about to relate that at times I read letters rather cursorily. Recently Emilio Coia, caricaturist and art critic, mentioned to me in passing, that he was really responsible for my Retrospective Exhibition of 1971. This was news to me, and I could hardly believe it. To substantiate his assertion he pointed out that he is even mentioned in the acknowledgements in the catalogue. I looked it up, and true enough, at the end of the acknowledgments is added, 'and to Emilio Coia'. It gives no clue as to why his name was included.

It was only when I began to look over the correspondence relating to the exhibition that I read,

"As you know Emilio Coia put the suggestion of an exhibition of your portraits to the Council, so I am enclosing a copy of my reply to him."

"As you know",—I did not know, for Emilio never mentioned to me that he had written to the Arts Council, nor did I realise how highly he judged my portraits. Personally I considered portraiture only one aspect of my sculptural activity, so I was not very enthusiastic about a portrait exhibition alone. The subsequent change over to one that would include all aspects of my work may have been the reason for my overlooking the fact that Emilio started the ball rolling.

This is by way of an apology to him, for by rights he should have been given the chance to write the introduction to the catalogue. Bill Buchanan with whom I was conducting my correspondence, and whom I saw regularly, could have reminded me about Emilio, but when I suggested Josef Herman, who knew my work well, he fully agreed.

Several venues were suggested, but they were not large enough to contain the type of exhibition I envisaged, the kind of retrospective I had in mind, when the Scottish Arts Council invited an exhibition from me in 1962.

The final result was an exhibition in the Royal Scottish Academy Diploma Galleries, containing sixty-five portraits, seventy compositions and figurative subjects, and forty drawings. It embraced the whole gamut of my output. It was a memorable show, second only to Epstein's Memorial Exhibition during the Festival of 1969.

It is only unfortunate that the catalogue was sub-standard. The Scottish Arts Council assistant who was asked to produce and arrange the exhibition was not sympathetic to me or my work, and I saw the catalogue only when it was being handed out to the critics at the Press View. It contained numerous errors which could have been corrected had I seen it in time.

The Private View coincided with a postal strike and all the invitations had to be delivered by hand. It was natural that many people were left out, and grievances ensued, yet it was surprising how quickly word went round that it was a show not to be missed. I did not want an official opening, but when President Zalman Shazar sent a cable of congratulations to the Scottish Arts Council, Bill Buchanan wanted it read out at the Private View. So during the forenoon a little ceremony was staged, and I had to make a few remarks in reply.

Josef had come up from London, and after lunch the two of us went back to the Gallery to see it in peace and quiet. "Benno, you have not wasted your life" was his comment. Nothing more satisfying could have been said to me at that moment, and I felt deeply touched, for it was a moment of fulfilment and of gratitude to all those who had helped me on my way.

It was arranged that the exhibition should also be shown in Aberdeen. As in the case of my 1962 Arts Council Exhibition, Bill Buchanan asked me to approach the Director of the Kelvingrove Art Galleries, Dr. Henderson, for a Glasgow showing, knowing he would not refuse me. I did not want to have to ask again for this huge exhibition, and the Arts Council conveniently forgot the McLellan Galleries, where it could have been seen to great advantage, and had been originally spoken of as a venue.

The trouble was, of course, that while the two cities are so close to one another that those interested could easily travel to Edinburgh to see it, this put it out of reach of the ordinary man.

In the spring of 1976, I travelled to London for the presentation of my bronze of Golda Meir to the Israeli Embassy there. I intended to return to Glasgow the next day. But it turned out that I took ill after the ceremony, with appendicitis, and my two days in London lasted seven weeks, staying with Cherna and her husband, with two operations in between.

On my return to Glasgow, I did not want to miss the occasion at the Glasgow Art Club, where Archie McGlashan, William Smith, Emeritus Professor of Architecture at Strathclyde University, and I were being made honorary members. I had to speak seated, and I was surprised to hear Harry Jefferson Barnes, the Director of the Glasgow School of Art, introduce me in a unique and beautiful oration, mentioning that it was time that Glasgow mounted a retrospective exhibition of my portraits—again my portraits. They all seemed to single out my portraits. Trevor Walden, the Director of the Glasgow Art Galleries, was present and took up the idea.

It took two and a half years for the project to fully materialise. Almost all the administrators in the Gallery were new, and did not know my work to any great extent. They were afraid, so it seemed to me, that a large number of portraits would make for a dull exhibition, and they allotted a small corner gallery in Kelvingrove, which could at most contain fifty pieces. I was surprised, and considered bowing out of the project, but finally allowed it to go ahead. By comparison, my 1971 Retrospective had included sixty-five portraits, apart from the compositions.

What was their surprise, when acceptances began to come in for the opening, in numbers they had never known before. They only had 650 seats, so many had to stand, while others were turned away from the door. Only then did they realise their mistake.

The show sparkled from beginning to end, and had they known the appeal my portraits had, they would have allocated me the large adjoining gallery. Not being one to push myself I had concurred with their proposals, though dismayed at them.

The portraits spanned fifty-eight years of my professional life, and notable amongst them was the family group, including a bust of my father as Lazarus.

As a youth, I had read a short story about Lazarus who was restored to life by Jesus. Lazarus dares not reveal his experience in the other world. His lips are sealed, he goes about as in a dream. Gradually his friends and the populace shun him, are afraid of him, and he feels isolated and forsaken to such an extent that in the end he walks out of his village into the wilderness there to die a second time.

It possessed me to such an extent that I had to get it out of my system in order to get on with some of my other compositions that clamoured to be done. I decided to portray his final act of going out into the wilderness. I represented Lazarus walking, one hand raised to his head and a finger pointing to his sealed lips, while the other hand points downwards to indicate that he is returning to the earth.

The life size plaster cast I exhibited in 1932, in the Glasgow Institute of the Fine Arts, and artists and critics judged that it was inspired by Rodin's 'St. John'. True, the pose resembled Rodin's work, and I had anticipated the criticism, yet decided to exhibit it, for its modelling was quite different from Rodin's, which the critics failed to see. A pose by itself means little. The Renaissance sculptors, including Michaelangelo used poses from antique Greek figures, and there are any number of walking poses in Egyptian and Greek reliefs.

I knew of course that to model life-size figures in Glasgow was a waste of time as far as selling was concerned. However, from the very beginning I had decided that I did not want to become a mantlepiece sculptor. I coined a paradox "One has to create unsaleable works to make one's work saleable". I was accused of plagiarism and later works were minutely studied to discover the source of my inspiration. After some time I cut off the lower part of my Lazarus and exhibited the half length in my one-man shows. Later still I performed an even greater surgical operation, and now only have the bust of it, which I did not want to destroy, because I used the features of my father's head for Lazarus, although much more stylised and chiselled. The trouble with sculpture is space, and the accumulation of work becomes a problem.

After my coronary we divided our house, and sold the top flat. Our son and daughter had left us to take up their own professions, married, and life held no more problems for us till Milly had a severe heart attack in the summer of 1971. She was one of those people who kept her health problems to herself, and was always annoyed when I tried to give her advice. She was compelled to undergo one operation in the early 1940's, and another in the early 1950's, but by then her heart had already been affected. She was always self sacrificing, never thinking about herself till illness laid her low.

Cherna, and Margaret, my sister-in-law, were planning a party for my eightieth birthday, and Milly determined not to miss it. She was progressing well, and was allowed to come home that forenoon from hospital. Nothing would have kept her in hospital, nor would I have endured such an event without her. She was happy to be home, and convalesced at home.

She only lived three months longer. I saw and spoke with her that afternoon, and five minutes later, when I was looking for her, I found her in our bedroom—dead.

I could write quite a little story about her last few hours alive, but to what purpose? I believe she died with happy thoughts on her mind, but I was prostrated and forlorn. She was laid out in her coffin in my studio, while we waited for Amiel to arrive from America. Her dear face haunted me, and I could not imagine ever being able to work in the studio again.

Well, a few days after the funeral a packing case arrived from the bronze foundry, containing a commissioned bust I had been awaiting anxiously for weeks. Amiel unpacked it and set it up for me to see. There are always little blemishes and imperfections on an untoned bronze, and without thinking I reached out my hand for a chasing tool and started tidying it up a little. Soon I was hard at it, while Cherna and Amiel looked on. Suddenly I turned to them and exclaimed, "Who could have thought I would be back at work so soon!" They smiled, and told me that no one would have been happier than Milly herself.

Yes, her presence does fill my studio, and home, but with encouragement and support, as always when she was alive, and she is forever in my thoughts.

As I have attained a venerable age, friends and strangers have begun to take my sculpture for granted, but cannot get over my youthful appearance, and have made me conscious of it. This has affected me, and for the past fifteen years I have worn my age as Joseph his coat of many colours, proud of my appearance and bearing.

Yet, when I go into my studio to work, the coat of many colours falls from my shoulders, and I feel young, full of energy and excitement, as I become absorbed in what I do, be it a composition, or a portrait. I live again a life with love in my heart that excludes the past and the future, and I hope that the inspiration and vision I have been given will stay with me as long as I live.

Index

Page references in **bold type** indicate that more than a few lines are devoted to the subject. Roman numerals denote illustrations. *bis* after a reference number indicates that the item is separately mentioned twice on the same page. *passim* denotes that the references are scattered. The author is referred to as BS throughout.

233

235

236

239

241